# INDO-EUROPEAN FIRE RITUALS

*Indo-European Fire Rituals* is a comparative study of Indo-European fire rituals from modern folklore and ethnography in Scandinavia and archaeological material in Europe from the Bronze Age onwards to the Vedic origins of cosmos in India and today's cremations on open pyres in Hinduism.

Exploring Indo-European fire rituals and sacrifices throughout history and fire in its fundamental role in rites and religious practices, this book analyses fire rituals as the unifying structure in time and space in Indo-European cultures from the Bronze Age onwards. It asks the question how and why was fire the ultimate power in culture and cosmology? Fire as an agent and divinity was fundamental in all major sacrifices. In Europe, ritual fires in relation to agriculture and fertility may also explain the enigma of cremation. Cremated remains were ground and used in fertility rituals, and ancestral fires played an essential role in metallurgy and the creation of cosmos. Thus, the role of fire rituals in culture and cosmology enables a unique understanding of historic developmental processes.

For students and academics studying Indo-European culture history from the Bronze Age onwards, this book has a broad interdisciplinary audience including archaeology, ethnography, folklore, religious and Indo-European studies.

**Anders Kaliff** is professor of archaeology in the Department of Archaeology and Ancient History at Uppsala University. Kaliff's main academic expertise is Scandinavian Bronze and early Iron Age with special focus on interpretations of funerals, ritual practice and cosmology. He has a broad international experience with excavations and research projects, among other places, in Jordan and Estonia. Kaliff is a working member of the *Royal Gustavus Adolphus Academy* and the *Nathan Söderblom Society*.

**Terje Oestigaard** is Docent in the Department of Archaeology and Ancient History at Uppsala University, Sweden. He started his early career with field-works in Nepal, India and Bangladesh before working with water, life and death along the Nile River for many years. Throughout his research, he has had a particular focus on funerals and rituals, in general, and cremations and sacrifices, in particular. In recent years, he has also focused on the rich Nordic ethnography and how this links to broader Indo-European questions and historic development processes.

# INDO-EUROPEAN FIRE RITUALS

## Cattle and Cultivation, Cremation and Cosmogony

*Anders Kaliff and Terje Oestigaard*

Routledge
Taylor & Francis Group

LONDON AND NEW YORK

Designed cover image: Lakh Batti ritual at Pashupatinath, Nepal, February 2022. Photo: Terje Oestigaard.

First published 2023
by Routledge
4 Park Square, Milton Park, Abingdon, Oxon OX14 4RN

and by Routledge
605 Third Avenue, New York, NY 10158

*Routledge is an imprint of the Taylor & Francis Group, an informa business*

*British Library Cataloguing-in-Publication Data*
A catalogue record for this book is available from the British Library

ISBN: 978-1-032-29293-9 (hbk)
ISBN: 978-1-032-29298-4 (pbk)
ISBN: 978-1-003-30091-5 (ebk)

DOI: 10.4324/9781003300915

Typeset in Bembo
by KnowledgeWorks Global Ltd.

Printed in the United Kingdom
by Henry Ling Limited

# CONTENTS

# FIGURES

# ACKNOWLEDGEMENTS

During the last 25 years, we have discussed cremation many times, and we have written about many funerary practices and fire rituals. It is impossible to thank all writers personally who have contributed to this book in one way or another, but we are grateful for everything we have learnt from their studies. Still, a few people need special thanks, in particular, Dr. Man Bahadur Khattri, Tribhuvan University in Kathmandu, Nepal, and Prof. Randi Håland and Prof. Kristian Kristiansen for long time inspiration. Also, Arnulf Osterdal gave valuable input to many European fire rituals. With regards to photos and illustrations, we thank Richard Holmgren (ARCDOC), Dr. Magnus Artursson (Gothenburg University) and Fredrik Larsson (National Historical Museums, Sweden). We also extend our gratitude to Prof. Jenny Larsson and the other members of the Languages and Myths of Prehistory (LAMP) Project, funded by Riksbankens Jubileumsfond, Sweden. Lastly, we thank the Department of Archaeology and Ancient History at Uppsala University and Sederholm travel grant (Uppsala University). Also, a special thanks to Routledge's highly efficient and competent production team.

# PREFACE

We met each other for the first time in 1998 in Stavanger, Norway. Anders had completed his doctoral degree in 1997 (Uppsala University, Sweden) on Bronze Age cremations in Sweden and Terje had just finished his MA thesis in 1998 (University of Bergen, Norway) with a focus on cremations in Nepal. Since then, we have cooperated and worked together, and fire and cremation have always been the main themes we have returned to over the years. In 2002, Anders visited Terje when he did fieldwork and studied cremations at the ghats along the Bagmati River next to the Pashupatinath Temple, Nepal. In 2010, Terje moved to Uppsala; this enabled a closer cooperation and more joint publications.

Throughout the years, there has been one particular question we have struggled with and always returned to – why cremation in prehistory? This book aims to shed light on this enigma, and as we argue – the Indo-European fires provide new answers and solutions to this returning and burning question.

# 1
# FIRE RITUALS AND THE INDO-EUROPEAN HERITAGE

## Burning questions

'The first age is called the Age of Burning', Snorri writes in *Heimskringla*:

> At that time all dead people had to be burned and memorial stones raised for them, but after Freyr had been interred in a mound at Uppsalir, many rulers built mounds as well as memorial stones in memory of their kinsmen. But after Danr inn mikilláti (the Haughty), king of the Danes, had had a mound built for himself and commanded that he should be carried into it when he was dead with his royal robes and armour and his horse with all its saddle-gear and many other goods, and many people of his line had later done the same, then the Age of Mounds began there in Danmǫrk, though the Age of Burning continued long after among the Svíar and Norwegians.
>
> *Snorri 2011: 3*

Following Snorri, the known prehistory or the old days, or more precisely the Indo-European era in Scandinavia, was the 'Age of Burning' (Figure 1.1). It was a unique fire regime which included major parts of culture and cosmology, but as Snorri points out, the fundamental core of this time era was the burning of the dead. In the history of archaeological thought, there are many enigmas, but one major question that has intrigued and haunted archaeologists for more than a century is the role of cremation. The answers to the ritualisation of fire in funerals and the religious rationalisation of burning the dead have not yet been found in European archaeology and ethnology. Turning eastwards to the Vedic and Hindu religious belief systems, the Indo-European tradition provides a wealth of information about not only

DOI: 10.4324/9781003300915-1

**FIGURE 1.1** Experimental cremation at Old Uppsala, Uppsala. Photo: Terje Oestigaard.

cremation, but fire rituals and sacrifices. The challenge is to convincingly establish a link between the Bronze Age Scandinavia and the Vedic India. This book is an attempt to do so.

While cremation as a funeral practice dates back to the Mesolithic in Scandinavia (Eriksen & Andersen 2016), the Indo-Europeanisation process represents a dramatic change in the fire regimes affecting all parts of culture and cosmology. From the Bronze Age onwards, a massive fire regime structures life from the cradle to the grave. With the migration of nomadic Indo-Europeans, forests were burnt to clear areas and to provide cattle with good pastures (Kristiansen 2007). When the historic farm was institutionalised around 1000 BC as far north in Sweden as the area of Stockholm and Uppsala (and beyond), slash-and-burn agriculture was an expansive and adaptive strategy enabling intensive colonisation of new lands (Larsson, Morell & Myrdal 1997; Welinder, Pedersen & Widgren 1998; Welinder 2011). In the same period, metallurgy represents the ultimate domestication and control of fire and extreme temperatures. Apart from bronzes, in areas of central Sweden, there are also evidences of iron already in Bronze Age period III (ca. 1300–1100 BC) and iron-melting with furnaces in period IV (ca. 1100–900 BC) (Hjärthner-Holdar 1993). The master of fire and the metallurgist seem to be a ritual specialist and a key player, respectively, in institutionalising Indo-European rituals and religion. There are also traces of cremations in furnaces uniting technology and cosmology. In the Bronze Age, cremation became the dominant funerary practice, and the intensive use of fire enabled ritual practices using the dead body and the bones in multiple ways.

Intriguingly, the ways cremations were conducted in Scandinavia are remarkably similar to the funeral rites described in the Vedas from the Indian sub-continent. Although the dates are debated, the Vedas are generally seen as composed around 1200–1000 BC, which directs the attention to the Indo-European links and knowledge transmissions in time and space with a particular emphasis on the Bronze Age.

Fire is instrumental and life-giving in all cultures, but particularly in cold environments with long winters. On the Eurasian steppes, as well as in Scandinavia, fire in its numerous forms and for various purposes has been fundamental in Indo-European cultures and traditions. Throughout history, fire has had a fundamental role in rites and religious practices; it is a mediator between the realms, but fire is also an embodiment of powerful deities. Controlling and mastering fire was the ultimate power inciting cosmic forces. Fire as an agent and divinity was fundamental in all major sacrifices. It is therefore not surprising that the enigmatic nature of fire has been seen as a divine character and even been regarded as a divinity in itself. Fire as a giver and destroyer of life can hardly be expressed in more powerful images than the description of the Vedic god Agni, a divinity representing and even being fire itself:

> Agni is brilliant, golden, has flaming hair and beard, three or seven tongues, his face is light, his eyes shine, he has sharp teeth, he makes a cracking noise, and leaves a black trail behind. He is fond of clarified butter, but he also eats wood and devours the forest. In fact, he eats everything. He is in particular a destroyer of demons and a slayer of enemies.
>
> *Staal 1983: 73*

Thus, this is a comparative study of Indo-European cultural history and the role of fire rituals as the unifying structure and historic trajectory in time and space from the Bronze Age onwards. In this analysis, we have two main objectives and main questions: How and why was fire the ultimate power in culture and cosmology? And how is it possible to use this shared Indo-European heritage of fire regimes to shed new light on cremation as a dominant funeral practice in large parts of prehistoric Europe?

An Indo-European study of fire rituals is one of the few themes that enable us to identify the long time frames from pastoral developments on the steppes to Scandinavian folklore and ethnographic studies of contemporary cremations in Hinduism (Figure 1.2).

Interdisciplinary Indo-European studies cannot be restricted by disciplinary boundaries, but have to use whatever relevant theoretical, methodological and empirical resources from any discipline. The great strength of interdisciplinary Indo-European studies is precisely that, because of a shared core Indo-European origin, it focuses on common structures and cultural features that are possible to identify across other differing cultural, religious, geographical and temporal variables and variabilities. Thus, in many cases, the core and origin will not be the

**FIGURE 1.2** Cremation at Pashupatinath, 2022. Kathmandu, Nepal. Photo: Terje Oestigaard.

most interesting, but the distribution, continuity and consequences of the very different and multifaceted Indo-European processes up to today, which have made world history and constituted large parts of Eurasia for millennia.

The main conceptual and methodological advantages of this study are the comparative perspective enabling new insights into specific cultural developments in varied regions and religions. The Indo-European framework places otherwise separate traditions into broader historic development patterns, and hence it is possible to identify the *longue durée* in the Indo-European cultural history (see Braudel 1980). In order to enable such a study, our approach includes archaeology, aDNA, history, ethnography, ethnology, linguistics, anthropology and religious studies. Thus, we may write a cultural history that is not restricted to only archaeological finds but present a comparative analysis that links the past to the present – from Ireland to India, Scandinavia, the Eurasian steppes and beyond.

## Fire in purgatory and hell

Throughout Europe, the common Indo-European heritage includes a wealth of ethnographic information and documentation of fire rituals and festivals (see Chapters 2 and 3). While many of these rituals were barely or only Christianised on the surface, they co-existed in parallel with Christianity as rural and agricultural festivals well into the 20th century, and some even up to today. The history of cremation, on the other hand, shows a diametrically opposite picture. While

Snorri identified the Age of Burning primarily with cremation, the church saw the burning of the dead as the ultimate pagan and heathen practice. The condemnation of cremation in the history of Christianity is omnipresent. The French king Charlemagne, or Charles the Great, introduced in the 780s death penalty for the Saxons if they cremated their dead, which was the same penalty for denying baptism and destroying churches (Nelson 2019: 197).

The European and Christian history of understanding the role of fire is a paradox. The absence of explicit elaborations of the qualities of the cremation fire is also remarkable because if there is one religious denomination in world history that has focused more on fire than any other, it is the Roman Catholic Church. In the history of Christianity, the eschatological fires in purgatory and hell were the most powerful cosmic means for purification and destroying sins. 'The cosmos is a machine for damnation and salvation. Soteriology is cosmology', Paul Ricoeur said (Ricoeur 2004: 268), and hell with its doors locked from the inside rather than the outside is the principle of cosmic retribution par excellence (Kvanvig 1993: 19). From the Middle Ages, the eternal punishment and damnation of sinners in hell played a fundamental role in Christianity (Sachs 1991, 1993). Also, as pointed out, 'If Heaven is spiritual, Hell is oddly fleshly' (Turner 1995: 3). The history of beliefs and perceptions of sin and Satan in Christianity is long (e.g. Russell 1977, 1981, 1988), but the Biblical absence of a torturing hell with fiery flames is also striking. In other words, the theological advancements and theoretical elaborations of the role of fire did not self-ignite but grew out of a common Indo-European stratum of worldviews and horizons of understanding (see Chapters 2 and 3). Thus, one has to differentiate between the cultural and collective background in history creating rational concepts of the role of fire in religion, on the one hand, and the specific forms and theological explanations Christian scholars developed in the Middle Ages, on the other hand. As usual, the church perceived existing ritual and religious practices and beliefs as pagan and true heresy while at the same time developing concepts of fire that never existed in Europe before or after – and never attained the same diabolic forms in any other religion (Figure 1.3).

In the Judeo-Christian tradition, there are at least five phases in the development of hell and notions of purgation. First, God penalised humanity with the Deluge; second, Sheol; third, Gehenna; fourth, the medieval torturing chamber of eternal fire, and final, the recent theological developments where hell is without fire but the pains of an eternal life without God's love is seen as hurting like actual fire (see Oestigaard 2003, 2009). The Deluge was a collective punishment here and now, and a penalty in this life rather than in an Otherworld realm cannot imply a heaven or hell with individual and eternal punishments (Segal 1997; Hachlili 2001). Sheol was a term used in the Old Testament to designate a kind of 'hell', but this signified more the concept of 'grave' with notions of judgements after death. Moreover, the character of punishment is also uncertain (Walvoord 1992: 16–17), and originally, it has been claimed, 'the realm of the dead, the rites connected with death and burial, as well as the destiny of the soul in the other

**FIGURE 1.3** Torturing fires in the Christian hell. Hortus Deliciarum by Herrad of Landsberg (1125–1195), Date: 1180. Public domain.

world, play no part in the religion of YHWH' (Kaufmann 1960: 311). In the New Testament, there are images of a fiery furnace – Gehenna – but this was a garbage dump outside Jerusalem where also bodies of criminals were burnt (Forsyth 2003: 201). Still, there are only 12 references to Gehenna in the New Testament, which include an 'unquenchable fire' (Mk 9:43), a 'pool of fire' (Rev. 20:13f.) and a 'fiery lake of burning sulphur' (Rev. 21:7–8).

The role of fire in the Christian hell and purgatory developed fundamentally in the 12th and 13th centuries, where purgatory was seen as a hell of limited time and suffering compared to the eternal abyss of everlasting torture in hell proper. In 1253, the church made a formal promulgation of the doctrine of purgatory in a papal letter. Part of the theological developments involved moving beyond metaphors and creating notions of a real three-dimensional and eternal cremato- rium (Le Goff 1984). Still, there were theological challenges that had to be solved concerning the nature of the divine and purgatory fires. If hellfire consumed like ordinary fire, sinners would burn up in hell and hence hell and the punishment would not be eternal. William of Auvergne, a 13th-century bishop of Paris, came up with a rational solution to this theological problem. Hellfire was different from the fire we are familiar with on Earth. Hellfire burned and tortured with- out consuming the dead bodies, and hence the damned would suffer in eternity. In purgatory, the fire worked as normal fire; it was designated to expiatory and purification processes (Bernstein 1982: 1993; Le Goff 1984: 245). In other words, the fires in purgatory and hell were fundamentally different; the first was a sign of hope and salvation, although painful, but the deceased would eventually reach heaven in a purified state, whereas the latter fire was eternal without mercy.

The purging fires took an extreme form in the European witch-craze from ca. 1450 to 1750. In Europe, there were approximately 90,000 witchcraft prosecu- tions and around 45,000 executions (Behringer 2004; Levack 2006). In Western Christianity, the witch became an incarnated and embodied form of pure evil in human shape and hence had to be burnt; erasing evil was a Christian duty. This theological development was unique and extreme because in other Christian denominations witches were closely associated with havocking weather and agrarian calamites. Among the Slavs, 'When prolonged drought set in and the community was threatened with famine and death, it was not uncommon, par- ticularly in parts of the Ukraine, for all the women, peasants and gentry alike, to be subjected to the swimming ordeal' (Zguta 1977: 229).

Throughout Indo-European history in Europe, a cosmic battle unfolded between various forces of nature, and the fertile and life-giving powers were always threatened by hostile and malevolent powers. This was the agricultural world from the cradle to the grave. Night battles between the good and hos- tile forces were omnipresent and omnipotent (Ginzburg 1983). This was also the world where werewolves and warriors partook not only in warfare against human and visible enemies but also against invisible enemies in nature. By engaging in cosmic battles conquering winter, infertility and malignant forces, humans overpowered evil (Kaliff & Oestigaard 2022).

Purifying and purging the land and thereby protecting and procreating life was essentially the primary role of the Indo-European fire rituals in Europe as documented in ethnography and historical sources throughout the continent during the last millennia. Thus, while the Christian witch-craze built on this common agricultural cosmology, the Western notion of an extreme hell and purgatorial fire was a perverted development of more profound and long-lasting

Indo-European beliefs and practices: the health and wealth of all people in agrarian societies. In an ecological world of hostile forces where the difference between individual and collective life and death was the direct result of successful or failed harvests, fire was an ultimate tool and power in cold environments characterised by snow, winter and frozen forces in nature for months each year. Death was literally seen in the absence of growth forces, and all life and well-being was dependent upon inciting and activating these forces at the right time for the right purposes. Fire was essential in these rituals and environmental engagements, which directs the attention to the early Indo-European research and the role of the sun in comparative studies.

## Fire: the sun or the soil?

All agricultural practices are dependent upon the right combination of the sun and water at the right time in right amounts for a successful harvest. Whether too much or too little of sun or water, or the wrong combination at the wrong time, it wreaks havoc and may immediately lead to hunger, starvation, suffering and ultimately death (Tvedt & Oestigaard 2016). In agricultural societies in Northern Europe, the winter was the greatest challenge and this particular water world poses particular challenges with regards to continuity between the seasons during the cold, dark and dangerous time (Oestigaard 2021a, 2021b, 2022a). This is the world where fire was the ultimate life-giver, but the role and relation between fire and water, and the sun and the soil, has hardly been seen as a fundamental axis and structure in prehistoric culture and cosmology.

The study of Bronze Age religion in Scandinavia is almost as old as the study of the Bronze Age itself, since the bronzes enabled Oscar Montelius to develop typology and chronology, and many of these objects were largely religious artefacts (Montelius 1885, 1895, 1917). Although many of the early interpretations focused on the sun and its relation to rain and thunder (Worsaae 1882; Montelius 1894, 1899, 1910), from the early days, studies and interpretations of an alleged sun-god have dominated archaeology (see Nordberg 2013). As J.P. Allen pointed out in 1892: 'When an archaeologist is in doubt he always falls back on the sun-god' (Allen 1892: 71). More than a century later, there is still nothing new under the sun, and some iconic finds like the Trundholm wagon have largely shaped this interpretative paradigm (Figure 1.4). Flemming Kaul argues that there was most likely a 'possible development towards a true sun-god or the expression of the sun as an anthropomorphic deity … [and] on the basis of the pictures on the bronzes it would seem that a development of a sun-god in Bronze-Age per. V was not impossible … we shall follow the sun on its cyclical journey from morning to evening and from morning to evening again' (Kaul 1998: 252, 259, see also Kaul 2004; Goldhahn 2019). As Kaul says: 'the minds of people of Scandinavia were almost obsessed with the religious ideas involving the voyage of the sun [in the Bronze Age] … Everything suggests that the sun was the most significant power which was worshipped' (Kaul 1998: 251).

FIGURE 1.4  The Trundholm Sun Chariot (ca. 1400 BC). The National Museum of Denmark, Creative Commons.

Although this interpretation of a sun-god and cosmology in the Bronze Age is largely based on iconography on bronze objects and circular rock-art motifs, this branch of Scandinavian archaeology has developed independently from Indo-European studies and the early ethnographic studies of sun cult and cosmologies (e.g. Müller 1856[1909], 1859). Thus, in the history of ideas, one has to understand the role of the sun in relation to fire and farming from an Indo-European perspective. 'Solar mythology primarily deserves the attention of folklore students for the role it played in the history of our subject' (Dorson 1955: 393), and an important scientific contribution was Max Müller's *Comparative Mythology* from 1856. From the Grimm brothers in the early 19th century onwards, the following decades were formative and instrumental in the consolidation of not only various scientific disciplines but also of Indo-European studies, and notable researchers include both Max Müller and Wilhelm Mannhardt. Still, as will be seen, the fundamental shortcomings of the solar paradigm became soon evident, and the sun was brought down to earth. Thus, both celestial and terrestrial perspectives originally had a strong Indo-European foundation, which included sun-gods and solar mythologies, on the one hand, and fertility gods and corn-spirits, on the other hand (Mannhardt 1865, 1868, 1875, 1877, 1884). Moreover, interpretations of the sun-god and cosmology faced criticism since the dogma basically lacked an empirical foundation. In fact, the main advocate of solar mythology, Max Müller, was ridiculed as a Sun-God himself. In 1870, the Anglo-Irish clergyman Richard Frederick Littledale published a highly satirical piece, which was reprinted in 1906 and 1909. The article has the title 'The Oxford Solar Myth':

> A VERY singular tradition, possibly due to the influence of classical Paganism in the course of study, still preserves, in the Oxford of the nineteenth century, the evident traces of that primeval Nature-worship whereby the earliest parents of the Aryan race marked their observance of the phenomena of the heavens. As so often occurs, the myth has assumed a highly anthropomorphic and concrete form, has gradually been incrusted with the deposits of later ages, and has been given a historical, or rather a biographical dress, which thereby veils, under modern names and ideas of the West, the legends current four thousand years ago on the table-lands of Transoxiana ... The symbolical name by which the hero was deified, even in our own days, is Max Müller ... The more scientific aspect of the question recognizes here the Sun-God, armed with his hammer or battle-axe of light, pounding and crushing frost and clouds alike into impalpability ... We require more exact data before we can with authority allege that Max Müller is indeed the Sun, or rather the Dawn, himself. But these data are accessible and abundant.
>
> *Littledale 1906: 279–280*

The parody goes on and on, and how unscientific and problematic this solar mythology was seen by the turn of the 20th century is best understood when Max Müller's well-known essay *Comparative Mythology* from 1856 was republished in 1909 by Abraham Smythe Palmer (Müller 1909). Smythe Palmer, who was a lecturer at Trinity College in Dublin, not only included Littledale's parody 'The Oxford Solar Myth' in the publication of Müller's work, but the satire was published before the actual Comparative Mythology!

Despite the fact that Müller's work still had academic relevance by the turn of the 20th century, it is nevertheless quite remarkable that Müller, in particular, and solar mythologies, in general, were so unpopular and stigmatised that one had to include satire and irony before publishing the actual work. One obvious reason is, of course, that saying that the sun is round and moves in daily and years cycles says absolutely nothing. However, although Max Müller has been criticised for everything by almost everyone (for an overview, see Dorson 1955), Müller was not simply a solar mythologist. Despite being ridiculed and seen as a caricature, Müller's primary focus was on comparative Indo-European mythology and not the sun itself: 'Müller tried to discover the underlying meaning of myth using philological principles that were widely accepted at the time, he can be regarded as the first person who tried to study myth using anything that even remotely resembled a scientific procedure. This in itself guarantees him a certain importance in the history of mythological studies' (Carroll 1985: 264). Following Müller, the whole purpose of comparative mythology was that 'a study of the traditions found in the Rig-Veda can shed light on the Aryan tradition from which the mythologies of various European cultures, notably including the cultures of Greece, Rome and the Germanic tribes, had developed ... Towards the end of his career, Müller [1892] claimed that his most important discovery in the area of myth lay in the equation Dyaus = Zeus = Jupiter — Tyr' (Carroll 1985: 266–267).

Ethnographically, it was difficult to shed light on an alleged sun cosmology in Europe. This has to be seen in relation to other scientific and empirical developments. The term 'folklore', for instance, was coined in 1846 and replaced the more awkward expression 'Popular Antiques'. Mannhardt played a fundamental role in this process and also pulling the sun mythology down to earth. Initially, he focused on heavenly bodies, in practice, the sun, but his own empirical investigation directed him to living customs and beliefs among the peasantry. In this predominantly comparative Indo-European agricultural context, it was not the sun that was at the centre, but fertility rituals and corn-spirits (Figure 1.5).

The ethnographic research focusing on empirical facts in European agricultural societies culminated and reached its climax with James G. Frazer and *The Golden Bough* (James 2017). Ackerman writes:

**FIGURE 1.5** Modern corn fields in front of the Bronze Age grave mound Håga (ca. 1000 BC), Uppsala, Sweden. Photo: Terje Oestigaard.

[Mannhardt's] great contribution lay in the way in which he forcefully broke the endless chain of theorizing by thinkers who were willing to pontificate forever about the nature of the primitive mind ... Instead of engaging in a priori reasoning, Mannhardt opted for the then novel alternative of gathering empirical folkloric evidence – specifically, by going out and patiently collecting and classifying hundreds of examples of behaviour of contemporary European peasants. Frazer extols Mannhardt's work for providing 'the fullest and most trustworthy evidence we possess as to the primitive religion of the Aryans'.

*Ackerman 1987: 81*

In other words, Frazer's *The Golden Bough* is not only about a terrestrial perspective and functional fertility gods and corn-spirits, but the interrelation and co-existence of gods working from above and beneath, and how life and agriculture is dependent upon the right combination of water and the sun throughout the year and season – and continuities between the seasons (Figure 1.6). Originally published in 1890, *The Golden Bough* comprised of two volumes (Frazer 1890a, 1890b), the second edition in 1900 was expanded to three volumes and the third edition from 1906 to 1915 had no less than 12 volumes. In 1922, the popular and abridged version was published (Frazer 1922), which for a century has never been out of print.

**FIGURE 1.6** Winter in Uppsala 2021 with snow covering the Bronze Age grave mound Håga (ca. 1000 BC), Sweden. Photo: Terje Oestigaard.

James Frazer was knighted in 1914 and received a string of honours, probably making him the most heavily decorated anthropologist of all times. When *The Golden Bough* was published, it was an ambitious study attempting to gather data from all over the world. Initially, it was enthusiastically received by fellow academics, but the academic popularity waned as the book became part of Western popular consciousness (Hunt 1997). As the years passed, the criticism became more devastating and there is hardly a thing Frazer and *The Golden Bough* has not been criticised for (e.g. Leach 1961, 1966, 1985; Lienhardt 1993). Ackerman says: 'Although in the first edition of *The Golden Bough* he says that his general subject is "the primitive religion of the Aryans" [i.e. the Indo-Europeans], in the second and third editions his subject in nothing less than the religious evolution of the whole of humanity'. He continues: '[Frazer] changed nothing because unfortunately he had learnt nothing' (Ackerman 1987: 84, 307).

However, as Edmund Leach also pointed out, 'it is the facts themselves that matter, not Frazer's interpretation of the facts' (Leach 1961: 81). And precisely because the facts matter, *The Golden Bough* is an invaluable source for understanding Indo-European practices in Europe. As Frazer himself pointed out in 1936, 'now, as always, I hold all my theories very lightly, and am ever ready to modify or abandon them in the light of new evidence. If my writings should survive the writer, they will do so, I believe, less for the sake of the theories which they propound than for the sake of the facts which they record' (Frazer 1936: v). Or with different words, 'Yet, sooner or later, every serious anthropologist return to the great Frazerian corpus' (Fortes 1959: 8).

It is only in recent years an agricultural perspective and cosmology have been integrated into the Indo-European cosmology in Bronze Age Scandinavia (e.g. Kaliff 1997, 2007; Kaliff & Oestigaard 2004, 2013, 2017, 2020, 2022). In this process, and in order to break out of the more than a century old and heavily criticised sun cosmology, one needs to focus on corn and fertility spirits (Frazer 1912a, 1912b), the evolution of kings (Frazer 1911a) and dying gods (Frazer 1911b), and not the least: fire. The ritual fire had a fundamental role in Frazer's interpretations and he devoted two volumes to the European fire rituals in a comparative context: *Balder the Beautiful Vol. 1. & Vol. 2* (Frazer 1913a, 1913b). While Frazer found the answer to all these puzzles in the myth about Balder and the mistletoe (Frazer 1913b: 76–94), a holistic theory that has been criticised, one may still be inspired by many of his thoughts and approach the topic from another perspective that is more familiar to most archaeologists, namely the family or farm tree where the first farmer or the clearer of the ground is buried in a mound. In many cases, following Frazer, this tree was an oak tree, but the further north one gets, there are inevitable variations around the same structuring theme. Whether gods, spirits or ancestors, in particular, old oaks have been seen as holy and not even fools dared to cut or harm these ancestral trees. Tree-spirits were deities of vegetation and the most powerful of them all. The trees contained life and this topic is literally rooted in Norse and Indo-European cosmology. And without trees and wood as fuels, no fire.

Later, Frazer also wrote a smaller volume on the *Myths of the Origin of Fire: An Essay* (Frazer 1930). Fire had a central part in the development and understanding of magic and scapegoats (Frazer 1913c), and it directly relates to his overall thesis about tree-spirits, the fundamental cosmology of oaks and the fires coming from within trees.

## Theories of fire festivals

In order to understand the role of fire, one has to answer the fundamental question Frazer asks: 'In what way did people imagine that they could procure so many goods or avoid so many ills by the application of fire and smoke, of embers and ashes? In short, what theory underlay and prompted the practice of these customs?' (Frazer 1913a: 329).

Broadly, there are two overall explanations or theories about fire festivals: 1) they are sun-charms and imitative magic ensuring and supplying sunshine for men, animals and plants by making fires, and 2) they are primarily purifying and protective means that ward off and destroy evil to ashes. In short, these two theories may be called the Solar theory and the Purificatory theory. While these two theories may at the outset seem contradictory, they are not:

> If we assume that the fires kindled at these festivals were primarily intended to imitate the sun's light and heat, may we not regard the purificatory and disinfecting qualities, which popular opinion certainly appears to have ascribed to them, as attributes derived directly from the purificatory and disinfecting qualities of sunshine? In this way we might conclude that, while the imitation of sunshine in these ceremonies was primary and original, the purification attributed to them was secondary and derivative.
>
> *Frazer 1913a: 330*

This, Frazer says, is the intermediate position between the two opposing theories and a view he argued for in the second edition of *The Golden Bough*. Wilhelm Mannhardt was once the greatest scholar emphasising the solar cosmology and theory, but as the work with the third edition of *The Golden Bough* proceeded, Frazer leaned more towards the Purificatory theory, although stressing that they are not mutually exclusive. His reasoning and arguments are therefore instructive, since 'A theory which had the support of so learned and sagacious an investigator as W. Mannhardt is entitled to a respectful hearing' (Frazer 1913a: 331).

The Solar Theory has its merits, in particular in the cold and cloudy climates in Europe. People have used charms to make sunshine and two of the greatest festivals among farmers throughout Europe coincided with the sun's cyclical turning points: the summer and winter solstices. During Midwinter, the Yule log and the birth of the sun may have been two sides of the same coin, or sun, 'if the kindling of the Yule log was originally a magical rite intended to rekindle the sun' (Frazer 1913a: 332). Moreover, 'The custom of rolling a burning wheel down a hill, which is often observed at these ceremonies, might well pass for an imitation of the sun's course in the sky, and the imitation would be especially appropriate on Midsummer Day when the sun's annual declension begins' (Frazer 1913a: 334). The swinging of a burning tar-barrel around a pole is another way of imitating the sun; the same is many need-fires produced by friction or the revolution of a wheel. In cold climates, sun-charms worked as opposite rain-making rituals, and Swiss children used need-fire on foggy days to clear away the must. In Scandinavia too, there are numerous testimonies of beliefs that fire rituals enabled weather modifications. Thus, 'the older view may have been not merely that the smoke and flames prognosticated, but that they actually produced an abundant harvest, the heat of the flames acting like sunshine on the corn' (Frazer 1913a: 337). In other words, the smoke and the bonfires fertilised the fields, but these powers were not limited to the vegetable world, but included animals and humans as well.

The Purificatory theory stresses other aspects, and the relation between the two may also be a matter of causes and consequences, rituals and responses, and means and matters. Without doubt, many ethnographic accounts describe sun-charms and weather modification rituals (Figure 1.7). However, it is not always clear what has been documented: the desired consequences of the ritual or ways

**FIGURE 1.7** The sun returns and rises at Old Uppsala, Sweden. 9 January 2021. Photo: Terje Oestigaard.

to cause these changes? Frazer says: '[it] is to be observed that the people who practise the fire-customs appear never to allege the solar theory in explanation of them, while on the contrary they do frequently and emphatically put forward the purificatory theory. This is a strong argument in favour of the purificatory and against the solar theory ... the conception of fire as an emanation of the sun, or at all events as linked to it by a bond of physical sympathy, is far less simple and obvious' (Frazer 1913a: 341). On the other hand, time and again, fire is told to burn and repel evil and witches. But this may also be an efficient way, in fact, the only way, to actively enable sun-charms to work. 'The burning wheels rolled down hills and the burning discs and brooms thrown into the air may be intended to burn the invisible witches' (Frazer 1913a: 345). Frazer thus concludes:

> On this view the fertility supposed to follow the application of fire in the form of bonfires, torches, discs, rolling wheels, and so forth, is not conceived as resulting directly from an increase of solar heat which the fire has magically generated; it is merely an indirect result obtained by freeing the reproductive powers of plants and animals from the fatal obstruction of witchcraft. And what is true of the reproduction of plants and animals may hold good also of the fertility of the human sexes. We have seen that the bonfires are supposed to promote marriage and to procure offspring for childless couples. This happy effect need not flow directly from any quickening or fertilizing energy in the fire; it may follow indirectly from the power of the fire to remove those obstacles which the spells of witches and wizards notoriously present to the union of man and wife.
>
> *Frazer 1913a: 346*

We will return to these festivals in depth in Chapter 3, where the Solar or the Purificatory theory will be discussed in relation to farming and the agricultural seasons before returning to cremation as a funeral practice, since it was basically the same fire that was used in farming and funerals.

## From Frazer and Müller to Indra and the Vedic fires

In the 19th-century Southern India, cattle were driven over hot ember, and the relation between pastoralism, farming and fire was explicit. At the fire festivals, three, five or seven men were chosen to walk through the fire. Before the fire-walk, they poured milk into an adjacent stream from cows that for the first time had calves that year. When the walk was concluded, it was a great feast for the participants, and the next day the land was ploughed and sown and it opened the agricultural season. Importantly, as Frazer points out, in India, there is little evidence that the fire-walk was a sun-charm, because in the arid and hot regions like India, farmers would rather wish to abate than increase the heat of the sun (Frazer 1913b: 9, 16).

Burning evil and the representatives embodying evil are somehow straightforward. In the European images and ritual practices, however, there are yet other practices, and one may also ask why the beneficent and good gods are burnt:

… when the god happens to be a deity of vegetation, there are special reasons why he should die by fire. For light and heat are necessary to vegetable growth; and, on the principle of sympathetic magic, by subjecting the personal representative of vegetation to their influence, you secure a supply of these necessaries for trees and crops. In other words, by burning the spirit of vegetation in a fire which represents the sun, you make sure that, for a time at least, vegetation shall have plenty of sun.

*(Frazer 1913b: 23)*

In a similar vein, when the god or representative of life-giving powers is killed by drowning, it is probably a rain charm. Thus, we are far away from any sun cult or worship of the sun as such, because it does not make sense among rational farmers, but the killing and sacrifices of gods represent a particularly unique way of conceptualising and taking control over the cosmic forces.

The role of rainmakers or ritual specialists engaging with weather modification is one of the most important religious roles and duties in traditional agricultural societies (Figure 1.8). In the abridged 1922 edition, Frazer writes: 'Of the things which the public magician sets himself to do for the good of the tribe, one of the chief is to control the weather and especially to ensure adequate fall of rain. Water is an essential of life, and in most countries the supply of it depends

**FIGURE 1.8** Sacrifice of Dómaldi at Old Uppsala after failed harvest and famine. Following Snorri Sturluson: 'In the first autumn they sacrificed oxen … The second autumn they held a human sacrifice, but the season was the same or worse. But the third autumn … Then the leaders held a council and came to an agreement among themselves that their king, Dómaldi, must be the cause of the famine, and moreover, that they should sacrifice him for their prosperity … and that is what they did' (Snorri 2011: 18). After the sacrifice, the harvest was bountiful. Creative Commons.

upon showers. Without rain vegetation withers, animals and men languish and die. Hence…the rain-maker is a very important personage' (Frazer 1922: 62). Importantly, as Frazer emphasises, most rain-making or weather-altering rituals and practices build on sympathetic magic in one way or another. 'Thus kings are often expected to give rain and sunshine in due season, to make the crops grow', he says, but 'Of all natural phenomena there are perhaps none which civilised man feels himself more powerless to influence than the rain, the sun, and the wind' (Frazer 1890a: 8, 13).

While Frazer mainly discussed Indo-European fire rituals on the European continent, Max Müller focused on India and the Vedic rites and conceptions. In *Lectures on the origin and growth of religion as illustrated by the religions of India*, Müller writes: 'Next to the fire, and sometimes identical with it, comes the sun', but in relation to thunder and the wind, he also points out some striking characteristics. 'We hear the noise of thunder, but we cannot see the thunder, nor can we feel, smell or taste it … Another precept, which chiefly depends on our senses of touch, though frequently supported by evidence of our ears, and indirectly of our eyes, is the *wind*' (Müller 1879: 200, 202–203). Different elements of culture and cosmos were visible and sensible to certain senses only, making them special, different and distinct from each other. Lastly, Müller writes about rain. Rain 'is not simply water, but water of which he does not yet know whence it comes; water which, if it is absent for a long time, causes the death of plants and animals, and men; and when it returns it produces a very jubilee of nature' (Müller 1879: 204). Water may thus represent both life and death and it bears many resemblances to the life-giving qualities of fire. Müller says (1879: 198):

> Now the fire may seem not only very visible, but also very tangible; and so, no doubt it is … imagine what it was to the early inhabitants of the earth … [it] must have marked a complete revolution in his life, he had seen the sparks of lightning, he had seen and felt the light and warmth of the sun, he may have watched even, in utter bewilderment, the violent destruction of forest by conflagration, caused either by lightning or friction of trees in summer …

Müller continues with the specific characteristics and mystical properties of fire and the flames:

> At one moment the fire was here, at another it had gone out. Whence did it come? Wither did it go? If there ever was a ghost, in our sense of the word, it was fire. Did it not come from the clouds? Did it not vanish in the sea? Did it not live in the sun? Did it not travel through the stars? … So many things could be told of him, how that he was the son of two pieces of wood; how, as soon as he was born, he devoured his father and mother, that is, the two pieces of wood from which he sprang; how he disappeared or became extinguished, when touched by water … how at a later time he

carried the sacrificial offerings from earth to heaven, and became a messenger and mediator between the gods and men: that we need not wonder
at his many names and epithets, and at the large number of ancient stories
or myths told of Agni; nor need we wonder at the oldest of all myths, that
there was in the fire something invisible and unknown, yet undeniable, – it
may be, the Lord.

*(Müller 1879: 199–200)*

Not only has the Vedic fire god Agni one of the longest continuities in the world,
but it is also one of the gods with the longest research history (Figure 1.9). As an
introduction to Indo-European fire rituals, we will present two very extensive

**FIGURE 1.9**  Small fire offering at the Dakshinkali Temple, Nepal. Photo: Terje Oestigaard.

and elaborate, although highly different, fire rituals from the Indian sub-continent. The first and most famous is the Agnicayana, which Frits Staal, together with a consortium of scholars, documented extensively in the coastal region of Kerala in southwestern India in 1975. The result is available partly as a monograph titled *Agni – The Vedic Ritual of the Fire Altar* (Staal 1983) and partly in the form of a documentary entitled *Altar of Fire*. When the film was shot, it was widely believed that this could be the last chance to experience the performance of this extensive and complicated Vedic ritual. Later, however, it has been revived and re-executed in Kerala. The actual Agnicayana performance in 1975 lasted for 12 days and the complexity required numerous priests orchestrating and building the fire altar with subsequent rituals. Thus, one may say that this ritual, to a large extent, is a priestly ritual on behalf of the principal devotee. Still, Vedic rituals are performed at different levels of complexity and in different contexts, from more mundane to highly elaborate ceremonies taking a long time to prepare and several days to complete. Even seemingly simple rituals can, however, contain a hidden complexity and involve great personal sacrifices, which relate to the other ritual we describe. The Lakh Batti ritual looks quite simple and not very extravagant, but in fact, it represents an extreme devotional penance and practice. The preparation for a Lakh Batti fire sacrifice may require more than 1,000 hours and this is mainly an individual or family ritual, although the fires are blessed by a priest prior to the offering. As such, these two fire rituals give an introduction to the importance, but also the different ways, huge fire sacrifice can be made and organised.

## Agnicayana – 'Piling up Agni'

Agnicayana is certainly one of the most advanced Vedic rituals, a ceremony including the building of an altar made out of more than a thousand fired clay bricks. The altar is built in the shape of a bird, which symbolises Purusa, also known as Prajāpati, i.e. 'the lord of living creatures', the first sacrificial victim of the Vedic creation myth. The performance signifies a re-creation of cosmos, even if the exact meaning of the different elements of the ritual remains obscure for the participants. One fundamental meaning is that the god of fire – Agni – is reborn on the sacrificial altar. Fire is regarded not only as a god, but simultaneously as a divine messenger. As a god himself, Agni also conveys sacrificial gifts to other gods at the same time. Although the deity Agni in recent Hinduism has been given a more hidden role, not least the name shows his centrality in earlier times. The name Agni has clear common Indo-European roots and can be compared with Latin *ignis*, Russian *ogon'* and Lithuanian *ugnis*. Agni is born, according to the Vedic account, from the pieces of wood in the fire drill used to light the ritual fire, the only way in which ritual fire may be lit, which is also a feature with a wide and general Indo-European distribution. During the preparation of the fire sacrifice, the person who initiates it is believed to be pregnant, bearing the fire god Agni, and the altar is believed to be the womb from which

Agni was born. Both the performance of agnicayana and the significance of the ritual have been carefully described by Fritz Staal in his large monograph on agnicayana (Staal 1983, Vol. 1).

The performance of agnicayana contains a complex cosmological symbolism, whose parts can be traced back to the creation myth, as depicted in *Puruṣasūkta* ('The Hymn of Puruṣa') from the Rig-Veda (10.90). Here, we are told how a primordial being, Puruṣa, is killed and cut into pieces, after which the cosmos and the different aspects of life are fashioned from the parts of his body. The fact that different elements in cosmos are believed to be identical with the body parts of the sacrificed primordial being is a fundamental cosmological idea. It means that an entity is created from the matter in another, alternative guises of each other. Meat and earth, for example, are believed to be of the same material substance and thus one can change into the other. In the same way, the bones, the hard part in the soft meat, are equated with rocks and stones, while hair is associated with plants. This myth has close equivalents in other Indo-European religious traditions, with the common feature that a primordial figure is sacrificed, and the world is created out of the body parts. This is a very important part of a common Indo-European cosmology (cf. Lincoln 1986), which we will also return to later.

In the preparation of the agnicayana, the bird-shaped altar is built of clay bricks in five layers, taking five days, one for each layer. The different layers correspond to the five main body parts of this first sacrifice of Puruṣa: marrow, bone, flesh, skin and hair. At the same time, they correspond to the five different zones of existence: the cosmological levels of earth, atmosphere and heaven, together with two transitional zones. Accordingly, material is taken from each part of creation in the construction of the fire altar: earth and water for the brick, grass (hair) to place on the altar and so on. The burnt clay bricks of the Vedic altar, as well as the material in the pottery used liturgically in the ritual, do not constitute just any material. Both bricks and ceramics are materials where fire is included, and they activate other materials in a very tangible way. Bricks are made by a combination of elements; earth, water and fire, giving it a profound symbolic meaning, which in itself constitutes a microcosm of creation. The same is true of ceramics. Through the transformation of the clay, it is believed that the god of fire – Agni – becomes active in the material, a crucial and meaningful part of the ritual. The ground where the altar is built is in advance prepared through ritual ploughing and through a symbolic burial: Five heads – of a human, horse, bull, ram and goat – are buried in the ground. Together with the burial of ritual objects, including pots, and the ploughing and sowing of the ground in preparation for the altar, this symbolises how the combination of elements contributes to the act of creation. In addition to the large bird-shaped altar, other altars and ritual buildings are built beside it. The buildings and other constructions prepared for agnicayana are deliberately burned down after the lengthy ritual is completed, ritually consumed by the main character of the performance himself, the god of fire – Agni (Staal 1983: 15–16, 73–139; cf. Lincoln 1986: 60–61).

**FIGURE 1.10** Agnicayana – Parts of the bird altar. From Gargeyapuram, Kurnool, India, 2015. Source: Collection of Shri Rajashekhara Sharma. CC BY-SA 4.0.

Agnicayana shows us an unusually grand and complicated ritual of burnt offering, which requires great efforts, resources and time (Figure 1.10). Importantly, there are general features that are also repeated in more common Vedic fire rituals, which are much less complex compared to agnicayana. These features emanate, as mentioned, from the underlying cosmological notions of a common Indo-European character. This means that equivalents can also (and should) be sought in other Indo-European contexts, even those that lack the early written evidence of the Vedic ritual. Rituals of this kind leave physical traces that are possible to detect by archaeological methods: altars, hearths, ritual waste, post-holes from the burnt-down ritual buildings and so on. As we will show, there are extensive archaeological evidences of fire-sacrifice as a general Indo-European phenomenon, not least in the ancient Scandinavian context. This applies both to material remains of complex fire rituals of a collective and formalised nature, as well as more everyday sacrifices. However, it is often difficult, based solely on material remains, to determine whether a fire was used for sacred, ritual purposes or had a secular function. Here, therefore, surviving folk beliefs and a comparative perspective are invaluable tools for the archaeologist. Furthermore, a mainly profane use of a fireplace need not exclude that it has also been used for rituals (cf. Kaliff 2007: 99–119). In particular, the hearth in the home may have been the scene of both sacred and profane activities that involved the use of fire as a medium.

## Lakh Batti – 'One hundred thousand lights'

The Lakh Batti ceremony is, in particular, a very popular rite in Nepal, and it is an ultimate offering to a deity showing the utmost dedication and devotion. It is a true sacrifice, but contrary to many other visual and spectacular sacrifices, the true value of the sacrifice is the personal commitments and devotions over time making this fire offering something special.

*Lakh Batti* (Nepali) literally means 'one hundred thousand lights' and in the ritual, devotees lit and offer 100,000 lamps to the chosen deity. These lamps are, in practice, the wicks, and in the fire ritual, there should be at least 100,000 wicks; this is the minimum, but the sacrificial gift may comprise more than 100,000 wicks. In Hinduism, the numbers five, seven and nine are auspicious, and the 100,000 wicks are placed in bundles on five, seven or nine clay pots. While this may not sound very impressive at the outset, each and every wick has to be handmade. Each wick is hand rolled out of cotton strings, and the time and dedication behind a proper Lakh Batti ritual is mesmerising. The wicks are made by twining a singular string around the fingers. Depending upon vows, the wicks have different sizes and also the thickness of the threads varies, and the minimum is to twine the string five times around the fingers, but many wicks are thicker. Thus, if the sacrifice is a gift to Shiva, the wicks can be made by twining five, nine, 11, 13, 16 or 21 times. The number seven is for ancestors and even Vishnu. Given the work burden behind a singular wick, the time it takes to complete a Lakh Batti ritual has no upper limits (Figure 1.11).

**FIGURE 1.11**   Lakh Batti along Bagmati River at Pashupatinath Temple, Nepal, 2022. Photo: Terje Oestigaard.

In 2022, one of the authors (Oestigaard) partook in a Lakh Batti ritual in Nepal. This year, Shivaratri, the main Shiva festival held at the Pashupatinath temple in Kathmandu, took place from midnight 1 March to midnight 2 March. This particular Lakh Batti ritual concluded a five-year cycle and as the last of five main fire sacrifices, it comprised of 150,000 wicks. It was said that if a skilled person worked efficiently, it is possible to make 200 wicks within an hour (twining 21 times), which means it takes 5 hours to make 1,000 wicks. Thus, 100,000 wicks take minimum 500 hours, and 150,000 wicks at least 750 hours, but in practice, it is difficult to work so hard and dedicated throughout the year, so it seems reasonable to estimate that only making the wicks had taken at least some 850–900 hours. Then, there were many other things that had to be done prior to the main sacrifice and fire ritual, which included arranging the pots whereby all wicks were soaked in sesame oil. Altogether, it seems reasonable to assume that by including all transport, arrangements and procurements in addition to the ritual part, the family members together had used at least 1,000 hours in preparations.

In 2022, it was estimated that there was about 1 million pilgrims and visitors coming to Shivaratri, and because of the crowd, priests came to the devotees' homes to bless and consecrate the Lakh Batti pots with wicks prior to the main event. Ideally, it should be done next to the fire altar where the pots are given, but during such big festivals, it is impossible in practice. Just before midnight, the family moved to Pashupatinath where they stood in a queue together with other pilgrims for about four hours. On Shiva's Night 1 March around 03.45, they reached the fire altar in front of the main gate at Pashupatinath and they cold lit the 150,000 wicks on the nine ceramic plates. Other devotees came with their Lakh Batti to the same altar, and each of the hundred thousand lights burnt for some two hours (Figure 1.12).

This is a very huge sacrifice and Shiva himself says that making a sacrifice to him on Shivaratri is very auspicious and greatly enhances the chances of receiving divine favours. By making such an offering, devotees may ask for wealth and health or prosperity in general. Thus, the ritual is mainly for the family members that have been devoted and dedicated and made so many personal sacrifices throughout the year. The real sacrificial value is not necessarily the presentation of the Lakh Batti itself, although important and a visual manifestation in front of the eyes of god, but the sacrifices behind and throughout the year while preparing the 100,000 lights.

Agnicayana and Lakh Batti are but two particular and extensive fire rituals in today's Hinduism, but they illustrate the depths and the pervasive role of fire in cult, culture and cosmology. They show us the presence of advanced rites, performed on a collective as well as an individual basis, and in both respects requiring great effort, resources and time. With fire as the means and medium, the Indo-European history gives testimony to innumerable rites that have been intrinsic to not only religion but, more fundamentally, to ecology and the ways living and livelihoods were parts of cosmology. The Indo-European fire rituals

**FIGURE 1.12**  Lakh Batti at the fire altar in front of the main entrance to Pashupatinath Temple, Nepal, 2022. Photo: Terje Oestigaard.

represent some of the most persistent and pervasive structures in history, precisely because of the role and importance of fire in all societies, and in particular in the cold north with long and dark winters. We will therefore start with the fires in homes and hearths.

## Contents

Chapter 2 analyses the European and Indo-European ethnography by discussing fire rituals and, in particular, the need-fire. Throughout Europe, the need-fire has been the most important and essential fire from the domestic hearth used to light the major bonfires. This was essentially a fertile fire and the production of this fire by friction has cross-culturally many associations to sexual intercourse. In the 19th-century folklore, there were still remnants of ancient Indo-European fire sacrifices. In remote regions in the southernmost part of Norway, daily and annual sacrifices were offered to the domestic fire on the farm. Food and beer were given to the hearth. The goddess or female ancestor embodying the fire and flames was called Eldbjørg (Eld = fire, Bjørg is a common female name). She was a wight and Mother of the farm. Also, there were remnants of a similar male spirit or ancestor, Eldgrim, and they seem to represent an ancient fire couple closely linked to the heart of the farm: the hearth. From Rome to Russia, the same beliefs are evident in the documented sources: the ancestor of the farm or the main deity lived in the hearth. Thus, fire rituals were intimately related to the ancestors and hence fertility and sexual associations, since they were links not only to the other world but also constituted the ancestral continuity and life forces from the cradle to the grave in agricultural societies.

Chapter 3 presents parts of the European ethnography and Indo-European fire rituals and traditions. Throughout Europe, the seasons of the year have been marked with elaborate fire rituals, and in particular the seasonal rituals focusing on the winter. There were four main seasonal and calendric fire rituals closely structured by the agricultural year: 1) the harvest rituals at the end of the summer and the beginning of the winter, 2) the midwinter sacrifice or the prehistoric jól at the darkest and coldest time of the year, 3) the ploughing and sowing rituals marking the end of the winter and the beginning of the summer and 4) the midsummer rituals with bonfires and fertility rituals structured around the life-giving waters in holy springs. This ethnography builds largely on 19th-century German folkloristic studies, like the works of Wilhelm Mannhardt and the Grimm brothers. In *The Golden Bough* (third edition 1906–1915, 12. Vols.), Frazer documented, synthesised and presented these major Indo-European traditions. We will contextualise the relevant rituals as an introduction and background to the archaeological material and funerary practices in Scandinavia.

Chapter 4 discusses parts of the archaeological material and cremation remains found in Scandinavia in general and Sweden in particular. From the Late Bronze Age onwards (ca. 1100 BC), cremation is the dominant funerary practice. The intensive use of fire and the mastering of heat can be seen in metallurgy and the smith's furnace, but cremation is first and foremost closely associated with cultivation and the fertility of the fields. Apart from fire regimes in agriculture clearing land for cultivation, a common feature throughout the millennia is finds of cremated human remains on the fields. Human bones have been scattered as part of agricultural rituals, and in many grave contexts grinding stones are found together with grains and crushed bones. In recent years, major archaeological contract excavations have documented contexts where grains and human bones have been made into bread and meals, which fit very well in the overall Indo-European tradition documented in later European and Scandinavian folklore. In an ancestral tradition, the fragmentation of the dead also puts emphasis on the unique characteristics of cremation as a funerary practice. In fact, it is not one, but many mortuary practices.

Chapter 5 analyses the Indo-European links between Europe and India in an ecological perspective. New results from aDNA research shed new light on this classic Indo-European issue, in which both descendants of the pastoral nomads on the steppe and the early farmers of Europe seem to play a role. Central to this scenario is that the Indo-European expansion takes place in different stages in a complicated process of East-West interaction drawn over a millennium or more. It is in this context that the ritual role of fire seems to be shaped hand in hand with the harsh living conditions and environments that characterised the early Indo-Europeans. The fundamental role of subsistence economies in the Indo-European traditions has structured historic developments from the first migration from the Pontic steppe – the area north of the Black and the Caspian Sea – 5,000–6,000 years ago. Whether settled agriculture, transhumance or nomadic pastoralism, throughout the millennia the winter season has defined large parts of wealth and well-being. Access to food and fodder have been critical resources during large parts of the year, and fire was the ultimate life-giver during the long, cold and snowy winters. Two pastoral cultures that may give clues to these historic developments are the early Iranians as well as the later Scythians in parts of central Asia. The Scythians were masters in metallurgy and the ancient Iranians developed particular concepts and religious practices around the purity of fire, which received their final form in Zoroastrianism. Given that the ancient Iranians share structural and cultural patterns with the Vedic civilisation, it creates a historic continuity between these Indo-European belief systems, but also to the much larger part of the Indo-European family.

Chapter 6 discusses Agni and the Vedic fire rituals. The worship of fire as a god (*Agni*) is central to Vedic religion. In the Vedic and Iranian view, fire is a substance that is active everywhere in cosmos. Fire is the fertile element in the cosmos; in the sky, in the storm and in the soil, and also in man and woman. Roughly one-fifth of the hymns in the *Rigveda* are dedicated to Agni – the god who personifies fire. Being a god himself, Agni is also the one who conveys the sacrificial gifts to the other gods. Vedic rituals are performed at different levels of complexity and in different contexts, from more mundane to highly elaborate ceremonies taking a long time to prepare and several days to complete, like the *agnicayana*. The divinities involved are Agni and Soma, in other words, fire and sacred fluid. The simplest ritual consists of a fire sacrifice to Agni (*agnihotra*). Three fires are needed: *gārhaptya*, the household fire, *āhavanīya*, the sacrificial fire, and *daksiṇāgni*, which is believed to give protection from evil. The Iranian fire ritual is in many respects like the Vedic complex. Thus, the sacred fire and the rituals surrounding it have defined large parts of cult and cosmology in different Indo-European cultural traditions.

Chapter 7 focuses on today's Hinduism and cremation as the dominant funeral practice. Cosmogony is the re-creation of the world, not only mythologically but also very concrete here and now. Cosmos is an ongoing process where cremation is a sacrificial act of destroying in order to create – exactly according to the pattern of the creation myth – and the fire also causes life-giving powers to flow. The body is essentially made of five elements – air, water, fire, earth and ether – and these elements also constitute cosmos. The cremation fire dissolves the elements to their cosmic origin from where they take new forms and life processes. Agni is not burning away the flesh of the body, but cooking it as a meal, which is given to the gods. The fire is life-giving, and the cremated ashes after the cremation are immersed in the holy water in the divine rivers. This last journey starts in Nepal and ends in Varanasi in India, which cosmologically is the holiest place not only in the Hindu world, but in the whole cosmos.

# 2

# HEARTS IN HEARTHS

## Ancestors and deities

## Food, fuel and family

'The domestication of fire has had far-reaching consequences, and it deserves to be ranked as the first great ecological transformation brought about by humans, followed very much later by two transformations of the same order. The emergence of agriculture and animal husbandry', Johan Goudsblom writes, and the uniqueness of fire compared to all other elements are remarkable: 'Humans could turn the destructive force of fire into productive use, and thus give it a purpose. The fact that fire is self-regenerating enabled them to preserve and reactivate it, something they could not possibly have done with either rain or wind' (Goudsblom 1992: 4–5). Fundamentally, our physical energy comes from two sources: food and fuel, and fire has been an important means in many food ecologies (Goudsblom 2015). In agriculture, fire rituals are intimately related to water and the right combination of water resources in relation to temperature. Hence, there is no wonder that symbols of fire and water are closely related (e.g. Bachelard 1968, 1988, 1994). Moreover, 'A person who sets a fire, who activates fire, magnifies but also controls and regulates the forces of the world' (Bachelard 1990: 69).

Agriculture is thus the key to understanding fire and water in relation to each other. The role of fire in seasonal rites and changing ecologies will be elaborated in Chapter 3; but before moving outdoor, we will stay indoors and put emphasis on the domestic fire in the hearth and cooking as a means and mediation of fire (Figure 2.1).

The analysis of cooking in anthropology has been associated with Lévi-Strauss and his works aiming to identify universals and the role of cooking in the evolution of humanity. His main argument is the role of fire in transforming food from raw to the cooked state, a process which he identifies with the emergence of humanity (Goody 1982: 17–18). From a structural point of view, Claude

DOI: 10.4324/9781003300915-2

**FIGURE 2.1** Reconstruction of a Viking hearth, Trelleborg Museum, Sweden. Photo: Terje Oestigaard.

Lévi-Strauss' analysed, in depth, the role of myths, the use of fire and cooking in his *Mythologiques, Vol. 1: The Raw and the Cooked* (1994), *Vol. 2: From Honey to Ashes* (1983), *Vol. 3: The Origin of Table Manners* (1990) and *Vol. 4: The Naked Man* (1981). In fact, following Lévi-Strauss in his 'A Short Treatise on Culinary Anthropology' from *The Origin of Table Manners*, cooking makes culture. In his discussion of the 'culinary triangle', Lévi-Strauss distinguished between three states: the raw, the cooked and the rotten. Cooking is a cultural transformation of the raw, and the rotten is a natural transformation. Hence, there is a double opposition between, on the one hand, the processed and the non-processed, and on the other hand, between culture and nature (Lévi-Strauss 1990: 478). Roasted being directly exposed to fire is non-mediated 'whereas boiled food is the product of a two-fold process of mediation: it is immersed in water and both food and water are contained within a receptacle ... The dividing-line between nature and culture ... places the roast and the smoked on the side of nature and the boiled on the side of culture, *in respect of means used*; and the smoked on the side of culture and the roast and the boiled on the side of nature, *in the respect of the results obtained*' (Lévi-Strauss 1990: 479–480, 490).

The role of food and cooking in constituting culture and cosmology is widely studied, and there is hardly a topic so heavily invested with symbolism and representations as food production and consumption, since food literally creates bodies and beings. By eating, everyone becomes and embodies the food; it creates identities and persona, and hence culture and cosmology (e.g. Caplan 1994;

Curtin & Heldke 1992; Goody 1982; Zimmerman 1982; Lupton 1996; Mintz 1996). Hence, given the pervasive role of fire and cooking in cult and culture, it is no wonder that the presence of pots and food is so essential in funerals as well (see Chapters 4 and 7). Goudsblom (1992: 7) also points out another important aspect of fire: '... the fire was always social: it could only be sustained by a group ... It was simply impossible to keep a fire burning for long without at least some social cooperation and division of labour in order to guard it and fuel it'. Throughout the Indo-European area, the social was not only a relation among the living, but the most important social relations constituted the inter-generational ties between the ancestors and the living – the dead and their children. Fire united the living and the dead.

## The need-fire and continuity through the winter

The fire festivals in Europe are of great age and probably some of the oldest continuous traditions existing on this continent. 'No account of the popular European fire-festivals would be complete without some notice of these remarkable rites, which have all the greater claim on our attention because they may perhaps be regarded as the source and origin of all the other fire-festivals; certainly they must date from a very remote antiquity' (Frazer 1913a: 269). Thus, Frazer points to the old Indo-European roots of these rites and fires, which have been known as need-fire. The origin of these fires seems to be pastoral societies with a focus on the health and wealth of cattle. In 1696, the method of kindling a need-fire was described in detail by Joh. Reiskius:

> When an evil plague has broken out among the cattle, large and small, and the herds have thereby suffered great ravages, the peasants resolve to light a need-fire. On a day appointed there must be no single flame in any house nor on any hearth. From every house a quantity of straw and water and underwood must be brought forth; then a strong oaken pole is fixed firmly in the earth, a hole is bored in it, and a wooden winch, well smeared with pitch and tar, is inserted in the hole and turned round forcibly till great heat and then fire is generated. The fire so produced is caught in fuel and fed with straw, heath, and underwood till it bursts out into a regular need-fire, which must then be somewhat spread out between walls or fences, and the cattle and horses driven through it twice or thrice with sticks and whips ... The poles that were used to make the need-fire, together with the wood that was employed as a winch, are sometimes burned with the rest of the fuel, sometimes carefully preserved after the cattle have been thrice driven through the flames.
>
> *Frazer 1913a: 271–272*

The need-fire was often called 'wild-fire' and was made by prolonged friction, and not by striking flint and steel. The size of the need-fires could vary significantly – from small sticks to large poles – and the inner heat and powers were ignited by a circling movement, usually involving ropes. Also, usually no other fire was allowed to burn in the village when the need-fire was kindled. Large need-fires on the continent were often made by oak and the bonfires kindled with this fire were composed of wood of nine different sorts. Need-fire could also be produced by the friction of nine different types of wood. In Scandinavia, the need-fire was named after the way it was produced, vrid-eld ('turned fire') or gnid-eld ('rubbed fire' or 'friction fire'). In the harsh northern conditions, most often these need-fires were small and literally a matter of life and death for people; in fact, among the Slavonic people, it was not called need-fire but 'living fire', highlighting the virtues of the fire (Frazer 1913a: 278–281).

In Wales, the hearth had a central place in the continuity of health and wealth, and this was an essential part of the fire. In the old days when women baked their bread in ovens heated with wood, the cleaning of the fire place afterwards was not only done meticulously but it was of fundamental importance that some of the wood ashes, together with a small charred stump, were left inside the oven. When the next fire was lit, it was this old stump and the wood ashes that were first ignited, and then new faggots were thrown into the oven and all burnt together. This practice had been done for generations, and hence the current baking-fires linked the fires from the past to the present (Trevelyan 1909: 33).

In a sense, this is a very practical and daily perpetual fire, and by using the charcoaled remnant from the last fire, it was a very direct way of keeping continuities back to time immemorial. Given that this practice and belief existed as late as the turn of the 20th century, it is reasonable to assume that this was a widespread tradition and common use of charcoal and fire in ancient times. Also, in practice, the perpetual fires were always latent and present even in hearths without fire, which puts emphasis on the ritualisation of these immanent forces in the wood itself. Wood and trees, in general, and oaks, in particular, contained embodied and immanent forces that could be incited and ignited.

## Eldbjørg and Eldgrim

In the Nordic ethnography, there are specific deities or spirits closely associated with or representing fire. In Norway, for instance, there seems to have been a particular fire sacrifice when children lost their milk teeth. The teeth were thrown into the fire followed by an utterance requesting Loke for new ones. Also, the skin of boiling milk was given to the fire and explicitly given to Loke. In the 19th-century documentation, it is uncertain whether Loke, the former Norse trickster-god, was living in the fire or the flames themselves were the deity (Figure 2.2). In the historic records, there is duality and ambivalence with regards to the fire as a mediator of the sacrifice or the actual recipient of the sacrifice. There is yet another spirit living in the hearth's flames, and that is Eldgrim or Ildgrim (*eld*, *ild* is fire). In many sources, he is presented as an ancestral spirit and even the founder of the farm, and as such, he should receive parts

**FIGURE 2.2** Depiction of Loke from the manuscript 'SÁM 66', Árni Magnússon Institute, Iceland. Public domain.

of everything that is cooked. The ancestral spirit should always taste everything first whether food or beer (Hauge 1965: 94–95).

In other sources, there is also evidence of a female ancestor or the mother of the lineage living in the hearth, namely Eldbjørg. In particular, in the lower parts of the Setesdalen Valley, the southernmost valley in Norway, the memories and traditions of Eldbjørg lasted well into the 20th century. Thus, together we have clear traces of an ancestral couple embodying and living in the fire – Eldbjørg and Eldgrim. The specific roles and characteristics of the male fire spirit and ancestor will be discussed later, and the Norwegian example of a female spirit and ancestor sheds new light on this unique cosmology literally at the heart of every household: in the hearth (Figure 2.3).

Although Eldbjørg demanded sacrifices throughout the year, she had a particular role in the preparation for Christmas. Whenever food was cooked, bread was baked, milk was churned and beer was brewed, everything was first given to Eldbjørg in the flames. If Eldbjørg did not taste first, it

**FIGURE 2.3** Inside a farmhouse in the Setesdalen Valley with the farmer having collected firewood. Painting by Olaf Isaachsen (1869). The National Museum, Oslo (NG.M.01177). CC-BY-NC.

could have devastating consequences for the members of the household and their well-being. When old women of the household gave small offerings to Eldbjørg, they said explicitly that the offering was to the wight. When screaming sounds from the water pot came just before the water started boiling, it was believed that it was Eldbjørg beating her children. From different places, there are stories about a mother with her children living in the hearth. As a guarding and ancestral mother, she had a prominent place in the most important rituals. Not only was it of utmost importance to first offer Christmas beer to the hearth, but the last day of Christmas was a celebration of Eldbjørg. Traditionally, Christmas ended on 7 January, alternatively called Knut's Day or the Eldbjørg Mess. This was also the day when the perpetual fire was saved and secured, and it was a celebration of the benevolent fire that would serve the household well in the coming year and do no harm to people and animals. Originally, the new fire was brought into the household on this day and everyone drank and proposed a toast in the honour of Eldbjørg (Olrik & Ellekilde 1926–1951: 254–259).

Also, in southern and western parts of Norway, Eldbjørg or the fire spirit served as an oracle prophesying about good and bad fortunes. The family members sat on the floor drinking beer, and afterwards they threw the bowl of beer behind their head. If the beer-bowl landed straight up, they would live the forthcoming year; otherwise, they would die. A more common tradition was to make a sacrifice to Eldbjørg and wishing for a prosperous year and that the fire would never extinguish the coming year (Celander 1928: 351–355).

There are yet other glimpses of the fire cult documented in rural ethnography. As late as the end of the 19th century, it is documented at several places that animals were slaughtered inside the farmhouse, not outdoor, with the exception of pigs. Oxen, cows and sheep were killed indoor in the farm's living room and the blood was collected in a bucket. Intriguingly, from southern Norway to Dalsland in Sweden and to Finland, there are evidences that this was not merely a profane slaughter, but indeed relics of ancient sacrifices. In Mandal, Norway, the animals' intestines were given to the fire, but in Søgne, the neighbouring area, blood was given to the hearth. In Sweden, a piece of the animal's meat was given to the flames, and in Finland, blood from the animal was given to the wight (tomten) who lived behind the stove (Lid 1923). Thus, here can be no doubt that the sacrifices were to the ancestral fire spirits living in the hearth: Eldbjørg and Eldgrim. While it seems certain that they were a couple and probably married, there is not much information about this hot relationship. The Scandinavian sources are silent about fire and sexual relations with regards to sacred marriages of the Indo-European fires, but this is a theme that is widely attested in classical sources from Italy to India.

## Marrying and merging Indo-European fires

The ways the fertilising and life-giving powers were culturally manifested and rooted in agriculture took numerous forms. On the one hand, there were numerous ways a sacred marriage between a human and the divine powers of vegetation or water took place, but on the other hand, in temples, the sacred marriage was the wedding of a bride as a virgin and fire as the divine bridegroom. This relates to the notion of the king's fire, because, in particular in early Latin kingship, the kings were seen as an offspring of mortal mothers and a fire-god. In Italy, the birth of Romulus himself was part of a flame like the male organ that hung over the hearth for days. Fire has also been seen as divine revelation and proof of royal genealogy and true kingship. In ancient Rome, Vesta was the goddess of the hearth and she personified more than any other deity the religious ethos of cult and culture (see Mueller 2004; Lorsch Wildfang 2006; Takacs 2008; Buchet 2019). Plutarch writes:

> [The Pontifex Maximus] was also the overseer of the holy virgins who are called Vestals. For they ascribe to Numa also the dedication of the Vestal Virgins and generally the care and worship of the inextinguishable fire which they guard, either because he considered the nature of fire to be pure and uncorrupted and so entrusted it to uncontaminated and undefiled bodies or else because he compared its fruitlessness and sterility to virginity. In fact, in all of Greece wherever there is an inextinguishable fire, as at

> Delphi and Athens, virgins do not have the care of it but women who are
> beyond the age of marriage.

*Plutarch, Numa 9.5*

From a comparative perspective focusing on fires and fertility rites throughout
the Indo-European region, Frazer is the scholar who provides the best ethnographic documentation. Following Frazer, the royal fire in the king's hearth
had to be ever-burning, and if it was extinguished, it was seen as a bad omen
that had to be expiated by sacrifices. In Rome, the sacred fires were tended by
virgins or priestesses of Vesta, called Vestals (Figure 2.4). These were unmarried

**FIGURE 2.4** Vestal virgins at an altar to goddess Vesta by Pieter Hendrik Jonxis, 1784,
Paris. Rijksmuseum, Amsterdam. Public domain (CC0 1.0).

women and, in many cases, it seems that these may have been the king's daughters (Frazer 1911a: 227–229). The Vestals had important functions in Rome's ceremonial life. Every year, pregnant cows were sacrificed to the Earth goddess, Tellus, in the so-called *Fordicidia*, a festival of fertility, on 15 April. In a bloody ritual, a calf was taken from its mother's womb after which the high priestess of Vesta burnt it and kept the ashes for further ritual use. Sacrificing a pregnant cow was a fertility charm enhancing the growth forces of both the seeds in the soil, sheep and cows. At the *Parilia* festival on 21 April, the ashes of the unborn calf were mixed with dried blood of a horse, which had been sacrificed in October, the Equus October, an animal sacrifice to Mars. The ingredients constituted the ritual substance *suffimen*, which was sprinkled on the bonfires of the *Parilia*, a festival devoted to purifying shepherds and their sheep ensuring their fecundity and a plentiful supply of milk (Frazer 1911a: 229; cf. Beard, North & Price 1998: 45–53). Frazer sees this ritual in light of ancient beliefs about fire-gods and the king's fire. 'Strange as at first it may seem to find holy virgins assisting in operations intended to promote the fertility of the earth and of cattle', writes Frazer, and continues, 'this reproductive function accords perfectly with the view that they were of old the wives of the fire-god and the mother of kings' (Frazer 1911a: 229).

There are yet other shadows of these Indo-European beliefs and practices. In many places, it has been a custom to lead a newly wedded bride three times around the hearth in her new home. On the one hand, this was obviously a way of introducing the new housewife to the ancestors who resided in the hearth's flames but there may also have been other fertility aspects involved, on the other hand. The ritual may have enabled the spirits to enter into her; being born again and various cultural aspects of this fertility charm are testified. In a similar way when a Slavonian bride enters her new house after being married, she is led three times around the hearth saying: 'As many sparks spring up, so many cattle, so many male children shall enliven the new home'. Fire rituals were also closely associated with water. In another South Slavonian tradition, 'When a wife wishes to have a child, she will hold a vessel full of water beside the fire on the hearth, while her husband knocks two burning brands together so that the sparks fly out. When some of them have fallen into the vessel, the woman drinks the water which has thus been fertilised by the fire' (Frazer 1911a: 232).

Following Frazer, there is an important homology between ancestors and fire-making, or more precisely how children are made, and he points out two important aspects. First, in many cultures, cross-culturally fire is seen as a child of the fire-sticks or the fire-drill. By rubbing the fire-sticks, a flame is born, and the parallels to sexual intercourse are clear. Moreover, the fire originating from within and female reproduction are also examples of innate growth. Second, wood, in general, or the ancestral tree, in particular, is the source fuelling the sacred fire, and hence life and death as living ancestors are immanent in the wood. These two principles or beliefs together give rise to numerous practices. The fire has been seen as male or female respectively, and one may also assume the fire-father was mainly associated with the male fire-sticks, whereas the fire-mother was intimately associated with the female sticks or the drill itself. The likeness to actual sexual intercourse makes this analogy very illuminating, and once perceived in this way, the life-giving properties and new births are constantly seen in flames and new fires (Frazer 1911a: 233–235).

> It is not hard to divine why the task of twirling the male fire-stick in the hole of the female fire-stick should by some people be assigned to married men. The analogy of the process to the intercourse of the sexes furnishes an obvious reason … As a virgin's womb is free to conceive, so, it might be thought, will be the womb of the female fire-stick which she holds; whereas had the female fire-maker been already with child, she could not be reimpregnated, and consequently the female fire-stick could not give birth to a spark.
>
> *Frazer 1911a: 239*

In practice, the wife of the household would rekindle lights and fires if needed, but there are also numerous stories and beliefs about the importance of perpetual fires. Keeping fires that never extinguish is obviously practical, but pragmatism cannot explain this alone. The possibilities to obtain a new fire without having to kindle it by friction seems to be an underlying structure in keeping a perpetual fire alive in villages. This could be the home and hearth of the village's headman, but there are also numerous stories in local farmsteads about always keeping the flames alive, particularly during the long and dark winter season (Frazer 1911a: 253–260). Thus, the ancient practice of leading the bride to the fire in the hearths originally seems to have been to make her fertile and to attain the generative virtues imbedded in the powers of the perpetual flames and fires. Also, bringing infants to the hearth has been a way of introducing and uniting the young ones with their ancestors.

In the *Grihya-Sutras*, another and more direct practice among the ancient Hindus is described. The bridegroom leads his wife around the fire saying: 'Mayst thou give back, Agni, to the husbands the wife together with offspring'. A very direct example seems to have been documented in temples, mainly in South India. Sometimes, a missionary was told, 'a scaffolding is erected over a fire. A man and a woman are got to copulate on it and allow the human seed to fall into the fire'. Alternatively, it may also relate to the more traditional beliefs that the fertilising virtues of the fire enter the woman; in practice, that she gets pregnant (Frazer 1911a: 230–231). This has to be seen in relation to *ojas*, or the source of the body's metabolic energy (Figure 2.5). This is the Jathara Agni, which is one of 13 types of fire in the body according to Ayurvedic philosophy: 'Only procreation is possible if it is expelled from the body, ejaculated during the sexual act. If it is retained within the body, stored instead of being wasted; the real creation becomes possible through ojas … Loss of semen means loss of ojas and thus loss of digestive powers' (Svoboda 1986: 260). As will be seen in Chapter 7, this cosmic

**FIGURE 2.5**  Sadhu conducing fire ritual at Pashupatinath, Nepal, 2003. Photo: Terje Oestigaard.

procreation is important in cremations with Agni's funeral fire as a vehicle and mediator, since a cremation is also a sexual union of cosmic and physical male and female elements. On the one hand, the ashes of the deceased after cremation are often referred to as 'bones' and they are the product of the father's semen, and hence a source of future fertility (Parry 1994: 188), and these 'bones' (or male semen) are immersed into the holy rivers and female waters, and hence new life may emerge. This has a parallel in another process, on the other hand:

> The semen is secreted from the food eaten. From the semen, the birth of another body is made possible. When the semen unalloyed is deposited in the vaginal passage during the prescribed period of cohabitation after the monthly menses, then the semen blow by the vital wind mingles with

the blood of the woman. At the time when the semen is discharged the individual soul with the causal body or unit of sense-organs etc. enters the vaginal passage fully covered and urged by its past actions. The semen and blood in the unified state become foetus in a day.

*Siva-Purana III, 22.14–16, p. 1542*

In Hindu temples, religious architecture and devotional iconography, there are many sexual expressions. It has been said that in the Hindu cosmology '[…] The entire world is based on the Linga. Everything is founded in the Linga. Hence, he who wishes for perfection of the soul shall worship the Linga' (Linga-Purana I, 73:6–7, p. 365). The Hindu mythology is full of sexual metaphors and stories about sex and violence (Doniger 1981, 1987). While this explicit language clearly defined gender relations and hierarchies, they were also expressive visualisation of cosmic and procreative forces. Shiva once said, 'O gods, O sages, you listen to my words with reverence. If my penis is supported in a vaginal passage there will be happiness. Except Parvati, no other woman can hold my penis. Held by her my penis will immediately become quiet' (Siva-Purana III, 12.45–46, p. 1300). Parvati – the Mother of the Universe – was stabilising the phallus by holding it and thereby creating welfare throughout the worlds. The linga and the yoni (female sexual organ) represent fire and water, respectively. Importantly, the linga or the male principle is '… the ontology of existence, placed on the yoni as its pedestal, [it] rises out of the yoni, the womb; it does not enter it' (Kramrisch 1981: 242–243).

Thus, the linga – the male regenerative organ or penis – is not prior to the womb or female principle, but arises from it (Figure 2.6). However, while the Mother is a priori and primordial, the control of female sexuality has been interpreted by male priests and pandits as ways of controlling Indra's tyrannical control of the rains, in particular, and the weather, in general. In certain temples, this has taken extreme forms, and if the Vestas have been seen as temple prostitutes in Italy, a similar tradition with temple prostitutes have been found in India. 'Although unchastity renders a woman impure, and thus unable to enter the inner sanctum or cook food, the sexuality of the courtesan is powerful for it combats the heart of asceticism. The sexuality of the courtesan ensures good rains and thus the prosperity of the realm' (Singh 1997: 149, see also Dubois 1899).

## Elements of life and death

While macro and micro cosmos constitute each other, it is only in Hinduism and classical antiquity that this thought has been fully elaborated into a coherent religious philosophy. In Hinduism, there are five elements with five substances or qualities: 1) firmament or aether with the quality of sound, 2) air with the quality of tangibility or touch, 3) fire with the quality of light and the property of various forms of colour, 4) water with the quality of taste and 5) earth with the quality of odour and smell. These elements and forces represent the nature

**FIGURE 2.6**  Linga with a dripping water bowl above, Pashupatinath, Nepal. Photo: Terje Oestigaard.

of the originator of creation, and hence it has a cosmogonic and creative force (Bhandar 1988: 8). As we can see, these five elements are in general agreement with the ancient Vedic beliefs, and thus also a clear heir to the common Indo-European creation myth where the elements correspond to the killed and dismembered primordial being. The elements are life-givers and that is why they are primeval; everything is made up of the elements. After death, new forms emerge from the same elements again and again, and as a result of death and transformations, these elements have the quality and the power to create new life: 'The ether, that is within and without the universe as well as that stationed in the bodies of living beings constitutes the powerful body of Siva [...]' (Linga-Purana II, 12:39–43, p. 647).

In death, at the moment life leaves the living, the eather, wind and lustre go upwards from the body whereas the water and earth go downwards where they get merged with their respective elements. In the very cremation, the fiery element of the body is united in the fire by the flames, air with air, the ashes are given to the water, etc. Turning from heaven to hell, there are various forms of punishment in Hindu notions of hell and the merging of elements are central in the penalties. In Hinduism, there are various descriptions of hell:

> Having their faces resembling cats, owls, frogs and vultures etc., they throw the man in cauldrons of oil and then light the fire. Some (are put) in frying pans, some in copper vessels, some others in cauldrons and others among sparks of fire. Some are placed on the tip of pointed pikes. Some are pierced in the Hell. Some are trashed with whips. Some are made to eat molten iron. The men are made to consume dust, excreta, blood, phlegm etc. and made to drink hot wine by the messengers of God of Death. The men are again pierced. They are tortured by mechanical devices and (the bodies are) eaten by crows etc. Hot oil is sprinkled over them and the head is pierced repeatedly.
>
> *Agni Purana IV, 371.24–28, p. 1039*

Turning from the East to the West, the pre-Socratic philosophers asked the question in the simplest form: What is the world made of? Thales said it was water or moisture, a substance available in three forms: solid, liquid or gas. Anaximander, a student of Thales, claimed that the primary substance was air because it is capable of being condensed into moist and water, and even further into solid substances like earth. The pluralists argued, on the other hand, that the four elements together constituted the ultimate and real world (Guthrie 1967: 25–29).

The pre-Socrates discussed which element or which combination of the elements was most basic to nature and cosmos (e.g. Allen 1966; Amaldi 1966). Even though there are traditionally four elements in the Greek philosophy, there is also a fifth element corresponding to the Hindu or Buddhist traditions. A passage from Philolaus says that 'there are five bodies in the sphere, the fire, the water, the earth, and air in the sphere, and the vessel of the sphere itself making the fifth' (Heath 1921: 158), and these are more to be understood of as elements in the universe than solid figures. The elements or the solids were, according to the Pythagorean school, mathematical figures. '*Pythagoras*, seeing that there are five solid figures, which are also called the mathematical figures, says that the earth arose from the cube, fire from the pyramid, air from the octahedron, water from the icosahedron, and the sphere of the universe from the dodecahedron' (Heath 1921: 159). Thus, the debate of which element was the most fundamental to nature was a scientific quest and mathematical task.

The elements could also merge together, like Heraclitus said: 'The death of fire is birth for air, and the death of air is birth for water' and 'For souls it is death to become water, for water it is death to become earth; out of earth water arises, out of water soul' (Kahn 1993: 47, 75). For Heraclitus, the world was constantly undergoing change and this universal condition was symbolised by water flowing in a river: 'You cannot step twice into the same river, for the waters are continually flowing on'. Similarly, fire was the most volatile of all things (Wheelwright 1959: 11, 30). Following Kirk,

> If, then, when the body dies the soul either becomes water or remains fiery, and becomes more fiery still, what is the factor which determines this issue? Clearly, the composition of the soul at the moment of death; the soul in life contains varying proportions of fire and moisture … if the amount of water at the moment of death exceeds the amount of fire, presumably the soul as a whole suffers the 'death' of turning to water: but if the soul is predominantly 'dry', then it escapes the 'death' of becoming water and joins the world-mass of fire.
>
> *Kirk 1949: 390*

The merging of elements was not only part of Western philosophy, but also included mythology and the divine world. Aristoteles seems to connect air with fiery aether or that air could be 'borne about' by winds and inhaled, and other philosophers equate aether and fire. Moreover, when 'the mystery cults contrast *aethereal* soul with the earth-born body it is safe to assume that the contrast is between the warm, bright aether of the soul and the cold, dark earth of the body' (Vlastos 1952: 118, fn. 94). Among the divinities, one may see similar unities and merges of elements. Zeus was fire, but cosmologically also aether (Scodel 1984: 19). The goddess Hera was sister-wife of Zeus, and, according to some of her mysteries, she united air with aether and aether with air, and also earth with water and water with air. This also resembles Heraclitus' philosophy where the elements where transmuted one into the other. The Aether of Zeus himself – the King of Gods and the sky and thunder god – was called 'the begetter of men and gods and Earth the mother of all' (Nilsson 1947: 174–175).

As will be seen later, the philosophy of the elements and the fundamental role of fire in this cosmogony are structuring cremation as a funeral practice in modern Hinduism (see Chapter 7), but one also finds many of the same elements in, for instance, Bronze Age Scandinavian cults and funerary practices (see Chapter 4). What is certain, though, is that the fluidity of the elements constituted not only the bodily juices, but also medical knowledge among scholars and scientists. A French doctor, for instance, said in 1788:

> I mean by this fire not a violent, tumultuous, irritating and unnatural heat which burns instead of cooking the bodily humors just as it does the foods; but rather that gentle, moderate, aromatic fire which is accompanied by a certain humidity having an affinity with that of blood and which penetrates the heterogeneous humors as well as the nutritious juices, separates them, wears them down, polishes the roughness and bitterness of their

several parts and finally brings them to such a degree of gentleness and refinement that they are adapted to our nature.

*op. cit. Bachelard 1968: 8*

While this is an elaborate and vivid description that perhaps was not shared by all, the bodily transmissions of fluids are essential in Hindu cosmology, which we will return to later. While the Scandinavian tradition cannot show a similar philosophy and cosmology structured around the elements and bodily fluids, they are still there albeit manifested and understood in distinctively northern ways.

## The elements in Scandinavia folklore

Johan Theodor Storaker (1837–1872) was a Norwegian teacher and collector of folklore who travelled across the country, and his premature death left a huge collection of documents that have been published posthumous mainly by the Norwegian folklorist Nils Lid. One of his most famous publications is *Naturrigerne i den norske folketro* (Approx: *The Kingdoms of Nature in Norwegian Folklore*, Storaker 1928), but another forgotten publication compiled by Nils Lid is *Elementerne i den norske folketro* (Storaker 1924), in English *The Elements in Norwegian Folk Beliefs*. While the four elements – air, fire, water and earth – were also a way of organising the documented ethnographic material, it is also clear that these elements represented real and constitutive life-worlds, and fundamentally what characterised these elements and materialities was first and foremost that specific wights or ancestors lived in these realms. Time and again, this is a theme that dominates the Nordic folklore. In the Norwegian tradition (e.g. Reichborn-Kjennerud 1928, 1933, 1940, 1944, 1947), the living dead and the ancestors manifested themselves in weather phenomena and as physical attacks on people from within and outside the body. Sickness was not a natural condition, but caused by magic, trolldom and malevolent ancestors and spirits. In Denmark too, concept about death, corpses and bodily fluids is heavily invested with qualities and inherent powers for the better or the worse (Troels-Lund 1900, 1984). Similarly, in Sweden many of the same perceptions are documented in-depth (Tillhagen 1977, 1984, 1989, 1991), and the shared cultural and cosmological strata of beliefs and practices is due to the common Indo-European heritage. The long historic trajectories are explicit and one has not to move far back in history to find traces of the Old Norse pantheon.

In the *Elements*, Storaker writes that Odin is explicitly a deity associated with flowing water, and, in particular, waterfalls, known as Fossekall or Fossegrim, where Grim is one of Odin's names. Loke, on the other hand, was the god of the fire and as with Eldbjørg, it was possible to hear when he was beating his children in the hearth. Also, Thor has been seen as the god protecting households and the hearth. Following folklore, fire originated from Thor's lightning, and therefore lighting would never harm a house where the fire was burning in the hearth or the stove (Storaker 1924: 79, 113, 126).

Storaker puts emphasis on two particular characteristics of fire: purification, on the one hand, and prophylactic and protective powers, on the other hand, and, in practice, they were intimately connected. These powers were central in all daily doings and matters. Everything that needed protection had to be blessed with fire. Water had to be carried in day time when it was light, because during the dark night dangerous beings and evil could follow the waters, but these malignant beings were warded off by putting a burning piece of charcoal into water bucket. Candles could also be used and evil was thrown away by using the fire or ashes from the stove. If food was made for workers outside the farmhouse, it was blessed and purified before taken outdoor (Storaker 1924: 87–89).

A particular feature having great relevance for understanding many prehistoric practices is the fact that the purificatory and protective powers of fire worked in objects *created* by fire. Although the heat from the pyre, fire or furnace was far away or had been extinguished a long time ago, the power of fire was still working in the objects because it was believed that they embodied and possessed the nature of fire. Thus, tare, gun powder and soothe, in general, had protective and purifying powers, but, in particular, objects made in fire were powerful (Figure 2.7). This included metal objects, but also pottery and even sherds from broken pots. The objects themselves were embodying powers because of the fire and they were, in practice, deified and active means against evil. Also, food contained extra powers, like bread, because not only was it made in oven, but also because barley, for instance, was a fertilising and life-growing seed. The powers lived on after its phase of production. Hence, horse-shoes protected the homes and cattle crossing iron were safeguarded from malignant beings and hostile forces. In the same vein, fire made by steel and flint was holier than ordinary fire, and this fire was called 'Kald-Eld' or 'Cold-Fire' (Storaker 1924: 96–99).

Even stronger and more holy than the 'Cold-Fire' was the need-fire, also having different names according to the way it was made ('turned fire' or 'rubbed/friction fire'). In Sweden, Gunnar Olof Hyltén-Cavallius (1863–68, I, §44) described how this fire was made in emergency cases, but it could not be called by its name, particularly not when making coal or tare. The fire was seen as a living being, but also as partly evil and dangerous because of its extreme powers. Hence, it was of importance to contain and control these mighty powers – on fields, in the hearth and the in smithy, and this could be done by tokens and sacrifices. The fire was almost always referred to as the 'heat'; 'beware of the heat'; 'borrow me heat' and so on. The most powerful need-fire was made in times of plagues and death, and it was made by turning a dry piece of oak clockwise (from the right to the left). Once ignited, the carrier of the fire shouted 'Gnideld! Gnideld!' (Rubbed fire! Rubbed fire!) when he came to new farms. Each household extinguished their old fires in the hearths and the new fire was lit by this holy fire made from the forces within the oak.

The role of fire in relation to death and ancestors is also seen explicitly in the prophesying role fire had in warning and predicting immediate and forthcoming

**FIGURE 2.7** Depiction of humans thrown in the furnace, 1907, Julita Gård, Sweden. Photo: Terje Oestigaard.

death. If one of the altar candles in the church extinguished during a wedding, it was a bad omen signalling that one of the couple would die. After extinguishing a candle that has been placed on top of a coffin, the direction of the smoke indicated who was next in line (Storaker 1924: 107–109). Not only fires, small or big, but also light in the sky was signalling forthcoming and sudden death. However, this was not ordinary light, but fire burning in the sky, sometimes in a clear manner, at other times with a cold and blue colour (Hagberg 2016: 32–34). Thus, from all of the Nordic folklore, the conclusion is the same: fire was intimately connected to powerful forces, ancestors and deities. Moreover, the presences of these powers and ancestors were unquestionable: these were reality. The dead was alive living with their heirs and descendants. But, this raises another question: how was the dead reborn and returning from death and the otherworld to the world of the living?

## Becoming ancestors and infants

The questions of how a baby is born and how the dead become ancestors are often seen as two separate questions, but, in fact, they are intimate and sometimes the same: how are ancestors born? Rebirth is often seen as identical to reincarnation, but a rebirth eschatology may take different forms. In the comparative study *Imagining Karma. Ethical Transformation in Amerindian, Buddhist, and Greek Rebirth*, Gananath Obeyesekere (2002) addresses this relation and develops new theoretical concepts and approaches enhancing the understanding of rebirth eschatologies and how rebirth and karma are interlinked. Obeyesekere distinguishes between three spheres. The main importance and difference is between what he calls 'ethicisation step 1' and 'ethicisation step 2', and then there is theoretically an otherworldly afterlife where nothing happens and in the world of ancestors they live their own lives without any rebirths. In other words, 'if the soul of a dead ancestor is brought back after death into the world of human association and this process is continued, one has a rebirth eschatology' (Obeyesekere 2002: 19).

If one starts with 'ethicisation step 1', Christianity serves as the prime example. The otherworld is split in two – a world of retribution ('hell') and a world of reward ('heaven'). Following the Christian thought, after death the dead rest in the grave and on Judgement Day God will send sinners to hell and the blessed to heaven. In practice, the dead are reborn to an eternal life in torments or divine pleasures. This is a very crude eschatology with only two options and otherworldly lives, and the consequences in the life hereafter are not correlated and fine-tuned to the deeds and doings in this life. In other words, how can limited good and evil in this life and world be rewarded with eternal salvation or damnation in the next and Otherworld? This is where 'ethicisation step 2' comes in and the theory of karma.

Karma depends upon ethicisation, which is a process by which 'a morally right or wrong action becomes a religiously right or wrong action that in turn affects a person's destiny after death', Obeyesekere says. Moreover, 'ethicisation deals with a thoroughgoing religious evaluation of morality that entails delayed punishments and rewards quite unlike the immediate or this-worldly compensations meted out by deities or ancestors' (Obeyesekere 2002: 75). The critical aspect of 'ethicisation step 2' is that the next rebirth is systematically reconditioned. 'If ethicisation is carried out to embrace the whole eschatological sphere constituting the otherworld (or – worlds), as well as the human world into which one is reborn, and if this is followed through into finite and infinite rebirth cycles, then one will have created a theory like that of karma' (Obeyesekere 2002: 82).

In practice, actions cause reactions and causes have consequences (Figure 2.8). Contrary to the Christian heaven and hell with immediate and absolute punishments of good and evil, in Indian religions immediate punishments are rare and never absolute or exhaustive. Any rewards or punishments are never totally fulfilled or completed, and there will always be some 'karmic' remains left; even the worst sinners suffering in hell have done some good things. Thus, even though there are 8.4 million (84 *Lakh*, an Indian unit equal to one hundred thousand) incarnations in Hinduism, even hell or the lower realms are temporary, and eventually even the worst sinner will be rewarded for the once good deeds committed, and hence gain a new and better reincarnation in upper realms.

**FIGURE 2.8** A devotee presenting a fire offering, Dakshinkali Temple, Nepal, February 2022. Photo: Terje Oestigaard.

That the lives in the lower realms are miserable is without any doubt. In the Agni Purana, for instance, there are descriptions of hells and the paths leading to Yama, the world of the God of Death and suffering: '(The lives) of doers of bad deeds (escape) through the anus and the organs of generation in the lower (region). The lives of yogins get out breaking the head by own will' (Agni Purana IV, 371.5, p. 1038). However, despite the filthiness, this is a temporary condition, and rewards will improve forthcoming incarnation, but this delayed process of rewards and penalties also creates physiological uncertainties, since a fortunate incarnation as a human today is no guarantee that incarnations in the lower realms are excluded (Obeyesekere 1968: 21).

If the Hindu rebirth eschatology and karma as the law of ethical recompense are the cosmic structures defining cremations and funerary practices on the Indian sub-continent today (see Chapter 7), and the Christian heaven and hell is an extreme version of 'ethicisation step 1', prehistoric concepts in Scandinavia and Bronze Age Europe are more difficult to identify. Not only a theoretical distinction between rebirth and reincarnation is lacking in research, but many of the interpretations of Bronze Age eschatology have been based solely on iconography and rock-art motifs. Given that the Bronze Age religion has rarely been seen as part of a proper Indo-European cosmology, many of the interpretations are rather speculative. As an example, Flemming Kaul argues strongly against reincarnation, but favours another rebirth eschatology. According to Kaul, the souls of the dead became part of the sun and are united in the celestial sphere whereby they shared the sun's destiny. The dead were the crew on the sun-ship's eternal journey on the sky and in the netherworld. The sun was dependent upon the dead souls and the dead souls were dependent upon the sun (Kaul 2005).

As will be seen in this analysis, there have never been such a sun cosmology in Indo-European religions, the Bronze Age included, although the sun was very important as part of agrarian practices, fertility rites and seasonal festivities (see Chapter 3). Moreover, if such a cosmological worldview existed, it cannot explain the pervasive ancestral cult. In practice, Kaul has created an otherworldly sphere for the dead totally separated from the lives of the ancestors: the ancestors live with the sun, not among the living, their families and as part of culture and society. All relevant comparative material and most archaeological sources testify to the contrary.

The question of an actual rebirth in Scandinavia is best illustrated by a story from the Icelandic *Flateyjarbók*. It tells about how the 9th-century King Olaf Geirstad-Alf or Olaf Elf of Geirstad was reborn as St. Olaf or Olaf II Haraldsson (c. 995–1030). While being buried in a mound, Olaf Geirstad-Alf instructed another Viking named Rane to open the mound and take the golden ring, knife and belt from him. The dead Olaf Geirstad-Alf was seated on a chair or throne in the middle of the mound, and he also instructed Rane to decapitate him whereupon he should put the head back on the corpse of the king. He was told to put the belt on the living queen Asta who had delivery problems. Following the instructions with regards to decapitating the king's head and giving the king's precious possessions to the queen, queen Asta gave birth to a strong boy who got the name Olaf. The boy received the sword Bæsing as a gift and he was now the old king reborn. He became St. Olaf.

This particular mythological story addresses a more fundamental problem not only about the role of ancestors and the possible destiny and rebirth after death, but also the relation to actual births and how a soul entered into the blood, bones and body of a baby in Scandinavian prehistory. A baby continues by definition two lineages of ancestors – the mother and father's sides – and hence comprises of a unique merge and marriage of two distinct genealogies of ancestors (Østigård & Kaliff 2020). The relation between the living and the dead was fluid and open, and, in particular, youngsters putting on masks during the main agricultural festivals became the ancestors, and the ancestors embodied the youngsters with masks (Kaliff & Oestigaard 2022).

The ethnographic record and earlier written sources are not giving a coherent picture of how ancestors and 'souls' were born. A cold and stiff corpse was certainly without heat and the inner fires characterising or giving life to the body. Also, the Norse concept of the human 'life-force' consisted of several distinctive features, which does not correspond to a 'soul' in the Christian or Hindu traditions, so it seems unlikely that the whole personality in its different forms was reborn in another human being. What is certain, though, is that the ancestors were alive and lived together with their heirs, and their home was primarily in the heart of the house: the hearth. Thus, we are back to the relation between fire and the sun, and all European ethnography is explicit with regards to the abode of the ancestors on farms and in homes; it was not in the sun, but a primary location was the fire in the hearth, and the Russian ethnography gives unique insights into this ancestral world.

## Domovoy – 'grandfather house-lord in the fireplace'

Domovoy is a central ancestral spirit living in the house and the hearth. In *Songs of the Russian People As Illustrative of Slavonic Mythology and Russian Social Life*, William R.S. Ralston (1872) gives a detail account of the Slavic perception of the house spirit. He has different appearances, and '[H]e is supposed to live behind the stove now, but in early times he, or the spirits of the dead ancestors, of whom he is now the chief representative, were held to be in even more direct relations with the fire on the hearth' (Ralston 1872: 120). In Galicia, it was believed that the souls of the dead haunted the hearths but there were also useful ancestors looking after the fields and the herds. Following folklore, Domovoy hide behind the stove all day, but when people were at sleep, he came forth and ate what was left or given to him. Wherever a fire was lighted, it was believed that Domovoy was present. Also, when hot water was thrown away, the ancestor was warned so he was not scalded and, in the same vein, people avoided to pass the night in a corn kiln because Domovoy could strangle the intruder. Although he is often described as having a human form or body, appearing as the proprietor of the house and even wearing his clothes, another embodiment was as a snake (Ralston 1872: 121–124). The house-spirit was generally benevolent, but he could also be angry and hot-tempered. While these are quite common characteristics of living ancestors, Ralston points out that the most peculiar aspect of Domovoy is the fire rituals associated with moving to a new house and making a new hearth. He elaborates:

> After everything movable has been taken away from the old house, the mother-in-law, or the oldest woman in the family, lights a fire for the last time in the stove. When the wood is well alight she rakes it together into the *pechurka* (a niche in the stove), and waits till midday. A clean jar and a white napkin have been previously provided, and in this jar, precisely at midday, she deposits the burning embers, covering them over with the napkin. She then throws open the house-door, and, turning to the 'back corner', namely to the stove, says, 'Welcome, *dyedushka* (grandfather) to our new home!' Then she carries the fire-containing jar to the courtyard of the new dwelling, at the opened gates of which she finds the master and mistress of the house, who have come to offer bread and salt to the Domovoy. The old woman strikes the door-posts, asking, 'Are the visitors welcome?' on which the heads of the family reply, with a profound obeisance, 'Welcome, *dyedushka*, to the new spot!' After that invitation she enters the cottage, its master preceding her with the bread and salt, places the jar on the stove, takes off the napkin and shakes it towards each of the four corners, and empties the burning embers into the *pechurka*. The jar is then broken, and its fragments are buried at night under the 'front corner'.
>
> *Ralston 1872: 137–138*

Thus, the fire is physically transferred from the old hearth to the new one. Domovoy was closely associated with protection and pastoralism, and people said: 'Dĭdŭska Domovoy, come and live with us and tend our flocks' (Máchal 1918: 241). In *The Mythology of all Races. Volume III. Celtic-Slavic*, Jan Máchal describes the same ritual in a slightly different way:

> Rites of a peculiar character are observed in case of removal into a newly built house. Before entering, the members of the family throw a cat, a cock, a hen, etc., inside, or on the threshold of the new home they cut off the head of a hen and bury it below the first corner of the room; while the first slice of bread cut during the first dinner is buried in the right-hand corner of the loft with the words, 'Our supporter, come into the new house to eat bread and to obey your new master'. If the family moves into a new home, they never forget to take their Domovoy with them, and for this purpose they proceed in the following way. An old woman heats a stove in the old house and scrapes the cinders out upon the fender, putting these at noon into a clean pan and covering it with a napkin. Opening the window

and turning toward the corner of the room where the oven stands, she invites the Domovoy to come into the new house, after which she takes the pan with the coal into the new home where, at the open gate, he is awaited by the master and the mistress with bread and salt in their hands. Bowing low, they again invite him into the new dwelling, and the old woman, with the master of the house, first enters the room, carrying bread and salt in their hands. The old woman puts the pan by the fireside, and removing the cloth, shakes it toward all the corners to frighten away the Domovoy and then empties the coals into the oven, after which the pan is broken in pieces and buried below the front corner of the room.

*Máchal 1918: 243–244*

The role of Domovoy or the Slavic god of the household as the deified progenitor of the kin sheds lights on prehistoric practices and beliefs shrouded in mystery and darkness. In his study of Slavic beliefs from 1918, Jan Máchal also presents various depictions of Domovoy. He is reported as being an old man with wrinkled face but having the size of a five-year-old boy. He could be portrayed and modelled as small clay statuettes that were kept inside the house in niches near the door or over the ovens, but Šetek or Skřítek, the Bohemian version of this father spirit, was portrayed in a more frightening and scary way (Figure 2.9). Although the Slavic people believed that the souls of fathers watched over their children and heirs, throughout the centuries the ancestral spirits became demonised and seen as 'unclean dead' or cursed by God. In particular, the Bohemian version of Domovoy, Šetek or Skřítek was demonised by the Church, and in his Christian representation he was portrayed as a hellish hobgoblin (Aveela 2018). This relation between the ancestral fire spirit or the 'Grandfather House-Lord in the fireplace' and the devil is intriguing, because it supports interpretations that parts of the Christian demonology and eschatological developments of hell were built, in fact, on existing Indo-European fire traditions and existing beliefs. Without the Indo-European heritage of fire and ancestors living in the hearth, the Christian concepts of hell would most likely have taken other forms, since the particular characteristics of the Christian hell is without parallels in any comparative religion.

## The devil and a royal fire

The answer to this puzzle is, in fact, found in the Bible, but not in God or Jesus, but the Devil. The Codex Gigas, also known as the Devil's Bible, is famous for two reasons; it is the world's largest preserved Bible from the medieval area – it is 92-cm long, 50-cm wide and 22-cm thick with a weight of 75 kg – but even more remarkable is the fact that it contains a full portrait of the devil. It contains of 310 leaves and the Devil is portrayed on page 577. According to a legend, the Bible was written by a monk who had broken his monastic vows. Being sentence to be walled up alive, he made an offer to create a book within one night that

**FIGURE 2.9**  Šetek. From *The Mythology of all Races* Vol. 3, facepage 244.

would glorify the monastery forever, but this was a task beyond any human capacity, so he made an ally, not with God, but Lucifer in exchange of his soul. The Devil completed the book as promised and the monk included a picture of the Devil in gratitude. Probably more historically, the Codex was created in the early 13th century by the Benedictine monk Herman the Recluse, in Podlažice monastery in today's Czech Republic. By the end of the 16th century, the Bible was part of the Habsburg ruler Rudolph II's collection, but during the siege of Prague at the end of Thirty Year's War (1648), the Codex was taken as war booty by Sweden and brought to Stockholm. In 1697, the royal castle in Stockholm caught fire and much of the royal library went up in the flames, but the Codex Girgas was thrown out of the window, and hence the Bible and the Devil was saved. Today, the Bible is at display in Stockholm at the National Library of Sweden.

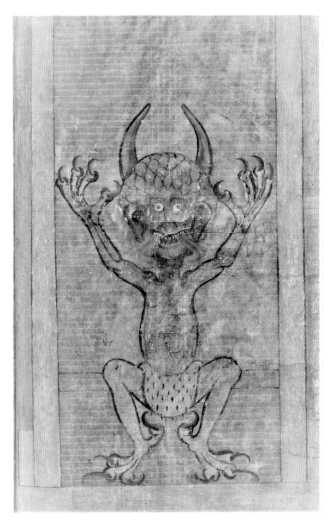

**FIGURE 2.10** The Devil in Codex Girga. Library of Congress, World Digital Library. Public domain.

The devil depicted in Codex Girgas is the Bohemian version of Domovoy, namely Šetek or Skřítek (Figure 2.10). Max Weber once pointed out that the early Christians perceived the rustic as the heathen (paganus) and historically the Church has always looked down upon peasants living in rural areas whereas religious thinking took place in churches and monasteries in urban areas (Weber 1964: 83). The word 'heathen' or *heiðinn* has an uncertain origin, but it may refer to 'homely' or the inherited religious tradition (Steinsland 1997: 14). And, at the heart of this homely tradition was the hearth and the fire, and the ancestral traditions that lived on for centuries despite Christianisation and urbanisation on the European continent. The homely fire spirits and ancestors contradicted everything the church preached and practised; not only was there a heritage of the living dead existing together with their heirs and descendants, but they were also believed to be more important and powerful than the Christian god in most matters that concerned the lives and livelihoods of farmers: the fertility of the field and good harvest. The seasonal rituals that ensured this prosperity were basically fire festivals in all their glory. It is no wonder why the Church perceived this fire and their main protagonists as hellish and devils, but the Indo-European traditions had throughout the millennia proved to be more successful and powerful than even the almighty god, who did not intervene in the farmers' seasonal rites and preparations for bountiful harvests.

In fact, some of humanity's earliest rituals seem to have originated in connection with the use of fire (Staal 1983: 19). Since Palaeolithic times, it has been one of the most important tools for human survival, shaping human culture as we know it. It gave humanity an opportunity to survive in environments where this would otherwise not have been possible, and fire enabled opportunities to prepare food in unprecedented ways maximising the nutrient content. In cold climates, the fire was not allowed to extinguish and the protection and powers of the flames were divine matters. Man had to preserve it carefully. This long period of time, in particular during the winter, human care for fire was a central element – perhaps the most important – in cult and culture, and it has undoubtedly shaped the view of life in profoundly fundamental ways. The focus on the preservation of fire, and the transport of it over long distances as part of a nomadic life, therefore came to shape some of the oldest rituals that are preserved. 'It is not far-fetched to suppose that man's sense of continuity was inspired by his experience with fire. When man at last discovered how to make fire himself, he continued to take extreme precaution to preserve and transport it … It is not surprising that fire and life were connected at an early stage, and that the preservation of fire came to be regarded as the preservation of life' (Staal 1983: 78).

Thus, the Indo-European fires have been fundamental in the constitution of culture and cosmology. 'Before there was Europe, there was fire', says Stephen J. Pyne and continues: 'In truth, civilization was impossible without fire; and the tended fire became Western civilization's most elementary emblem of itself. In their symbiosis, fire and civilization each took on the attributes of the other' (Pyne 1997: 3–4). The Indo-European civilisations developed in unique ways because of the ways fire and water constitute agricultural cultures and cosmologies.

# 3

# SEASONALITY AND FIRE FESTIVALS

## The agricultural seasons and challenges

Throughout European history, farmers and pastoralists have at all times kindled bonfires at specific dates. Bonfires in the rural world were always part of the seasonality and the farmers' world of soughing, ploughing and harvest – and the cattle and pastoral livelihoods. It is impossible to understand the pervasive and fundamental role of fire in Indo-European traditions without understanding the ecological, environmental and economic contexts of the people conducting these rituals, and that is the agricultural world.

The winter and weather defined lives from the cradle to the grave, because if the harvest failed and the husbandry died, the immediate result was absolute and without mercy; hunger, famine and possible death. The length of the growth season was the fundamental parameter (Charpentier Ljungqvist 2015, 2017; Huhtamaa 2018; Huhtamaa & Helama 2017), because a delayed spring with late snowfalls or early night frost in the autumn could wreak havoc on any harvest. In a similar vein, too little or too much rain or sun at the wrong time of the year could jeopardise the year's supply of food and consequently threaten the lives and livelihood of humans and animals alike (e.g. Tvedt 2016, 2021). Thus, the cultural and cosmological challenges were at least twofold: on the one hand, a fundamental challenge in agrarian societies was the continuity between the seasons and how the growth and life-forces from one season were transferred to the next through the cold, desolate and barren winter (e.g. Nikander 1916; Celander 1920; Lid 1928). On the other hand, another challenge was the ways and means by which humans could engage, incite and partake in controlling these cosmic flows of forces defining large parts of cult and culture in practice (Lid 1933: 39–40; Kaliff & Oestigaard 2020: 294–295; Oestigaard 2021a, 2021b). Fire was the most essential means and methods since it was directly related to the growth forces and the sun's role and function in agriculture in relation to water.

DOI: 10.4324/9781003300915-3

Thus, the agricultural world of humans and animals determined the lives and livelihoods – and, in this rural life-world, fire festivals created continuity and wealth. As the following presentation of the European fire festivals will show, they were intimately structured around the agricultural season and the pastoral cycles, which may explain the relation and difference between the various fire festivals in Europe. Given that the ecology differs as well as two millennia of Christian influences have impacted on the original Indo-European traditions in various ways, it is nevertheless remarkable how persistent these agro-ritual beliefs and practices have been. It is a testimony of the fundamental role that agriculture and subsistence strategies for living and surviving have played in structuring and defining culture and cosmology (Figure 3.1).

Agriculture and many divinities and ancestors work the same way in practice; it is about procreation and enabling and controlling vital life- and growth forces. Fire was instrumental in these daily and divine processes, and broadly one may differ and identify two ecological and ritual traditions. On the one hand, there are fire festivals in relation to the cycle of the sun and its solstices – midwinter and midsummer – and the equinoxes – spring and autumn. In practice, these rituals are largely defined by the winter and the agricultural season of sowing (spring) and ploughing and harvesting (autumn). On the other hand, in the Indo-European traditions there are also major festivals around 1 May and 1 November, which are not related to the agricultural season of fields and harvests. These were the defining days in the pastoral world when the animals were brought out from the barns after a long winter and when they returned back home to the farms after a long period of summer grazing. Whether pastoralism, transhumance and agriculture, the major fire festivals were fundamentally

**FIGURE 3.1**  Agrarian fertility ritual and ploughing. Aspeberget Tanum Bohuslän, Sweden. Photo: Åsa Fredell, 2002.

*Source*: www.shfa.se.

linked to the agro-pastoral world. Without these rituals, the health and wealth of humans and animals were at risks. Fire was a means for fertility and protection.

## The Midwinter fires

If the sun reached the highest climax on the celestial vault on Midsummer Eve before starting declining and descending, at Midwinter, the bottom was reached and time and the sun stood still at the darkest and coldest time of the year before the sun slowly started returning and gaining strength. Both the light and the temperature were in stark contrast to each other and although it was the same sun, the processes at work were fundamentally different. The historic Scandinavian Christmas celebration or prehistoric *jól* was a time of great midwinter sacrifices (Figure 3.2). The solstice at the darkest time of the year was a dangerous time and, from time immemorial, it seems that this was not only the most important ritual time of the year (see Kaliff & Oestigaard 2022), but also that the pre-Christian winter festival and sacrifice were complex celebrations of ancestors and the dead, farming and fertility, and the return of the sun by overpowering hostile and malevolent cosmic forces (Wegelius & Wikman 1916). During celebration of the ancestors (e.g. Feilberg 1904) or the agrarian and fertility rituals (e.g. Celander 1928, 1936, 1955; Nilsson 1936), fire was the fundamental agent and mediator.

Frazer says that it has been long established that 'the Yule log was only the winter counterpart of the Midsummer bonfire, kindled within doors instead of in the open air on account of the cold and inclement weather of the season' (Frazer 1913a: 247). However, despite important similarities, there were also

**FIGURE 3.2** Section of 'Midwinter sacrifice' by Carl Larsson (1915). The National Museum, Stockholm. Public domain.

significant differences in recent times. While the Midsummer bonfires were public spectacles outdoor, the winter celebrations indoor were primarily private or domestic festivities around the hearth in the house. During pre-Christian times in Scandinavia, there can be no doubt that important rituals were conducted outdoors. At the same time, it is clear that Yule, in particular, was a festivity where central elements were traditionally performed indoors. Celebrating Yule outdoors was perhaps seen more as an anomaly. In *Haraldskvæði* (Hrafnsmál 6), it is said about the Norwegian king Harald Fairhair: 'He will drink Yule at sea if he decides the matter' and not be 'bored from youth, by fireside basking, indoors sitting, with ladies' warm bower and wadded downy mittens' (Snorri 2011: 65). It is difficult to say anything certain about the size of outdoor pyres in the winter and the scale of these rituals, but as seen in Chapter 2, major rituals and sacrifices were held indoor. Most animals, even horses and oxen, were sacrificed inside farms and in royal halls with blood being spilled on walls and in the heart of the home: the hearth. This puts emphasis again of the hearth and the domestic fire, and from the perspective of seasonal fires, the continuity of the fire and the notion of a perpetual fire were fundamental in securing continuity between the seasons and keeping the forces of regeneration alive, especially during the cold and dark winter.

Since the hearth was the heart of the house, the Yule-log was a foundation in the household's life and well-being throughout the long and difficult time. The laying of the new log as the foundation of the hearth and health was pivotal. In Germany,

> A heavy block of oak-wood, generally a stump grubbed up from the ground, is fitted either into the floor of the hearth, or into a niche made for the purpose in the wall under the hook on which the kettle hangs. When the fire on the hearth glows, this block of wood glows too, but it is so placed that it is hardly reduced to ashes within a year. When the new foundation is laid, the remains of the old block are carefully taken out, ground to powder, and strewed over the fields during the Twelve Nights. This, so people fancied, promotes the fruitfulness of the year's crops.
>
> *Frazer 1913a: 248*

Moreover, this fire and the ashes from the Yule-log had special qualities. 'In some villages near Berleburg in Westphalia the old custom was to tie up the Yule log in the last sheaf cut at harvest' (Frazer 1913a: 248). Moreover, it was generally believed that the ashes from the last parts of the log protected the house against thunder and lightning, but also fire, burglary and other misfortunes. If the ashes were mixed with water, it was also believed to have vital medical qualities. In some cases, the ashes were also used by the ploughman in spring because this process caused the seeds to thrive and grow (Frazer 1913a: 248–251). In many parts of Wales, parts of the old Yule-log were kept until the next Christmas for 'good luck'.

> It is then put into the fireplace and burnt, but before it is consumed the
> new log is put on, and thus 'the old fire and the new' burn together … in
> the past the observance of this custom was to keep the witches away, and
> doubtless was a survival of fire-worship.
>
> Trevelyan 1909: 28

The Yule-log was often a young oak tree cut down by young men, sometimes
before Christmas. In Herzegovina and Montenegro, it was custom to cut the tree
on Christmas Eve, which usually was an evergreen oak, but sometimes an olive
tree or a beech. The belief that the Yule-log kept throughout the year protected
the household against fire and especially lighting seems to relate to old Indo-
European beliefs about oak trees being associated with the god of thunder and
lightning (Frazer 1913a: 263–265).

While we have mainly focused on rituals and ecologies north of the Alps
with long and cold winters and an agricultural summer season with rain, the
Mediterranean climate is opposite with dry summers and wet winters. If the
cold climates in the north favoured indoor festivals and sacrifices, in the city of
Agnone in the Molise region, not far from Rome, one of the oldest fire festivals in the world sill existing today is a collective celebration performed on 24
December. It is called *'Ndocciata'* from *'ndocce'* – torches – and in the Christmas
procession, enormous torches are carried through the city (Domenico 2002:
227). Originally, it was an ancient rite celebrating the winter solstice and the
torches were put together by men in groups of two, four, six, eight and up to 20
wearing ancient costumes. The tradition goes back to the Samnite tribe and it
belongs to the Indo-European era before Christianity, but it is striking that this
pagan fire festival has lived in parallel with Christianity, given that the Vatican
and the heart of Catholicism are literally next door.

## The Lenten fires

In Belgium, the north of France and many parts of Germany, there was a custom of kindling bonfires on the first Sunday in Lent. In Belgium, for a week or
a fortnight before the 'day of the great fire', children went from farm to farm
collecting fuel. If anyone refused the request, the children would come back the
next day trying to blacken the farmer's face with ashes from an extinguished fire.
If a village should be protected from conflagrations, seven bonfires had to be lit,
and if snow and ice were still covering the fields, the fires were lit on the frozen
land. The pole set up in the middle of the pile was also called 'the witch' and the
fire was kindled by the last married man in the village. In many villages, it was
custom to sing and dance around the bonfire and leap over the fires to ensure
good harvests and happy marriages in the forthcoming year (Frazer 1913a: 107):

> [...] girls thought that by leaping over the fires without being smirched
> they made sure of a happy marriage. Elsewhere in order to get a good

husband it was necessary to see seven of the bonfires from one spot. In Famenne, a district of Namur, men and cattle who traversed the Lenten fires were thought to be safe from sickness and witchcraft. Anybody who saw seven such fires at once had nothing to fear from sorcerers. An old saying ran, that if you do not light 'the great fire', God will light it for you; which seems to imply that the kindling of the bonfires was deemed a protection against conflagrations throughout the year.

*Frazer 1913a: 108*

In the Ardennes, it was also the last married person who kindled the fire whether a man or a woman. This person was called the master of fire. In this fire, cats used to be burnt or roasted to death by being held over and while the animal was burnt, shepherds drove their flocks through the smoke and flames to ensure that their herds were protected against witchcraft, malignance and other sicknesses. It was also believed that the livelier the dance around the fire, the better the harvest would be (Frazer 1913a: 109).

The explicit fertility aspects of the fire rituals were evident in many places in France. When the pyre was half burnt, the farmers kindled torches at the expiring flames and brought them to their fields, gardens and fruit trees. 'In some villages the people also run across the sown fields and shake the ashes of the torches on the ground; also they put some of the ashes in the fowls' nests, in order that the hens may lay plenty of eggs throughout the year ... Here the application of the fire to the fruit-trees, to the sown fields, and to the nests of the poultry is clearly a charm intended to ensure fertility' (Frazer 1913a: 112). This, Frazer interprets, is a way of directly supplying the fields with the sun's heat, but he also highlights another aspect. The fire was not primarily intended to stimulate growth and reproduction but to burn away and destroy evil or all malignant forces threatening the growth of crops and the fertility of animals, whether these came in the shapes and bodies of vermins or witches. In agricultural rites, it is therefore difficult to clearly separate and identify the Solar theory and the Purificatory theory (Frazer 1913a: 112–113).

Thus, in any fertility rites, there are at least two processes at work. On the one hand, it is to incite and activate the positive, fertile and life-giving qualities; but on the other hand, and in many cases equally important, it is to combat and kill the malevolent, destructive and dangerous forces threatening life. The latter included not only spiritual and malevolent ancestors but also very practical termination of pests, rats, mice, darnel and smut. In practice, the use of torches and ashes could fulfil both purposes, and the difference was not necessarily so important, since procreative fertility forces could not blossom by itself. If they were attacked by physical or spiritual enemies and hostile powers, the growth powers would wane.

In the Eifel Mountains in Germany, on the first Sunday before Lent, young people went from house to house and collected straw and small wood. The direction the smoke blew from the pyre was a sign of plenty and prosperity, and the specific corn fields the smoke went towards were believed to indicate an abundant harvest. On the same day, a great wheel was made of straw and three horses dragged it to the top of a hill. At nightfall, young boys set fire to the wheel and let it rolling down the slope (Frazer 1913a: 116). In Tyrol, a human figure was fastened in the top of the tree of the pyre. This figure, made of old clothes and stuffed with gun powder, was called the 'witch'. At night, the spectacle was set on fire and boys and girls danced around it and sang rhymes, which included the strophe 'corn in the winnowing-basket, the plough in the earth'. In Swabia, this person was explicitly referred to as the 'old wife' or 'winter's grandmother'. She was fastened to the pole and also this figure was seen as a 'witch'. At the same time as the witch or the old forces of the winter were burning, young people threw blazing discs into the air. These discs were round pieces of wood measuring a few inches in diameter. The edges were notched and imitated the rays of stars and the sun. In the middle of the disc, it was a hole and the disc was attached to a wand, often made of hazel. The disc was thus set on fire and flung into the air. The burning disc flies in the air in a lengthy fiery curve before it reaches the ground; they were like a continual shower of falling stars. This was popular among the youngsters and a single person could throw 40 or 50 burning discs into the air during a night, and the discs should be thrown as high as possible. Importantly, 'The charred embers of the burned "witch" and discs are taken home and planted in the flax-fields the same night, in the belief that they will keep vermin from the fields' (Frazer 1913a: 117).

Similarly, in the Rhön Mountains on the borders of Hesse and Bavaria, a wheel wrapped in combustibles was kindled and rolled down the hills followed by young people running to the fields with burning torches and brooms. It was said that the purpose was to 'drive away the wicked sower'. In the neighbouring region, it was believed that the fields where the burning wheels rolled on were safe from hail and storm. In some regions, it was not only wheels made of straw but also old proper wheels that was covered in straw.

> The more bonfires could be seen sparkling and flaring in the darkness, the more fruitful was the year expected to be; and the higher the dancers leaped beside or over the fire, the higher, it was thought, would grow the flax.
>
> *Frazer 1913a: 119*

These bonfires on the first Sunday in Lent where an effigy was burnt has to be seen in relation to the ceremony 'Carrying out Death' or the 'Burying of Death' (see also Kaliff & Oestigaard 2022). In Central Europe, 'Being condemned to death, the straw-man is led through the village, shot, and burned upon a pyre. They dance round the blazing pile, and the last bride must leap over it. In Oldenburg on the evening of Shrove Tuesday people used to make long bundles of straw, which they set on fire, and then ran about the fields waving them, shrieking, and singing wild songs. Finally they burned a straw-man on the field …' (Frazer 1913a: 120). The relation between the sacrifice of infertile forces and the forthcoming prosperity and harvest is seen in the effigy being called 'witch', 'old wife' or 'winter's grandmother'. This image has clearly been incorporated in Christianity and it shows what was at stake: getting rid of the ultimate evil.

## The Easter fires

Fire festivals were usually held on Easter Eve or the Saturday before Easter Sunday. In Catholic traditions, it was custom to extinguish all lights in the churches and then make new fires. Sometimes, this was done with flint and steel; at other times, by a burning-glass. This fire was used to lit the Easter candle, and the latter fire was used to lit all the other lights in the church. In Germany, there was also a tradition at many places to kindle a bonfire outside the church on a nearby open space. The fire was consecrated and people brought sticks of oak, walnut and beech, which were charred in the fire. These charred sticks were brought home by the peasants and some of them burnt in a new fire together with prayers to God that the farms should be protected from fire, lightning and hail. From this newly erected fire of charred sticks, every house received a 'new fire'. Some of the sticks were placed in the fields, gardens and meadows with wishes of a good and prosperous year saved by God from blight and hail (Frazer 1890b: 251). These fields and gardens were believed to throve and be more fertile than others and not harmed and attacked by vermin, mice or other pests. Intriguingly, 'The charred sticks are also applied to the plough. The ashes of the Easter bonfire, together with the ashes of the consecrated palm branches, are mixed with the seed at sowing. A wooden figure called Judas is sometimes burned in the consecrated bonfire' (Frazer 1890b: 252).

In Germany, the bonfires were blazing simultaneously and as many as 40 fires could be seen together.

> It is a fine spectacle to watch from some eminence the bonfires flaring up one after another on the neighbouring heights. As far as their light reaches, so far, in the belief of the peasants, the fields will be fruitful, and the houses on which they shine will be safe from conflagration or sickness … people used to observe which way the wind blew the flames, and then they sowed flax seed in that direction, confident that it would grow well.
>
> *Frazer 1913a: 140*

Remains from the bonfires were used to protect houses from being struck by lightning. The ashes were believed to increase fertility and also to chase away mice, and when mixed with the cattle's drinking water, the animals thrived and they were protected from plagues. When the flames of the bonfires died down, young and old alike leaped over them, and even cattle were sometimes driven through the glowing remains and charcoaled woods (Frazer 1913a: 140).

There were different beliefs and practices associated with the bonfires. Many of the rituals surrounding the Easter fires also involved rolling down fires on wheels from the mountain sides and throwing discs up in the air. In the Harz Mountains, squirrels were burnt in the Easter bonfire; at other places, bones were burnt. The ashes after the bonfires were often collected by old folks who preserved and used them as a remedy for the ailments of bees. In Upper Franken, they also burnt a straw-man called Judas, as a clear sign of how a superficial transfer to Christian tradition has been made, without the symbolic meaning having changed significantly. 'The whole village contributed wood to the pyre on which he perished, and the charred sticks were afterwards kept and planted in the fields on Walpurgis Day (the first of May) to preserve the wheat from blight and mildew' (Frazer 1913a: 143). In Upper Bavaria, on Easter Saturday there was a celebration called 'burning the Easter man'. On Easter Monday,

> the villagers gathered the ashes and strewed them on their fields; also they planted in the fields palm-branches which had been consecrated on Palm Sunday, and sticks which had been charred and hallowed on Good Friday, all for the purpose of protecting their fields against showers of hail.
>
> *Frazer 1913a: 144*

The close resemblance to human sacrifice is striking. Sometimes, a profane fire was used on Easter Eve instead of a consecrated fire. The village lads collected firewood in the afternoon and carried the sticks to a corn-field or on top of a hill. 'Here they piled it together and fastened in the midst of it a pole with a cross-piece, all wrapt in straw, so that it looked like a man with outstretched arms. This figure was called the Easter-man, or the Judas' (Frazer 1890b: 252). The Eastern and Lent Fires, in fact, have many similarities, not least in the sense that evil – in the form and embodiment of a figure who in both cases was called Judas – was burnt.

## The Beltane fires

In the Scottish Highlands, bonfires were known as the Beltane fires and they were kindled as part of great ceremonies on 1 May. The tradition continued well into the 18th century, and the sacrifices in ancient times have been associated with Druid festivals, and more academically, pastoral societies. Also, traces of human sacrifices are particularly evident with regards to this festival. John Ramsay, laird of Ochtertyre, wrote extensively in the last quarter of the 18th century about this ritual tradition. Following Ramsay's account, the Beltane or May Day was the most considerable of the Druidical festivals. In Gaelic, this festival was called *Beal-tene*, the fire of Bel. Frazer says: 'Bal-tein signifies the *fire of Baal. Baal* or *Ball* is the only word in Gaelic for a *globe*. This festival was probably in honour of the sun, whose return, in his apparent annual course, they celebrated, on account of his having such a visible influence, by his genial warmth, on the productions of the earth' (Frazer 1913a: 150). In the old days, the sacrifices took place in the open air and most often on hill tops; but in the 18ᵗʰ century, the ritual took place in local hamlets or the grounds where cattle had their pastures. The young folks made a pile of wood which they kindled with forced-fire or need-fire, and this was an act rekindling the world. The night before, all the fires in the country were extinguished, and on the morning the day the ritual was taking place, they prepared the materials for the sacred fire.

Ramsay describes in detail how the fire that was used to kindle the bonfire was made: 'A well-seasoned plank of oak was procured, in the midst of which a hole was bored. A wimble of the same timber was then applied, the end of which they fitted to the hole … In some places three times three persons, in others three times nine, were required for turning round by turns the axle-tree or wimble'. Intriguingly, whether the fire was holy or not, the ritual participants had to be pure: 'If any of them had been guilty of murder, adultery, theft, or other atrocious crime, it was imagined either that the fire would not kindle, or that it would be devoid of its usual virtue'. The fire was not ordinary fire, but coming from the heavens:

> This fire had the appearance of being immediately derived from heaven, and manifold were the virtues ascribed to it. They esteemed it a preservative against witchcraft, and a sovereign remedy against malignant diseases, both in the human species and in cattle; and by it the strongest poisons were supposed to have their nature changed.
>
> *Frazer 1913a: 148*

When the bonfire was kindled, food was eaten and the participants sang and danced around the fire. Later, there was a sacrifice of a cake to the fire, which closely resembled a sacrifice, given that it was laid flat on the ground, and it was symbolically quartered and seen as dead. Ramsay says:

> There is little doubt of these inhuman sacrifices having been once offered in this country, as well as in the east, although they now pass from the act of sacrificing, and only compel the *devoted* person to leap three times through the flames; with which the ceremonies of this festival are closed.
>
> *Frazer 1913a: 152*

The Beltane fires were closely associated with shepherds and cowherds. In one area, the fire was not called bonfire, 'They were called bone-fires. The people believed that on that evening and night the witches were abroad and busy casting spells on cattle and stealing cows' milk' (Frazer 1913a: 154). It may be noted that the word 'bonfire' actually means bone-fire, derived from a Late Middle English word referring to a fire in which bones are actually burnt (cf. Kaliff 2007: 166). The Beltane fires were burning away the witches and hurting animals and people alike. There were yet other fires. John Pinkerton wrote in 1808 about the Scottish Highlands:

> There was an ancient custom in the island of Lewis, to make a fiery circle about the houses, corn, cattle, etc., belonging to each particular family: a man carried fire in his right hand, and went round, and it was called *dessil*, from the right hand, which in the ancient language is called *dess* ... There is another way of the *dessil* or carrying fire round about women before they are churched, after child-bearing; and it is used likewise about children until they are christened.
>
> *Frazer 1913a: 151*

The making of the Beltane May fire is also instructive. From Wales, Marie Trevelyan writes:

> Charred logs and faggots used in the May Beltane were carefully preserved, and from them the next fire was lighted. May fires were always started with old faggots of the previous year, and midsummer from those of the last summer. It was unlucky to build a midsummer fire from May faggots. People carried the ashes left after these fires to their homes, and a charred brand was not only effectual against pestilence, but magical in its use. A few of the ashes placed in a person's shoes protected the wearer from any great sorrow or woe.
>
> *Trevelyan 1909: 23–24*

In Wales, bonfires were also kindled on Midsummer Eve and Halloween (31 October), but the Beltane fires in May were the most important. It was generally held that the bonfire lighted in May or in Midsummer protected the lands from witchcraft and sorcery and as a consequence the harvest would be bountiful. The ashes were also seen as powerful charms. Thus, Frazer points out a fundamental function of the bonfires: 'it appears that the heat of the fires was thought to fertilise the fields, not directly by quickening the seeds in the ground, but indirectly by counteracting the baleful influence of witchcraft or perhaps by burning up the persons of the witches' (Frazer 1913a: 156–157). Again, it seems that the powerful and fertilising forces in the ground were hindered by malignant powers harming and blocking life and vitality. Thus, the most important rituals were those combating and eliminating evil and thereby enabling the good forces to prosper by themselves.

The first of May was seen as a particular day when dangerous forces were alive and active, and hence there were urgent needs for protection. The elves and witches were especially active and they harmed humans and animals. Bonfires functioned as the ultimate protection by chasing away witches and safeguarding against diseases (Frazer 1913a: 157). Bonfires on the night before first of May – Walpurgis Night – were particularly a common tradition in Scandinavia, which is

**FIGURE 3.3**  Bonfire in Uppsala 1 May 2022: Photo: Terje Oestigaard.

still very much alive in the Swedish Walpurgis Night bonfire (Valborgsmässobål). Although the lighting of these bonfires nowadays mostly constitutes a festive way of welcoming spring, traditionally bonfires protected animals, crops and people from evil forces (Figure 3.3). As far as the fires were concerned, evil forces were kept away during the coming fruitful season (Kaliff 2007: 164–166). In practice, this also seems to imply that goodness and the procreative forces in the world were natural or at least immanent in nature, but these were threatened by the active and deliberate actions of hostile forces that jeopardised human lives and welfare. Thus, the most efficient way of procuring fertility was to fight evil powers; another tradition that was echoed in Christianity.

In Wales, as Marie Trevelyan points out, the May Day festivities were not complete without the traditional fight on horses between Summer and Winter. This tradition is also found all over Scandinavia (e.g. Magnus 1998; Olrik & Ellekilde 1951). In Wales, two companies of men or youngsters were formed, one group representing Winter and the other Summer and respectively dressed with heavy furs and coats, and white clothes and flowers. Then there was a mock battle between the forthcoming Summer and the dying Winter. 'A good deal of horse-play went on, but finally Summer gained the mastery over Winter', says Trevelyan and continues: 'Then the victorious captain representing Summer selected a May King and the people nominated a May Queen, who were crowned and conducted into the village. The remainder of the day was given up to feasting, dancing, games of all kinds, and, later still, drinking' (Trevelyan 1909: 25–26).

Although the Beltane fires were the most distinguished, fires on the Eve of May have been a common tradition throughout Europe – from Sweden to Switzerland and beyond. In Scandinavia, there are evidences that fertility and fire were two sides of the same coin. In springtime when the cattle were released from the winter-barn, it was a custom to let the cattle pass by burning charcoal and smoke on the way to the pastures. Another more explicit way of symbolising fertility was a direct imitation of birth. In some villages, the farm's housewife stood in the barn's door on two ladders and all cattle passed through her thighs as if she gave birth (Olrik & Ellekilde 1951: 1160–1161).

## The Midsummer fires

Throughout Europe, the great season for fire festivals has been the summer solstice, Midsummer Eve or Midsummer Day. The Midsummer Day was the climax of the sun's yearly journey on the celestial vault, but it was also a sign of the darker times to come. Usually, the summer solstice was a time of joy and festivities, but the turning of the sun also manifested the human power-lessness in the face of the forces and cyclic changes of nature. There are also documented beliefs that the midsummer air was poisoned and that the bonfires intended to drive away noxious dragons copulating in the air and poisoning wells and water by dropping seeds. While such stories are exceptionally fan-ciful, the eclipse of the sun was a particular bad omen and a more visible sign. During the eclipse, it was believed that poison fell from heaven and cattle were kept in the stalls, the fields were not sown, and people avoided business and practical tasks. The reason was, in the same way as water was believed to be poisoned at midsummer, that during the eclipses a monster attacked the sun or the moon (Frazer 1913a: 161–162).

The Midsummer festivals usually consisted of rolling burning wheel down slopes, or in the waters, but there were also more specific rituals as part of the bonfires: 'Cattle were driven through the fire to cure the sick animals and to guard such as were sound against plague and harm of every kind throughout the year. Many a householder on that day put out the fire on the domestic hearth and rekindled it by means of a brand taken from the midsummer bonfire', Frazer writes. The customary tradition of trundling a burning wheel over the fields was believed to fertilise and incite the growth powers in the earth. The fertility aspects were especially important and structuring major parts of the festivities: 'In many parts of Bavaria it was believed that the flax would grow as high as the young people leaped over the fire. In others the old folk used to plant three charred sticks from the bonfire in the fields, believing that this would make the flax grow tall' (Frazer 1913a: 165). Also, this aspect of procreation may be seen in relation to another tradition, namely the practice of lovers to run over the fire hand in hand. This was also seen as a declaration of a forthcoming wedding, and the crossing of fire together was seen as tantamount to a public betrothal (Frazer 1913a: 168).

A special ritual and sacrificial practice was documented at Rottenburg in Swabia in the year 1807 or 1808. It was about the expulsion of evil and, in this particular case, it was associated with Christianity. Groups of boys went from house to house in the town begging for firewood.

> In each troop there were three leaders, one of whom carried a dagger, a second a paper banner, and a third a white plate covered with a white cloth … they expressed an intention of roasting Martin Luther and sending him to the devil; and for this meritorious service they expected to be paid … In the evening they counted up their money and proceeded to 'behead the Angel-man'. For this ceremony an open space was chosen, sometimes in the middle of the town. Here a stake was thrust into the ground and straw wrapt about it, so as to make a rude effigy of human form with arms, head, and face. Every boy brought a handful of nosegays and fastened them to the straw-man, who was thus enveloped in flowers. Fuel was heaped about the stake and set on fire. When the Angel-man, as the straw-effigy was called, blazed up, all the boys of the neighbourhood, who had gathered expectantly around, fell upon him with their wooden swords and hewed him to pieces.
>
> *Frazer 1913a: 167*

At midsummer, the bonfires, rolling wheels from hillsides and the discs thrown into air were quite similar to the festivals during spring, but there were also specific practices at certain places. 'At Edersleben, near Sangerhausen, a high pole was planted in the ground and a tar-barrel was hung from it by a chain which reached to the ground. The barrel was then set on fire and swung round the pole amid shouts of joy' (Frazer 1913a: 169). In Scandinavia, there are some Bronze Age rock-art depictions that can be interpreted in this light and given the long Indo-European trajectories and continuities; it is not unreasonable to assume that similar kinds of fire festivals took place some millennia ago (Figure 3.4)

Many of the particular rites were directly related to the welfare of the cattle and the prosperity of the fields. From a specific fire made by the friction of two sort of wood – oak and fir –, a bonfire was made: 'The boys light torches at the new fire and run to fumigate the pastures. This is believed to drive away all the demons and witches that molest the cattle. Finally the torches are thrown in a heap on the meadow and allowed to burn out. On their way back the boys strew the ashes over the fields, which is supposed to make them fertile. If a farmer has taken possession of a new house, or if servants have changed masters, the boys fumigate the new abode and are rewarded by the farmer with a supper' (Frazer 1913a: 170).

In Russia along Volga, a specific Midsummer festival may give further insights into the prehistoric way of sacrificing and worshipping the forces of nature. Published in 1776, the account describes the rites: 'A sacred tree in the forest, generally a tall and solitary oak, marks the scene of the solemnity. All the males

**FIGURE 3.4** Barrels swung around a pole as part of a prehistoric fire ritual? Gerum 1 Runohällen Tanum, Bohuslän. Documentation by Bertil Almgren, 1955.

*Source*: www.shfa.se.

assemble there, but no woman may be present. A heathen priest lights seven fires in a row from north-west to south-east; cattle are sacrificed and their blood poured in the fires, each of which is dedicated to a separate deity', writes Frazer and continues: 'Afterwards the holy tree is illumined by lighted candles placed on its branches; the people fall on their knees and with faces bowed to the earth pray that God would be pleased to bless them, their children, their cattle, and their bees, grant them success in trade, in travel ...' (Frazer 1913a: 181).

From Aix in France, there are glimpses of the ritual leadership organising the Midsummer rites and bonfires. In Aix, a nominal king was chosen among the youngsters based on his shooting skills at a parrot. The elected ritual king selected his officers and escorted by a train of participants, he lit the bonfire and was the first to dance around; and the following day, he distributed money to the participants. He reigned as a king for a year and, during this time, he enjoyed some privileges, like some specific hunting rights (Frazer 1913a: 194). In other

**FIGURE 3.5** Corn-mother with the last sheaf as a harvest crown. Jan Nepomucen Lewick, 1841, Poland.

*Source*: Creative Commons.

places and cases, a woman was seen as the corn-mother having the last sheaf as a harvest crown on her head celebrating a bountiful harvest (Figure 3.5).

Also, the ritual and holy qualities of the ashes are worth emphasising. From Wales, it is reported: 'It was also believed in former times that the bon-fires lighted in May or Midsummer protected the lands from sorcery, so that good crops would follow. The ashes were also considered valuable as charms' (Davies 1911: 76). This represents not only a unique and fundamental resource for daily and practical magic among farmers, but it links the fires and the ashes from communal bonfires to cult and continuities in everyday life. This, we believe, may also have been a vital and important part of prehistoric cremations. The spreading of bones in the arable land is well-known in Scandinavia. From prehistoric and archaeologically documented contexts, cremated bones are found deposited in agricultural land. From later folk beliefs, it is documented that bones or soil were sometimes taken from graves and cemeteries because this process was believed to enhance the fields' fertility. The bones of the dead were generally considered to have a very strong and inherent power in Scandinavian folk beliefs, something which in all likelihood goes back to central pre-Christian ideas. In fact, the connection to the common Indo-European creation myth, with the disintegration of the primordial being and the inherent creative power in its body parts, is very likely a prehistoric source. The deposition of burnt bones in arable land, in addition to deposition of bones in water, is one of the most reasonable explanations for the fact that most of the cremated bones from pre-Christian cremation graves are missing. The bones have been used for other purposes in active ancestral cults (Kaliff 1997: 72–78, 2007: 154–161; Kaliff & Oestigaard 2022: 117–120).

## The Halloween fires

The most common and important fire festivals among the Celts were on the eve of May Day and six months later, the last of October or Allhallow Even, more popularly known as Halloween or All Saint's Day. While the Midsummer and Midwinter sacrifices coincide with the sun solstices and represent one way of organising culture after the calendar of nature, the festivals and fires by the beginning of summer (the first of May) and the beginning of winter (the first of November) represent not only another way of organising society and the calendar, but fundamentally they represent other ecologies, livelihoods and adaptation strategies. From an agricultural and farming perspective, in May the seed had been in the soil for a long time and the harvest was reaped and fields lie bare when November knocked on the door. Among pastoralists and cattle herders, on the other hand, first of May and first of November were important days and represented the days when cattle were driven out on the fields and summer pastures and the time when they returned home or back to the farm for their winter stalls. Thus, May Day and Walpurgis Night in May and the Feast of All Souls at the beginning of November were historically related to pastoral and cattle communities (Figure 3.6).

Frazer sees this as the original calendar: 'Hence we may conjecture that everywhere throughout Europe the celestial division of the year according to the solstices was preceded by what we may call a terrestrial division of the year according to the beginning of summer and the beginning of winter' (Frazer 1913a: 224). This is also testified in the old runic calendar having only two periods: summer and winter. The winter lasted usually from 15 October or 1 November to 15 April or 1 May, and the next half year was the summer. In practice, the old calendar was a pastoral calendar based on animals and their pastures.

In other words, in major parts of Europe, the Indo-European stratum that developed among pastoral groups have the longest time trajectories and later Christian perceptions veiled a thin cloth around the All Hallows Day and made it a festival of the dead. But, the dead and the ancestors were also alive.

**FIGURE 3.6** Cattle at Ale's Stones, Sweden. Photo: Terje Oestigaard.

It seems that the fire festivals in November defined the New Year, and hence they may have been more important than the Beltane fires in the spring. If All Saint's Day and New Year's Day were the same day, 'the annual kindling of a new fire takes place most naturally at the beginning of the year, in order that the blessed influence of the fresh fire may last throughout the whole period of twelve months' (Frazer 1913a: 225). This night, at the transition from summer (autumn) to winter, was a time when the departed souls and the ancestors returned to their old homes to warm themselves by the fire and to be provided by their kinsmen and descendants. The ancestors – the past lives – and the cattle – the future lives – were one: 'Did not the lowing kine then troop back from the summer pastures in the forests and on the hills to be fed and cared for in the stalls, while the bleak winds whistled among the swaying boughs and the snow drifts deepened in the hollows? and could the good-man and the good-wife deny to the spirits of their dead the welcome which they gave to the cows?' (Frazer 1913a: 226). It was a day or the night when the living and dead returned whether as humans or animals.

In the Scandinavian tradition, the belief in the return of the dead ancestors to their old home was placed to the winter solstice or the celebration of Yule. A strong surviving tradition has existed in the Nordic countries until recently, documented in writing since the middle of the 18th century, when the Swedish priest Petrus Gaslander describes the rites and perceptions in detail. These beliefs are similar to the Celtic counterparts associated with All Saint's Day, a holiday that in Scandinavia has been much less important than Yule. Until the middle of the 20th century, it was instead on Christmas Day that graves were traditionally decorated in Scandinavia, and only in recent decades has the tradition of lighting candles on the graves on All Saint's Day been common. In both Celtic and Nordic traditions, there was historically a custom to provide food as well as bed and housing to the dead relatives. Another similarity is that on Halloween and Yule people tried to predict the events of the coming year by divination rituals. The time was the end of the old year and the beginning of the new in both traditions (e.g. Kaliff 2007: 191; Oestigaard & Kaliff 2020: 265–277).

The winter fire at Halloween was quite similar to the Beltane fires in May. Young people from the hamlet made the bonfire and, around it, a circle of stones was placed and there was one stone for each family in the hamlet. These were used for divination. 'When the fire had died down, the ashes were carefully collected in the form of a circle, and a stone was put in, near the circumference, for every person of the several families interested in the bonfire. Next morning, if any of these stones was found to be displaced or injured, the people made sure that the person represented by it was *fey* or devoted, and that he could not live twelve months from that day' (Frazer 1913a: 231). Similarly, in the northern part of Wales every family made a great bonfire and when it was nearly finished, everyone threw a white stone into the ashes, which they had marked. Then, they said their prayers and went to bed for the night. Next morning as soon as they got up, they started to search for the stones. If any of them were missing, it was believed that the one who threw those stones would not see another Halloween, or in other words, he would die in the forthcoming year (Frazer 1913a: 239).

A corresponding Scandinavian tradition, recorded in Bohuslän in western Sweden in 1746, was to drink Eldbjørg's toast. This was a divination ritual centred on the hearth's female spirit or ancestor, which took place at the end of the Christmas celebration on either the 13th or 20th day after Christmas Eve. After the toast, the drinking bowl would be thrown overhead backwards. If the bowl overturned, the person who threw it would die during the coming year; but if it instead stood upright, the person would live on (Celander 1928: 351–354; Oestigaard & Kaliff 2020: 276–277). Continuity throughout the year and the seasons was a defining aspect of cult and cultures. The end of the summer and the beginning of the winter were of great importance in Indo-European traditions, which is also reflected in similarities in rituals connected to animal husbandry and agriculture.

From the mountain regions in Norway, the return of the animals in the autumn was a time of festivities and celebrations. This tradition is vividly described in the late 19th and early 20th centuries, and while the release of the animals during the spring was a time of happiness and prosperity, since humans and animals had survived the challenging winter, the return signalled successful food security and forthcoming safety in the difficult time to come. Importantly, this was a celebration of women and, in particular, the milk-maiden, who was hailed as a queen for a day upon her safe arrival with the animals from the summer pastures (Solheim 1952: 604–623).

## Fire sacrifices – burning animals and humans

The literature on sacrifice is extensive and definitions and practices of sacrifice are vividly discussed and challenged from empirical, methodological and theoretical perspectives (see Oestigaard 2022b); but for the time being, we will follow Frazer and his analysis. In our common understanding of ritual hierarchies and religious structures, killing a god is an absolute crime and the worst violation of taboos and cosmic laws. Still, this has been a fundamental principle in prehistory as well as testified in ethnography, and herein is a religious logic explaining how the world and cosmos were perceived to work and function. Killing and sacrificing the effigy as a symbol or the animal or human in person was not a heinous crime, rather the contrary. In practices, they were vehicles or messengers that were the main powers in cosmos rejuvenating the life-giving forces. There was no external or simple sun or water god, but it was possible to incite, activate and participate in these powers by sacrificing an effigy symbolising or embodying these spirits or deities. In a world of magic, nothing comes from nothing and there was no free lunch. In other words, if these spring and harvest rituals should work, there was a price to pay. This relates to the direct testimonies of human sacrifices to the fire and water, in particular on Midsummer Day, but also on other occasions, in general. If divinities and life-giving spirits could be killed and sacrificed at certain calendrical rites, these beings were placed higher in the cosmological hierarchies than mere humans. Thus, Frazer asks: 'Why were men and animals burnt to death at these festivals?' (Frazer 1913b: 41). This question can be divided and elaborated by a range of more specific questions.

> It remains to ask, What is the meaning of burning an effigy in these bonfires? The effigies so burned … can hardly be separated from the effigies of Death which are burned or otherwise destroyed in spring; and grounds have been already given for regarding the so-called effigies of Death as really representations of the tree-spirit or spirit of vegetation. Are the other effigies, which are burned in the spring and midsummer bonfires,

susceptible of the same explanation? It would seem so. For just as the fragments of the so-called Death are stuck in the fields to make the crops
grow, so the charred embers of the figure burned in the spring bonfires
are sometimes placed in the fields in the belief that they will keep vermin
from the crop.

*Frazer 1890b: 274*

Frazer finds the answer precisely in the fire rituals and the powers whereby they
broke the evil forces of witchcraft and warlocks by burning and destroying them.
Not only was evil terminated, the forces that hindered fertility to blossom, but
the transformation of cosmic evil to goodness was a source for future life that
was ritually activated in the seasonal rites and festivals (Figure 3.7). From a theoretical point of view, this was a central aspect of Marcel Mauss' classic work
on sacrifice which he wrote with Henri Hubert in 1898, *Essai sur la nature et la*

**FIGURE 3.7**   The agricultural seasons and continuity in rites and practices. Illustration:
Richard Holmgren, ARCDOC.

*fonction du sacrifice*, or in English *Sacrifice: Its Nature and Function* (Hubert & Mauss 1964). The sacrifice of gods in agrarian rituals is often quite different than divine sacrifices in other contexts. Hubert and Mauss write:

> This singular value of the victim clearly appears in one of the most perfected forms of the historical evolution of the sacrificial system: the sacrifice of the god. Indeed, it is in the sacrifice of a divine personage that the idea of sacrifice attains its highest expression … We shall see how the agrarian sacrifices were able to provide the point of departure for this evolution. Mannhardt and Frazer already saw clearly the close connexions between the sacrifice of the god and the agrarian sacrifices.
>
> *Hubert & Mauss 1964: 77*

They elaborate the important differences between divinities and sacrifices of victim gods and agrarian gods. First, the relation between the sacrificed god and the victim (the animal or the last sheaf cut during harvest) is intimate and, in practice, homogenous. 'The spirit of the corn … is almost indistinct from the corn that embodies it … As soon as it is immolated, it is diffused once more through the entire agrarian species to which it gives life, and so again becomes vague and impersonal … This independence is further increased when the sheaf is replaced by an animal victim' (Hubert & Mauss 1964: 78–79). This is also precisely what Frazer describes in *The Scapegoat* (Frazer 1913c). A scapegoat is 'on the one hand, the evils are invisible and tangible; and, on the other hand, there is a visible and tangible vehicle to convey them away. And a scapegoat is nothing more than such a vehicle' (Frazer 1890b: 202). In the process of sacrifice, it 'effects an exaltation of the victims, which renders them directly divine … He must still possess his divine nature in its entirety at the moment when he enters again into the sacrifice to become a victim himself' (Hubert & Mauss 1964: 49, 81). Or, as they phrase it: 'The notion of sacrifice *to* the god developed parallel with that of sacrifice *of* the god' (Hubert & Mauss 1964: 90).

The role of fire in sacrifices becomes clearer when one sees the dual process at work in sacralisation and desacralisation, following Hubert & Mauss again: 'Now actually in any sacrifice of desacralization, however pure it may be, we always find a sacralisation of the victim. Conversely, in any sacrifice of sacralisation, even the most clearly marked, a descralization is necessarily implied, for otherwise the remains of victim could not be used. The two elements are thus so closely interdependent that the one cannot exist without the other' (Hubert & Mauss 1964: 95). In a fire sacrifice, for example of an ordinary animal, the fire purifies the animal so it is fit for the gods: it is a process of sacralising. The process of desacralising works the other way around, like for instance when the agrarian gods or divinities embody in the last sheaf. The holy or divine becomes mundane and ordinary, and it is possible to use in daily matters and for practical purposes, like a meal (Robertson Smith 1889). Furthermore, in a tradition where the fire itself constitutes a deity or a spiritual being – such as the Vedic Agni, as well as Eldbjørg and Eldgrim in the Nordic folklore – the complex connection between the fire sacrifice process and the recipient of the sacrifice becomes more noticeable.

During epidemics and plagues, animals were sacrificed alive in the fire, and a common explanation has been that is saves the herd from the spells cast on them. This notion also challenges the concept of sacrifice, because the animal killed and burnt on the pyre was embodying evil or concentrating the power of the witches. In 1862, Sir Arthur Mitchell writes about Scotland: 'for the cure of the murrain in cattle, one of the herd is still sacrificed for the good of the whole. This is done by burying it alive. I am assured that within the last ten years such a barbarism occurred in the county of Moray' (Frazer 1913a: 324).

By burning the animal to ashes, the actual malignant powers threatening the herds were completely destroyed. Not only was the animal killed, but the witches were burnt. 'Hence if you burn the creature to ashes, you utterly destroy the witch and thereby save the whole of the rest of the flock or herd from her abominable machinations', says Frazer and continues: 'And the same train of reasoning that justifies the burning alive of bewitched animals justifies and indeed requires the burning alive of the witches themselves; it is really the only way of destroying them, body and soul, and therefore of thoroughly extirpating the whole infernal crew' (Frazer 1913a: 305).

While the European and Christian witch-craze is not the main theme of this study, particular notions and ways of believing the fire may purge out evil have clear Indo-European roots and builds on the logics of how the Indo-European need-fires worked. Frazer uses the example of how the farmer Michael Cleary burnt his wife Bridget in 1895 (see also see Bourke 2001):

> Bridget Cleary [was burnt] alive over a slow fire on the kitchen hearth in the presence of and with the active assistance of some neighbours, including the woman's own father and several of her cousins. They thought that she was not Bridget Cleary at all, but a witch, and that when they held her down on the fire she would vanish up the chimney; so they cried, while she was burning, 'Away she goes! Away she goes!' Even when she lay quite dead on the kitchen floor (for contrary to the general expectation she did not disappear up the chimney), her husband still believed that the woman lying there was a witch, and that his own dear wife had gone with the fairies ….
>
> *Frazer 1913a: 324*

Bridget, who was only 25–26 years old when she was murdered, was described in popular media as the last witch burnt in Ireland and the subject of the last witch-craft trial. However, she was not accused of being in pact with the Devil, quite contrary. *The New York Times* reported: 'She did not fall a victim to the belief in witchcraft or in demoniacal possession – neither has any real hold in Ireland.

She perished owning to the belief in the fairies, a belief to this hour singularly prevalent … Cleary and 'the neighbors' evidently believed that the being they tortured was not Cleary's wife, but a changeling … He said when he set fire to her: 'You will soon see my wife come down the chimney', believing that the fairies would snatch away the tortured fairy and restore his real wife' (*The New York Times* 1895a). Michael Cleary was sentenced to imprisonment for 20 years for the bestial murder of his wife (*The New York Times* 1895b).

There are many striking aspects of this tragedy, not only the rather lenient punishment for such a horrific crime but also the strength and pervasiveness of these beliefs only some 125 years ago. From an analytical point of view, however, it may give some unique glimpses into the logic of the Indo-European cosmology and the beliefs in the ritual and sacrificial fires. While the belief that witches represented evil and were in pact with the Devil is omnipresent, the alleged dangers of fairies is remarkable; but, it gives a testimony to the ontological realities of various beings in a now forgotten world. Following Hubert and Mauss, it also shows the dual role of fire in sacralising and desacralising sacrificial victims. On the one hand, the fire was believed to have purifying qualities; but on the other hand, protection was achieved by burning away malevolent powers. From this perspective, one may summarise some key elements of these Indo-European fires as a heuristic tool before approaching the funeral flames in prehistoric cremations. This reasoning rests on a reasonable assumption, namely that many of the perceptions and qualities associated and ascribed to ritual and sacrificial fires in other contexts also applied to the cremation fires. As seen, humans and animals have in some cases been treated in the same way in the sacrificial fires. In other words, these were the ritual fires defining the rituals and sacrificial victims, not the opposite. This enables a comparative approach where the Indo-European fire is the source and solution to an understanding of rituals and sacrifices, funerals and cremations included.

## Cremations, concepts and collective actions

The Hindu cremation will be described and discussed in depth in Chapter 7, but based on the European ethnography and shared Indo-European tradition, one may flesh out some preliminary understanding and interpretations of continental cremation practices, in general, and the Scandinavian funeral flames, in particular. Frazer says: 'Indeed we may assume with a fair degree of probability that the need-fire was the parent of the periodic fire-festivals; at first invoked only at irregular intervals to cure certain evils as they occurred, the powerful virtue of fire was afterwards employed as regular intervals to prevent the occurrence of the same evils as well as to remedy such as had actually arisen' (Frazer 1913a: 299). If the need-fire, and the way it was produced, represents the original fire – a cosmic or cosmogonic fire – then this has potential implications for the cremation fire, since funerals are literally links between the living and the dead, this world and the otherworld. As seen in the ethnographic examples, the major bonfires were lit in the afternoon or after dawn and they illuminated the dark night and the stars of heaven. The cosmic role of this need-fire is seen in the notion that it represents a unity, which cannot be broken. Following Frazer,

> The curious notion that the need-fire cannot kindle if any other fire remains alight in the neighbourhood seems to imply that fire is conceived as a unity which is broken up into fractions and consequently weakened in exact proportions to the number of places it burns; hence in order to obtain it at full strength you must light it only at a single point, for then the flame will burst out with a concentrated energy derived from the tributary fires which burned on all the extinguished hearths of the country.
>
> *Frazer 1913a: 298*

If this also represents a prehistoric reality, it gives indications of collective practices and rituals. It is reasonable to assume that the cremation fire was one of the most important cosmic fires, and hence the religious structures regulating and prescribing the lightning and use of this fire was strictly controlled, not necessarily by ritual specialists or a priesthood, but by collective and cultural sanctions and taboos. On the one hand, if the prescribed rule was that all domestic fires should be put out before the cremation fire was lit, not only would the absence of villagers in the funeral be noted, but more importantly lights from houses or smoke from the hearth would expose those who violated the collective norms. From a practical point of view, extinguishing the domestic fire would also have been an effective way of making homage to the deceased and paying tribute, and, in this way, a huge hinterland may have partaken in the funeral even at long distance from the actual cremation. On the other hand, as seen with the seasonal fire festivals documented in European ethnography, there were hardly any reasons not to follow the collective and cultural rules, rather the contrary. These fires were for the benefit of the community and part of the agricultural world enabling and securing a good harvest and continuity between the agricultural seasons. This directs the attention to the use of the cremation fire, not only in the actual funeral of the deceased, but more importantly among the descendants and villagers afterwards.

The need-fires may also give some other clues. The collective scale of some of these need-fire rituals was quite staggering. From the western islands of Scotland, a plague haunted people and murrain the cattle in the community. All fires in the parish were extinguished and no less than 81 unmarried men came together to produce the need-fire. This great number of men was thought necessary for the design and success of the ritual. They used two great planks of wood and nine of them were employed at turns to rub one plank against the other until it caught fire. From this new and powerful forced fire, each family was supplied with a new fire. With this new fire, immediately a full pot of water was heated and afterwards the water was sprinkled on the people suffering from the plague and the cattle that had murrain. And, according to not only tradition, but more importantly to experience, these rites and fires proved successful (Frazer 1913a: 289). Beltane fires were also made by friction of wood, and as Frazer points out,

> It deserves, further, to be noticed that in North Uist the wood used to kindle the need-fire was oak, and that the nine times nine men by whose exertions the flame was elicited were all first-born sons. Apparently, the first-born son of a family was thought to be endowed with more magical virtue than his younger brothers.
>
> *Frazer 1913a: 295*

An intriguing aspect of these fire rituals is not only that all the fires in the households and villages had to be extinguished and put out when the major ceremonial fires were made, but also the ethnographic evidences that every house received a 'new' fire from the collective bonfire (Frazer 1890b: 251). From this perspective, it seems reasonable to assume that the funeral fires were the original fire lighting and heating up every household. In particular, when a member of the family or the household died and was cremated, this would have been a very direct way

**FIGURE 3.8** Cremation fire consuming the body and burning a ceramic pot. Experimental cremation, Old Uppsala, 2013. Photo: Terje Oestigaard.

of making the hearth an ancestral shrine back home where the ancestors lived in the flames. In this sense, the fire place was a direct continuity of the funeral pyre and the deceased as an ancestor embodied the flames and was present in the fire (Figure 3.8). The dead lived in the hearth, like Eldbjørg, Eldgrim and Domovoy.

The collective efforts of making the Vedic fire rituals and altars will be discussed in Chapter 6, which also includes taking back home the ritual fire to the individual households, but also the European ethnography provides important information about the size and scale of these fire rituals. The public and collective attendance in, for instance, midsummer festivals, or funerals of important people like kings or chiefs, was probably huge, although the exact number of participants would of course vary from funeral to funeral or festival. The information from Scotland that 81 unmarried men came together to produce the need-fire in the case of a collective emergency is intriguing, but also the Beltane fire was made by groups of nine-by-nine men. This was only the share number of participants in the lightning ceremony of this cosmic fire.

Among the Slavonian people, the role and function of these fires were explicitly seen as a protector or shield: 'They regard it simply as a barrier interposed between their cattle and the evil spirit, which prowls, like a hungry wolf, round the fold and can, like a wolf, be kept at bay by fire', says Frazer and continues:

> the conception of the need-fire as a barrier set up between the cattle and a dangerous spirit is clearly worked out. The spirit rides the cow till he comes to the narrow pass between the two fires, but the heat there is too much for him; he drops in a faint from the saddle, or rather from the horns, and the now riderless animal escapes safe and sound beyond the smoke and flame, leaving her persecutor prostrate on the ground on the further side of the blessed barrier.
>
> *Frazer 1913a: 282, 285–286*

As will be seen later, this purificatory and procreative function of fire by protecting and being a mediator between this worldly and the otherworldly realms is a deeply rooted Indo-European belief and practice. In essence and as a consequence, this is also a divine quality and fire has been seen as a distinctive god or divinity as well as a mediator and messenger between humans and gods. In death, not only is the deceased in a highly vulnerable position, but in the transformation from this world to the next as an ancestor, all good forces that helped ensuring a benevolent future for the living and dead were utmost important sources and forces in this cosmic drama. Fire was one of the most important agents in this transformation.

# 4

# CREMATION AND CULTIVATION IN THE NORTH

## Fire in the North

Historically, fire rituals and fire sacrifices have not been much discussed in Scandinavian archaeology, despite the fact that many finds and numerous sites indicate that such traditions were common (e.g. Bellander 1938; Nylén 1958; Hyenstrand 1968; Thörn 1996). This was partly due to a lack of interest in ritual and cult, characterised by the spirit of the times, and partly to a prevailing view of the ancient Scandinavian cult and cosmology. In this view, fire rituals and fire sacrifices were not present, or at least not having a dominant place and importance.

In recent years, this has changed. This is due to a shift in focus in Scandinavian archaeology in recent decades, in terms of interest in religion and ritual in general, and a greater awareness among field archaeologists that finds showing traces of fire rituals are in fact abundant. Above all, a number of major archaeological excavations in eastern Central Sweden of complex, ritual archaeological sites have been excavated (e.g. Kaliff 1996; Hjärthner-Holdar, Eriksson & Östling 2008; Artursson, Karlenby & Larsson 2011; Artursson, Kaliff & Larsson 2017). A large amount of archaeological documentation has been added, not least through the extensive contract archaeological activities that have been conducted in Sweden in recent decades. Various traces of fire rituals have proved to be very prominent finds indeed. This is especially evident in remains from the Bronze Age, particularly the late part of the period, 1100–500 BC, but with examples already from the third millennium BC and with continuity until the end of pre-Christian times.

Today, a large source material speaks for a widespread tradition of fire rituals in ancient Scandinavia with close parallels in various other cultural contexts of Indo-European origin. With the exception of some publications by the authors

DOI: 10.4324/9781003300915-4

(e.g. Kaliff 1997, 2005, 2007; Kaliff & Oestigaard 2004, 2013, 2017), attempts to place this material in an overall context have largely been lacking, partly because of a reluctance to conduct comparative Indo-European studies. The aDNA breakthrough paved way for renewed research on the Indo-Europeans (Haak, Lazaridis & Reich 2015; Allentoft, Sikora & Willerslev 2015); but prior to these studies, Indo-European approaches were by and large viewed with strong scepticism by the majority of the archaeological community. Now this has changed dramatically and based on a now (again) generally accepted interpretation of Indo-European cultural dissemination, and a well-documented archaeological material that has been added in recent years, we want to highlight the Scandinavian finds in such an overall perspective.

An important part of the archaeological material consists of remains after cremations and depositions of burnt bones. However, traces of fire rituals in the archaeological material are much more common than just in funeral contexts. Remains of fire altars with traces of sacrifices, seasonal fires linked to agriculture as well as ritual activities connected to the hearth of the home, are other find categories that are included which indicates a much more general and widespread use of various fire in cult and cosmology. These rituals have been deeply rooted and integrated in culture and society and thus represent very long continuities and historic trajectories. This in turn has resulted in the fact that in many cases the traditions have been preserved until recent times, even if in a partially modified and Christianised form, in the form of folk beliefs, including notions of the magical and healing power of fire, sacrifices to the hearth of the home and not least seasonal fires.

From the Late Bronze Age onwards (c. 1100 BC), cremation is the dominant funerary practice in Scandinavia (e.g. Kaliff 1997, 2007). However, this is not a sudden transition from an earlier inhumation practice. In fact, cremation occurred already in the Mesolithic; but from the beginning of the Bronze Age onwards, cremation became more common. The intensive use of fire and the mastering of heat can also be seen in metallurgy and the bronze smith's furnace, which was an important aspect of the Bronze Age society. There are clear links between mastering the fire in metallurgy and the development of cremation as a funeral ritual that includes both the refined technical ability to master temperature and the analogy between the fire's transformation of metal as well as of bodily remains. Fire's ability to transform cold dead material into liquid, hot metal, with potential to form new objects, is an easily transferred metaphor for the fire's transforming and life-giving qualities of the dead. It is in turn a metaphor that is very close to basic features of the common Indo-European cosmology, based on the creation myth, with body parts transmuting into new elements.

At the same time, cremation is closely associated with cultivation and the fertility of the fields. In the form of clearing fires, the fire's close association to fertility goes back to the introduction of agriculture, already during pre-Indo-European times. Nevertheless, there is evidence that the ritual significance of fire may have played a special role in early Indo-European contexts, not so much related to the clearing of farmland as to the clearing of new pasture for animals. The latter is closely linked to nomadic herdsmen and fits well with the early Indo-European communities of the Eurasian steppe, especially when expanding into forested areas (Figure 4.1).

There are signs that extensive clearing took place already during the first expansion from the Yamnaya at the beginning of the third millennium BC as a part of the process that led to the emergence of the Corded Ware culture.

**FIGURE 4.1** There is evidence that the ritual significance of fire played a special role in early Indo-European contexts and Bronze Age Scandinavia was no exception. Fire started by drilling – symbolically born from another material – has been an enduring method to lit sacred fire, until modern times used for curing disease and crop failure. Drawing by Richard Holmgren, ARCDOC, from Kaliff 2007, Figure 14, p. 188.

Not least in Jutland, Denmark, pollen analyses provide very tangible evidence for a clear deforestation and the emergence of open pastures (Andersen 1993; Kristiansen 2007). Nevertheless, the strong cosmological and ritual significance of fire in its capacity as a clearing fire is most clearly established in the Vedic tradition. The spread of Vedic, seminomadic immigrants across the northern part of the Indian peninsula took place in the wake of an extensive initial clearing of pastures by fire (Staal 1983: 97–105). This early clearing of land has such a strong symbolic significance that it was incorporated into many sacrificial rituals still surviving in Vedic-Hindu ritual tradition. The close connection between fire and the clearing of pastures and arable land is present already in the early Vedic culture: 'The Vedas swarm with cattle and often mention agriculture' (Staal 1983: 99). We will return to this aspect of fire in Chapters 6 and 7.

Agriculture was introduced in the area that makes up the present-day Sweden, or geographically more precisely the southern third of the country, as early as 4000–3800 BC, with a northern border crossing from Bohuslän in the west to northern Uppland in the east, which coincides with a very clear boundary between climate zones. This border has ever since been relevant throughout history dividing southern and northern Sweden, although agriculture in more recent times also occurs far to the north. The revolution in secondary products took place later than the introduction of agriculture itself, sometimes during the period 3000–1500 BC, in other words as part of the Indo-Europeanisation of southern Scandinavia. The advent of historical farms with permanent, manured fields happened even later, ca. 1000–800 BC (Welinder 2011: 23, 43; Kaliff & Oestigaard 2022: 91–92; Oestigaard 2022a).

There is every reason to believe that the Indo-European features in Scandinavia basically correspond to those that were originally brought from the steppe and existing as common features in most branches of the Indo-European cultural tree. At the same time, Scandinavia's northern location and special natural geographical and climatological conditions mean that an adjustment must have taken place already at an early stage. Undoubtedly, this also left its mark on beliefs and rituals. The adaptation may certainly have included an incorporation of older beliefs and rituals from pre-Indo-European, Neolithic Scandinavia, as well as a modification of basic Indo-European features. Finding out the relationship and proportions between these common Indo-European features and local older cultures is a challenge in the study of all branches of the Indo-European cultural tree, in a manner similar in principle to exploring the specifics of languages.

By comparison, the results of linguistic research in combination with archaeology have made it probable that the transformation from Proto-Indo-European to Pre-Proto Germanic reveal a hybridisation between an earlier Neolithic language, spoken by the Funnel Beaker people, and the language of incoming migrants. This is shown, among other things, by the fact that linguistic terms of non-Indo-European origin linked to agriculture were adopted by the incoming Indo-European-speaking groups, still not fully fledged farmers. 'The most plausible, and perhaps the only possible, context for this to have happened would be the introduction of Proto-Germanic by the intruding Yamnaya groups. Archaeologically, this adoption can be understood from their interaction over several hundred years with late Funnel Beaker groups still residing in eastern Jutland and on the Danish islands, where they maintained a largely agricultural economy' (Kristiansen, Allentoft & Frei 2017: 340).

The ecology of Scandinavia, with long cold winters forced everyone to stay put in the coldest months and they needed to put aside food for humans as well as fodder for the winter in advance (Ericsson 2002: 63). Although there might have been seasonal migrations to good pastures during summer, as historically in Scandinavia's mountainous regions, the clearance of forest suggests a more sedentary life. Large herds in Scandinavia had few options for migrating across huge areas due to ecological reasons and limitations, and historically the cattle were confined to their stalls during the long northern winters (Frazer 1922: 341). Also, as early as the latter part of the Bronze Age, a climate change created harsher living conditions (e.g. Armit et al. 2014).

While agricultural rituals are usually closely related to the fertility of the fields and the cultivation of these according to the seasons, pastoral communities are more focused on access to water and the growth of pastures. However, the adaptation to the changing seasons and the vulnerability of the forces of the weather are conditions that are common to both farmers and pastoralists. In the northern climate of Scandinavia, the ecology locked the inhabitants in a predominantly agrarian worldview. After a long winter where the animals had starved in order to survive, the primary concern was food, both for humans and animals. The long, snowy winters posed the greatest danger. Hence, pastoralists and agriculturalists faced the same challenge, since humans and animals depended upon a long growth season (Kaliff & Oestigaard 2022: 92–94).

## The elements and cosmology

Apart from using fire for clearing land for agriculture, a common feature throughout the millennia is finds of cremated human remains on the fields (e.g. Ericsson 2002; Petersson 2006). Human bones have been scattered as a part of agricultural rituals, and in many grave contexts grinding stones are found together with grains and crushed bones. These are often found in close proximity to deposits of burnt bones, features that are conventionally considered to be the grave itself. However, the Scandinavian burial sites are extremely complex, and not least during the Late Bronze Age there are extensive sites where depots with cremated human bones are located in direct connection to sacrificial closures that also contain other material such as animal bones and not least grain. Grinding stones are found in both of these types of features – the depots with human bones and those with other material remains. It is obvious that the crushing and grinding itself has been considered of great importance for the remains of the bodies of the dead – the burnt bones – as well as for grain and other sacrificial offerings.

In both cases, the material has been ground in a similar way and the tools used have been deposited on the site (Kaliff 1992: 99–103, 1997: 88–89; cf. Karlenby 2011) (Figure 4.2).

In recent years, some major archaeological excavations in eastern Middle Sweden have documented contexts where grains and human bones have been made into bread and meals, which fits very well in the overall Indo-European tradition documented in later European and Scandinavian folklore (e.g. Artursson, Karlenby & Larsson 2011; Artursson, Kaliff & Larsson 2017). In an ancestral tradition, the fragmentation of the dead also puts emphasis on the unique characteristics of cremation as a funerary practice; in fact, it is not one, but many mortuary practices. Cremating the dead body at various temperatures whereby the fire clears the bones from the flesh enable a wide range of rituals and uses of the bones. On average, not more than 10–20% of the deceased's burnt bones are buried in what often are labelled 'graves' in a conventional archaeological terminology: the rest of the bones are used in different rituals for other purposes (cf. Kaliff & Oestigaard 2017).

A further aspect of the cremation ritual in its Scandinavian design is its close relation to fire sacrifice in general, a relationship that is particularly well

**FIGURE 4.2** In Scandinavian Bronze Age cremation graves, grinding stones are often found together with crushed bones and grains. There is reason to assume a powerful symbolic meaning in this, as part of eschatological beliefs connected with agricultural rituals. Illustration of Bronze Age grinding stones together with grain and a human skull. Photo: Terje Oestigaard.

documented in the Vedic tradition, but seems to be central to several traditions with Indo-European roots. In fact, the similarities between Scandinavia and the Vedic cult are surprisingly big, evident both in terms of cremation practice and the less frequently noticed fire offerings and associated altar constructions. Given that the Vedic ritual tradition itself is apparently older than the establishment of Vedic culture in northern India, this is perhaps not as strange as it may first appear to be. The term Vedic generally refers to the culture and beliefs that the Indo-Aryan tribes already carried with them when arriving to northern India in the 2nd millennia BC. Although the Vedic ritual can hardly be said to represent an original common Indo-European stage – as suggested by some early researchers but later abandoned – it is probably the closest equivalent, and definitely the richest evidence, that can still reflect this oldest phase. There is much to suggest that the Vedic tradition originated north of India, on the steppes of the border between Europe and Asia, in the so-called Sintashta culture and its successors around 2000 BC (e.g. Anthony 2007: 408–411; Kuzmina 2008: 163–168, 217–223). This cultural context, in turn, has a very huge impact on the spread of both religious, cultural and technological innovations through a complex interaction between East and West, not least actualised through discoveries within aDNA (e.g. Saag, Vasilyev & Varul et al. 2021: 1–30). In fact, there are close similarities between Vedic cultic practices and the traditions that have prevailed in completely different geographical areas, not least in parts of Eastern and Northern Europe, including Scandinavia, which we will look at in more detail in Chapter 5 (Figure 4.3).

The power of perseverance in Vedic tradition is not due to the practices and beliefs being written down in manuals at an early stage. On the contrary, the knowledge was transmitted orally, and so is the tradition even today. A similar scenario is realistic also for prehistoric Scandinavia with a ritual practice based on a strong oral tradition transmitted from one generation to another. A time perspective from the Bronze Age to the Late Iron Age, a period of more than 2,000 years, is thus not unreasonable for the preservation of many rituals, nor, as we have already seen, their survival in even more recent times as part of folklore. Taking such a long-term perspective seriously is therefore crucial when interpreting ancient Scandinavian ritual tradition and the religious beliefs and rites.

The presence of close ritual similarities in different Indo-European cultural areas reflect common cosmological ideas, which in turn reflect parts of the Indo-European creation myth. This is at least the most probable interpretation in order to explain close similarities of this kind, analogous to the relationship between Indo-European languages. As with languages, however, we can hardly expect exact similarities between rituals and cosmology in the Vedic and Scandinavian traditions, respectively, but basic and structural similarities are likely to exist – and have existed.

Sacrificial rituals are considered to be a particularly central element in Indo-European ritual traditions, which would be in line with the fact that they probably received important parts of their design as a reflection and materialisation

**FIGURE 4.3** Grinding has a long lasting significance in the Nordic tradition and its deep symbolic impact can still be seen in the Old Norse poem Gróttasöngr (the song of Grótti), where two slave girls – Fenja and Menja – are forced to grind out wealth for the king from a magic grinding stone. Engraving by George Pearson after W. J. Wiegand. From Goddard, J. 1871. *Wonderful Stories from Northern Lands*. Longmann, Green, and C, London, p. 93.

of the common Indo-European creation myth. Through comparative analysis, a basic, common Indo-European cosmological myth has been reconstructed (cf. Lincoln 1986). The very core of this story – in its various versions – contains a theme where a primordial being is killed – sacrificed – and its body is dismembered. As a result, the world and all living beings, including man, are shaped out of the body-parts. This particular theme seems to be important for how both sacrificial and funeral rituals have been formed among different Indo-European peoples, not least does it apply to fire-sacrifice and cremation.

Based on summaries of David W. Anthony (2007) and Martin L. West (2007), the basic Indo-European creation myth reads approximately like this: From the beginning, *Manu, the first man, existed together with his twin brother *Yemo. The creation of the world begins when Manu sacrifices his twin-brother. Thereafter, with the help of some significant celestial deities – reconstructed as the Sky-Father, the Storm-God and the Divine Twins – Manu creates all parts of nature as well as the human race out of the body parts of his killed brother. This act constitutes the very first sacrifice, which all later sacrificial rituals reflect. This first sacrifice constitutes the origin of the world, and each sacrifice performed by men serves to re-create it. It is a story of fundamental importance and thus with a potential for outstanding survivability over time and in space. This also applies to its possible expressions in the form of rituals which leave physical traces that can be studied with archaeological methods.

According to the historian of religion Bruce Lincoln (e.g. 1975, 1976, 1981, 1986, 1991), not only the creation of the physical world, but also the emergence of the whole structure of Indo-European society, is given its meaning through the creation myth. Important consistent aspects of the common creation myth are found in the ancient Scandinavian as well as in several other Indo-European traditions, not least the Vedic. A particularly prominent feature is the episode in which different variants tell how the world is created from the dismembered body of a primordial being, who was killed by the first gods. The story corresponds and creates a homology between different natural elements and body parts in humans and animals. Man's sacrifices take place as a microcosmic repetition of the creation, and are thus performed according to the pattern of the myth. Not least animal sacrifices have been designed as a reflection and repetition of this treatise, but as already mentioned, the treatment of the dead fits well into the theme of the myth. In the same way as the myth gives meaning to creation, it also explains the perception of death and how the bodies of the dead should be taken care of. Rituals that include fire can, as we shall see, correspond particularly well.

The Scandinavian – Old Norse – version of the myth is found in the Eddic poem *Grímnismál* (40–41), which describes how the cosmos were created from the body parts of the giant *Ymir*, killed by the first gods. A similar mythological tale is *Purusasūkta* from the ancient Indian *Rigveda* (10.90), the oldest part of the ritual manuals and poems that followed the early Indo-European immigrants to India. In this story too, the world is created when the gods cut up a cosmic giant, *Purusa*. It is this narrative that is the archetype for the

**FIGURE 4.4** The giant Ymir is attacked and torn apart by the first gods, who then create the world from Ymir's body parts. This is the Old Norse variant of a common Indo-European creation myth. Illustration by Lorenz Frølich (1820–1908).

Vedic sacrifice as well as for death rituals. The agreements between the two Indo-European versions are related, although not exact, but the overall picture is supplemented by other Norse and Old Indian myths. Bruce Lincoln (1986) has described these creation myths as one of the world's most successful ideological systems, which has survived with a very wide geographical spread (Figure 4.4).

The homology – the belief that one entity is created using the matter in another entity – is one basic cosmological idea that appears in the common mythical theme. Meat and soil, for example, are considered to be of the same material substance and can therefore be converted into each other, and the same also applies to blood and other body fluids in relation to water. Accordingly, bones are equated with the stones in the earth and with rocks and mountains, while hair is associated with plants. The cosmological belief in homology makes the myth of a ritual death and division of a body a narrative that can be easily transformed into ritual practice and structure. The ritual can then be perceived as a microcosmic repetition of the creation process where not only the sacrificed animal or object, but also the body of a dead person, is dissolved and returned to the natural elements that are in themselves identical to the body parts from the first being. In this way, human ritual adds power to the very process of creation in a very concrete way, and in the case of underlying perceptions to both sacrifice and cremation, the connection to the structuring homology is evident.

Furthermore, it is of fundamental interest for understanding the concept of death in Indo-European tradition the very etymology concerning the word for death itself. The proto-Indo-European verb *mer- combines the sense 'to die' and 'to reduce to small pieces'. Such semantics have strong implications for the understanding of death, and also include the way in which the body crumbles into smaller pieces after death (Lincoln 1986: 119). After death, the body breaks down into numerous constituent parts, which then are believed to transform into the elements and their macrocosmic alloforms according to the creation myth. Thus, the transformation on the pyre is seen as the last sacrifice that all human beings must perform to ensure the continued existence of the universe. Like all sacrifice, death is a repetitive, ritual act. Each death repeats every other death and every other sacrifice: above all the first sacrificial death, which effected the creation of the universe. Whenever people die, their bodies re-create the universe at large. In the Vedic world of beliefs, cremation was perceived in this way. In all probability, there was a parallel in the Nordic Bronze Age culture, something that the nature of the archaeological finds strongly suggests. During the cremation, the body is separated in its original elements; to fire and air (through the smoke), to water (by pouring water on the pyre and eventually immersing the burnt remains into water) and to earth (by taking a piece of flesh and burying it in ground).

Cremation is a ritual that clearly illustrates this process as it dissolves the body and brings its constituents back to the original elements. Crushing or grinding the bones after the cremation will make an even more powerful illustration of this cosmic mythology. The bones clearly express a microcosmic version of the decomposition of the primordial being from the creation myth, and the grinding stones – the tools with which the further fragmentation of the bodily remains is performed – likewise acquire a powerful symbolic meaning in this context. Thus, there is a clear ritual logic in that the bones and these tools are deposited together in grave deposits as well as on the cremation site itself (cf. Kaliff 2007: 137–139) (Figure 4.5).

**FIGURE 4.5** The vast majority of the burnt bones found in Scandinavian cremation graves are very fragmented, having been further crushed after the fire. The picture shows burnt bones of typical appearance, contrasted with an unburned lower jaw. Photo: Terje Oestigaard.

## The ancient Scandinavian fire altar

Vedic fire altars are built of burnt clay bricks in five layers, corresponding to the body parts of the primordial being, and material is taken from different parts of creation. A particularly complex and magnificent example is the fire offering agnicayana, 'Piling up Agni', which we have already described at the beginning of the book. Vedic cremation pyres are similarly built out of wood in five layers, in accordance with the same cosmological symbolism, where the cremation platform has in principle the function of a sacrificial altar. The clay bricks for the altar are fired in kilns as are the liturgical pots (Staal 1983: 94–130). The effect of the fire on the material is crucial and meaning-bearing. Through the transformation of the clay, fire is believed to become active in the material. Altars made of clay has no known equivalent in Scandinavian tradition, but instead we have the presence of burnt stone, a material with a potentially similar cosmological meaning. Burnt stone, especially in combination with water, receives a corresponding symbolic meaning to the Vedic bricks, made out of clay, water and fire (e.g. Zimmer 2009: 185; cf. Kaliff 2007: 121–134). Heating stones and making them crack by pouring water on them results in a material with a visible and tangible impact, which clearly shows how it has become a combination of elements: rock, water, fire and also air.

A particularly interesting feature in this context are the so-called 'burnt mounds' (or 'heaps of fire-cracked stones'). These are significant monuments that are largely built of burnt stone, which to the exterior may resemble burial mounds. Burnt mounds constitute a rather common feature in Scandinavian Bronze Age contexts. Some features show evidence of being used as cremation places (Nylén 1958; Kaliff 1994) and they often contain deposits of cremated bones. In fact, as many as in between a quarter and a third of the cases in regions in central Sweden where systematic studies have been conducted contain cremated material (Rundkvist 1994; Noge 2009).

It has previously been argued that these structures may constitute a Scandinavian variant of Indo-European fire altars (Kaliff 2005, 2007), a ritual tool that in various forms could be expected to exist throughout the whole Indo-European area (cf. Staal 1983). Both the design of these burnt mounds – often with intricate, hidden interior constructions – and the deposited material they contain make an interpretation of them as sacrificial contexts very plausible. Despite this, there has been a tenacious notion among archaeologists that burnt mounds are primarily piles of waste or discarded cooking stones, useful primarily as indications of Bronze Age settlements (e.g. Gustawsson 1949; Wigren 1987; Jensen 1989). The dismissive attitude that many archaeologists have long shown for this type of archaeological structures is strikingly illustrated in the following lines, taken from British archaeology, but definitely also reflecting Scandinavian archaeology:

> Burnt mounds are, individually, among the most boring sites with which a field archaeologist must deal. Apart from new data and a new spot on the distribution map, individual sites have little to contribute to our understanding of the past.
>
> *Barber & Russell-White 1990: 59*

However, this stage is now over, and the time has come to see the Scandinavian burnt mounds (and most probably British equivalents!) as what they really are: a main candidate to be the Nordic version of a common Indo-European sacrificial altar. This is certainly not true for all features labelled as burnt mounds, which in fact is a collective, operational term developed to describe the shape and construction of the material structure, not its interpretation and meaning. The morphological variation among the excavated burnt mounds indicates that the features that go under this name can in fact constitute traces of rather different activities. The term encompasses quite different types of constructions, even those that probably constitute only piles of waste. In order to see the difference, an excavation is often required. However, when it comes to features with a particularly intricate design, including complicated internal stone structures – spiral patterns or concentric circles – as well as a disparate and enigmatic find material, we are entering a whole new world. It is these clear ritual features that are of particular interest in this context, although there are also many enigmatic and dubious cases.

The possible intention of burning stone and adding water, as with the clay, would have been to combine the elements in a favourable way. When visibly transformed, it worked as a confirmation that the fire, as well as the divine powers associated with it, had now become active in the material itself. This corresponds closely to the Vedic ritual and the beliefs associated with it:

> Fire together with water cracks stone more effectively than fire alone. In a doctrine of elements this could be perceived as the fire and the water combining to release energy from the stone and the rock. Burnt mounds, besides their association with fire, are also linked to water. Evidence for this comes from their topographic location, and from the fact that many of the stones in the mounds seem to have split in water. The effect of water striking the red-hot stone may have been what was ritually intended. Both the sound and the sight of the union of the water and the red-hot stone could be regarded as living proof of the way the elements combine and change ....
>
> *Kaliff 2007: 123–124*

Burnt mounds occur in very different contexts, also the features that are clearly ritualistic in nature. They are frequently documented on sites designated as cemeteries, but often on settlement sites as well. They are particularly common in southern and central Sweden, but with examples also in the northern parts of the country as well as in Norway and Finland. Importantly, they are particularly common in eastern central Sweden with the largest concentration located in the province of Uppland, north of the Lake Mälaren valley. The majority of the excavated monuments are dated to the Bronze Age (c. 1700–500 BC.) with most dates to the latter part of the period. In total, however, they show a much longer chronological spread, from the Late Neolithic to the Viking period, a time span of 3000 years. Many individual mounds also have a long period of use, with several centuries passing between the earliest C14 dating and the last, within the same mound (Jeppsson 2019 for overview) (Figure 4.6).

Typically, the burnt mounds contain a large amount of fire-cracked stone, usually together with soot and charcoal. Still, there is a relatively broad variation, which has resulted in misunderstandings when comparing the interpretations of different excavated sites. A closer study of different types of mounds reveals the differences. Some burnt mounds seem to be unorganised deposits of burnt stone and other residual material while others are very complex structures. In the former cases, the well-established interpretation as 'rubbish heaps' may well be true, as mentioned, while other structures give a completely different impression. The latter contain elements such as stone kerbs and complex inner stone structures in forms of circles, spirals and stone foundations under the filling. Many burnt

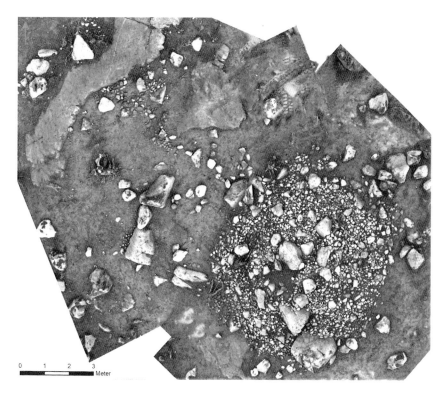

**FIGURE 4.6**  Burnt mounds often show advanced inner constructions, not visible before excavation. Beneath a filling of fire-cracked stone hides complicated stone structures. Burnt mound from Nibble in Tillinge parish, Uppland, with the over-lying packing of burnt, shattered stone front cleaned. After Artursson et al. 2011, Fig. 5:34, p. 238

mounds also contain material that, at first sight, may seem contradictory. Apart from fire-cracked stone, soot and charcoal, there are pottery, grain, seeds and grinding stones and sometimes also traces of metallurgy. Bones – both burnt and unburnt – from various animals, and in many cases also humans, make up the absolute majority of the find material, with cattle as the most dominant species, followed by sheep and goats and to a lesser extent pigs, horses, dogs and domestic birds and more (e.g. Ullén 2003: 243–256; Wigh 2008: 371–389; Larsson 2014: 295–298; Björck 2014: 214–216; Artursson et al. 2017: 66–68). The finds that meet us in the burnt mounds constitute to a large extent what one might expect as traces of a sacrificial place. Human bones also occur frequently.

A comparative study of 31 burnt mounds of eastern central Sweden – all pro-fessionally documented in recent times and excavated from the 1990s onwards – shows a long dating span in total, from around 1400 BC up to the beginning of the Common Era. Based on the analysis, a main division into three categories was made, labelled A, B and C. Category A includes complex features that have been used for a long period of time, often located in central positions on settlements. Activities such as sacrifices, human burials and ritualised cooking as well as special crafts such as bronze casting were performed here. Category B consisted of slightly less complex mounds, often found on the outskirts of the sites. In these features, cooking was the central activity, often with signs of ritualised activities, sometimes also supplemented with burials and traces of craft. Category C, finally, was found in the outermost parts of the sites, and consisted of relatively simple burnt mounds. In these mounds, cooking seems to have been the sole main function and the mounds were in use during a relatively short time (Larsson 2014: 125–127; Artursson et al. 2017: 131).

Although the extensive bone material found in the burnt mounds is a well-known archaeological feature, it has traditionally been interpreted as a profane residual product (e.g. Elfstrand 1995; Ullén 1995). An illustrative example site is Sneden in Litslena Parish, province of Uppland, excavated in the 1990s. The largest structures excavated here were almost 15 m in diameter, and primarily interpreted as large-scale butchering places, although ritual connotations were not ruled out. Particularly one of the monuments stands out, covering a back-filled water well, dated to the early Iron Age, 400–200 BC (Fagerlund 1998: 80–85). The combination of burnt material and the underlying water well are phenomena with clear cosmological connotations, typical of the common Indo-European background based on the creation myth. In the filling of both the mound itself and the back-filled well, a large bone-material was found, including remains of domesticated animals but also humans. Bodies had been cut up, parts were burned and parts were deposited together with stone, soil and water in various combinations. Another example of a well with similar filling was discovered on the nearby Bronze-Age settlement site of Apalle, also in Uppland. In this case, the burnt mounds lay adjacent to a well, located centrally on the site. The find-material consisted mainly of animal bones, with cattle as the dominant species, followed by sheep and goats. The slaughter age of the animals varied greatly, indicating that these animals were killed for reasons other than having reached the perfect age for slaughter (Ullén 2003: 259–261).

A good example of a site with burnt mounds in a clear ritual context is Ringeby in the province of Östergötland, excavated 1993–1994 and dated to the Late Bronze Age and the earliest phase of the Iron Age (ca. 1000–400 BC). Four burnt mounds were documented, all with constructions and deposited material that clearly showed a ritual context, beside extensive traces of other ritual activities: about 60 deposits of burnt human bones, cremation sites, hearth pits and a small cultic building. Unburnt bones from mainly cattle, sheep and goat were found in the mounds, together with cremated bones of animals and humans as well as remains of metal craft and pottery. More recently excavated sites from the province of Uppland show a similar pattern. Illustrative examples are Ryssgärdet (also named Onslunda) and Sommaränge skog in Björklinge parish and not least Nibble in Tillinge Parish – to date the largest Bronze Age cultic site excavated in Scandinavia – as well as Skeke and Björkgärdet in Rasbo Parish (Forsman & Victor 2007; Hjärthner-Holdar, Eriksson & Östling 2008; Artursson et al. 2017). At Nibble, Skeke and Björkgärdet, extensive sacrificial activity was documented, including fire sacrifices and ritual cooking (Artursson, Karlenby & Larsson, 2011: 421–423; Larsson 2014: 163, 299–300; Björck 2014: 214–216). The Skeke site was used as a settlement as well as a cultic site with a continuity of more than 1500 years from about 1100 BC until the mid of the first millennium AD. A large and centrally located burnt mound played a particularly important role during the major part of the history of the settlement. Beginning as a burial site, this mound was used as an important ritual monument for centuries (Figure 4.7).

**FIGURE 4.7**   The same burnt mound as in Fig. 4.6, with the underlying stone structures in the form of concentric circles excavated. After Artursson et al. 2011, Fig. 5: 34b, p. 239

At both Skeke and Nibble, water wells were found directly adjacent to cooking stations, cult houses and burnt mounds. The water may have had a direct functional significance in cooking, but were probably associated with ritual qualities as sacred water emanated from the ground. There are also strong indications that the burnt and fire-cracked stones in the mounds were further cracked by the addition of water to the heated material. When water was poured on the heated stones, it corresponded closely to the symbolic liquid that was put on the Vedic altar, through which it was believed that rain and fertility were generated (cf. Kaliff 2007: 121–134). The combination of water and fire is also present in the Vedic cremation ritual. By pouring water on the burning pyre, Agni is prevented from having to strong impact on the dead body. There has to be balance between the various elements, and none of them – in this case the fire – must dominate too much. The food prepared on the Nibble and Skeke sites consisted of ingredients with a relatively small variation: Mainly meat from cattle and sheep/goats and more rarely pigs and horses, as well as cereals such as barley, wheat and small quantities of hazelnuts (Artursson et al. 2017: 132). That ritual meals formed an important part of the ancient Scandinavian sacrifice were clearly attested also in the Old Norse sources. Although these texts were written down only during the medieval period, there is every reason to believe that the importance of sacred meals has very deep historical roots (e.g. Hultgård 1996; Näsström 2002: 182–184). The ritual cooking works as an important part of the sacrificial ritual itself, as an interaction between man and divinity.

Despite the distance in time, there are good reasons to connect the archaeological finds of burnt mounds of the Bronze Age with a cultic feature mentioned in the Old Norse written sources, namely *hörgr* (or *hǫrgr*). This term sometimes refers to a rock, but also seems to have been able to consist of a structure of stone, sometimes of wood, and probably reflecting a sacrificial altar. In the Eddic poem *Hyndluljóð* (10), there is an account of the worship of the goddess Freyja taking place at a hörgr of stone. The poem is only preserved in a manuscript from the 14th century, but it has been considered to contain a realistic description of a sacrificial scene (Hultgård 1996: 29–32; cf. Vikstrand 2001; cf. Kaliff 2007: 113–114).

The hörgr may originally have been a natural place in the form of a rock or an assembly of stones, but later developed into a proper altar structure. Cultic sites of the type exemplified above, in the form of the named excavated sites from eastern Central Sweden, are often built on rock plateaus, where the original rock is 'built on' and reshaped by adding rocks and building cairns and burnt mounds. In this way, the features on the sites strongly resemble the description that also fits in with a hörgr, as a natural rock which was built on with additional stones, probably in order to further strengthen the power of the place. At most of these documented ritual sites, large amounts of stone have been piled up beside areas of natural rock. The phenomenon also includes large boulders, sometimes weighing 10 tons and more, which have been moved and placed over pits with burnt, deposited material. No practical, functional reason for this procedure can be found, so it is clearly the traces of a ritual, so important that almost a superhuman effort has been devoted to it. Clear examples of this were found at both Nibble, Skeke and Ryssgärdet in Uppland as well as at Ringeby in Östergötland. Geographically close to the latter was yet another similar site, namely Klinga in Borg's parish, excavated 1989–1990, which was one of the first sites where this phenomenon was observed. This site was mainly characterised as a cemetery from the Bronze and Early Iron age, located on a ridge of natural rock, where stone and quantities of boulder clay had been brought as an apparent 'improvement' of the natural rock surface (cf. Kaliff 1992, 1997; Stålbom 1994).

Another fascinating site, this time from the western part of Sweden that clearly illustrates how stone was collected to re-shape a rock formation, is Svarteborg in Bohuslän. The site measured 37 × 34 m and consisted of a stone-lined rampart shaped around an oval natural rock formation. This site shows a particularly long continuity of ritual use from the Early Bronze Age up to the Late Iron Age, with traces of ritual fires, cremation burials and also rock carvings. In the filling of the stone settings, built on the rock surface, there were scattered bone fragments, or deposits of small concentrations of bone. This site was interpreted by the excavators as being built in agreement with cosmological ideas, suggesting that different cosmic levels and elements met here: earth, sky and underworld (Munkenberg 2004: 17–36, 54–60). This corresponds very well with Indo-European perspectives (cf. Kaliff 2007: 177–178). These places can be described as 'improved' natural formations where a mountain or a moraine formation has been given a more characteristic appearance or a more symbolically charged content (Figure 4.8).

Sacrificial rites in ancient Scandinavia, as well as in the Vedic context, seem to have been performed at various levels of complexity, from everyday sacrifices in the hearth of the home to the construction of advanced altars for burnt offerings. As we have seen, there is in particular one type of archaeological remains that clearly manifests the myth physically on a large scale, namely the burnt mounds. If we are looking for an ancient Scandinavian equivalent to the great Vedic fire sacrifices with advanced altar constructions – of which the agnicayana ritual described in Chapter 1 is the best known and thoroughly documented, then some of these features – the burnt mounds – are indeed very good candidates.

> The fire-cracked stone in the burnt mounds/fire altars would thus correspond to the Vedic idea that Agni was born on the fire altar. A further parallel, which in my opinion may be of great explanatory value, is that the stone was burnt to transform it in such a way that the fire became active in the material itself. This would correspond closely to the Vedic ritual as it was performed, for example, in the agnicayana, although there it is clay that is fired to make the brick used to build the altar. The brick then contains a combination of elements – earth, water, and fire – which gives it a profound symbolic meaning. If the burnt mounds are created by heating stone and then making it crack by pouring water on it, the result is a material that may have been perceived as a similar combination of

**FIGURE 4.8** Natural rock formation, added and improved with large amounts of loose stones and boulders, both natural stone and burnt and shattered stone. Some stones are arranged in the form of kerbs or concentric stone circles. Part of the excavation area at Klinga in Borg's parish, during the 1989 survey. Photo Anders Kaliff.

> elements: rock, water, fire, and perhaps also air ... Here it is simple to see a symbolism that corresponds very well to that manifested in the great Vedic fire sacrifice.
>
> *Kaliff 2007: 123*

As the ancient Scandinavian fire sacrifices seem to be based on the common Indo-European cosmology, there is no reason to doubt that this tradition had a very long and enduring continuity in a similar way as its Vedic equivalent. In the latter, as we have seen, this is closely linked to the particularly conservative tradition of oral, verbatim transmitted ritual manuals. An at least partly comparable example, Old Norse oral narrative tradition was by all account a prominent feature also of Scandinavia. There is much to suggest that this oral narrative art, probably largely performed in bound verse form, may have constituted a corresponding strong conservative culture-bearing tradition. An extremely important difference is, of course, that the Vedic tradition has a living continuity into today's Hinduism and that the Vedic literature has thus remained highly relevant. Corresponding continuity in religious superstructure does not exist in Scandinavia where Christianity, a millennium ago, became a dividing line in history. Here, the tradition has only sporadically been able to live on in popular customs, stories and rhymes, often in opposition to public religion and society. The rich and unique Icelandic evidence, in the form of Eddic poems, skaldic verses and sagas, is an exception, and even this is extremely fragmentary in a comparison with the Vedic equivalent. The existence of a very enduring conservative ritual tradition from the Bronze Age to the Viking Age should therefore not come as a surprise.

## Sacrifices and funerals

Although Scandinavian fire sacrifice rituals have been performed in very different environments; settlement sites, significant natural sites and burial sites, the latter are of special interest. As we have already seen, there is every reason to assume a close connection between the cremation ritual and burnt offerings, similar to the Vedic tradition. Archaeological finds clearly indicate a very close relationship between burial ritual and sacrifice also in the ancient Scandinavian context. This is evident from the remains of both activities within the same archaeological contexts, but not least also in the form of features that show a combination of traces of both cremation and burnt offerings. Thus, archaeological sites with remains of cremation platforms and deposits of burnt bones are also particularly important for studying remains of fire sacrifice rituals in a broader sense.

In the cremation fire, the dead person's body disintegrates and merges into the various elements in a corresponding way to sacrificed animals or objects in a fire sacrifice (e.g. Lincoln 1975, 1986). Cremation becomes, as in the Vedic version, the last sacrificial act of the dead. This belief may have been strengthened even more if the cremation was also carried out in the same environment, and even with the same cultic tools that were used for other fire rituals. Thus, sacrificial altars can have a double role in this respect as there are strong indications in the Scandinavian archaeological material that these may also have functioned as cremation platforms. In that case, it would be another close parallel to the Vedic ritual where the cremation platform is ideally designed in the same way as the square fire altar (Kaliff 2007: 78–79) (Figure 4.9).

Of particular interest in this context is the frequent occurrence of cremated human bones in burnt mounds, finds which are seldom interpreted as primary burial sites. On the contrary, the bones have sometimes been interpreted as reburials in older mounds (Rentzhog 1967; Hyenstrand 1968; Wigren 1987), an interpretation that does not explain why these mounds were built in the first place. Viewed from a comparative perspective, most finds suggest that the connection between the cremated bones and the burnt mounds are more multifaceted with the human remains rather reinforcing a sacred place than having been placed there only because the mound had an advantageous 'grave-like' shape. According to this scenario, the bones constitute a very clear manifestation of a

**FIGURE 4.9** Reconstruction of a Scandinavian Bronze Age cremation, performed on a smooth rock surface with rock-carvings next to a shoreline. The reconstruction is based on archaeological finds of cremation sites combined with inspiration from comparative Indo-European examples, particularly Vedic ritual. Drawing: Richard Holmgren. ARCDOC, after Kaliff 2007: Figure 6, p. 100.

central motif in the Indo-European creation myth, the part of the story where the bones of the primordial being are transformed and become the rocks and stones of the earth.

A couple of systematic analyses have been made of the presence of human bones in burnt mounds, but without making any connection to Indo-European belief systems. The archaeologist Anna-Sara Noge (2009) conducted a detailed study of 98 excavated burnt mounds in the northern part of the Lake Mälaren Valley in eastern Sweden aiming to explain why human bones were deposited in them. The study showed that such finds occurred in about a third (32%) of the mounds. These mounds generally deviated from the vast majority, especially with regard to the presence of internal structures. Clear internal structures were more common in the burnt mounds with human bones and about half of these had internal stone circles or kerbs covered with a filling of burnt and fire-cracked stones. A similar study was previously done by Martin Rundkvist (1994), analysing 42 burnt mounds in the eastern part of the Lake Mälaren valley. Of these mounds, slightly less than 24% contained human bones. The vast majority, 80% of the mounds in this study, were built during the Bronze Age, and burials occurred only in the mounds dated to this period. Both studies are consistent in terms of the fact that burnt mounds with human remains more often feature kerbs and interior stone circles.

Illustrative examples of burnt mounds of this kind were present at several of the sites mentioned above. At Nibble in Tillinge parish, Skeke and Björkgärdet in Rasbo parish, as well as at Ryssgärdet (Onslunda) in Björklinge parish, all in Uppland, but also at Ringeby in Östergötland, human bones were present in the burnt mounds. Furthermore, the findings from Ringeby provided strong support that burnt mounds also had a function as cremation platforms, which is an interpretation that does not contradict a parallel function as sacrificial altars (Kaliff 1994, 1997). As shown by the Vedic analogy, cremation platforms and fire altars have many traits in common and a similar ritual significance.

A number of these ritual sites also show a long continuity with the aforementioned sites Nibble, Skeke and Björkgärdet as good examples, both in the case of cremations and sacrificial rites (Artursson, Kaliff & Larsson 2017: 121–134). The burning of the dead often took place on an individual cremation site that seems to have been used only once, but in a few cases on a more permanent platform, used repeatedly over a longer period of time. Pyres and cremation platforms with so-called air pits – a construction intended to increase the air supply to the fire – have been found in a large number of sites of this type (see, among others, Kaliff 1995: 41ff, 58ff; Arcini 2007; Arcini, Höst & Svanberg 2007; Svanberg 2007; Artursson, Karlenby & Larsson 2011: 195f). In cases where cremation sites have been used only once, the cremated individuals appear to have been buried on or near the spot where the cremation was performed. In some cases, grave goods in the form of food, whole animal bodies and objects followed the dead on the pyre. A varying amount of the burnt bones were collected after the cremation and sometimes also remains of grave goods. In other cases, the burned bones have been placed in a ceramic vessel or other types of containers, but more commonly only a selection of bone fragments were deposited in more or less clear concentrations (Figure 4.10).

In several cases, special cult buildings were erected for the funeral rituals and for recurring ritual feasting. Ritual demolition and burial of cultic or

**FIGURE 4.10** Some burnt mounds show clear traces of having been used as platforms for cremation pyres, alongside a role as sacrificial altars. This is probably deeply rooted in the Indo-European view of cremation as a form of burnt offering, perhaps most clearly expressed in the Vedic ritual. Photo showing such an example from the grave and cultic site Ringeby, during the excavation 1993–1994. Photo: Anders Kaliff.

ancestral houses has in some cases taken place when the ceremonies have ended or when new monuments were erected, with good examples from the Nibble site. Furthermore, parts of the demolished buildings on this site have been deposited in adjacent to burnt mounds or alternatively in pits or in stone formations. In some cases, the pits have been sealed with large boulders, weighing several tons. Another very clear example is Skeke. During the early phase of the Skeke site, two cremation pyres were built, presumably just before 1000 BC. One adult person of unknown sex and a young woman were cremated on the respective pyres. A few bones from the adult individual, altogether 14 fragments from different parts of the body, were buried next to a large boulder. The boulder itself was incorporated in a burnt mound, in the documentation material named A83. Nearby, the young woman was buried in an inconspicuous pit, containing a relatively large amount of burnt bones. As grave gifts she received a bronze dagger, some stone and flint tools and parts of ceramic vessels. The buried person next to the boulder received only parts of simple pottery and food – cattle, sheep/goat, fish and barley – as grave gifts. The bones of the adult, buried next to the

**FIGURE 4.11** Reconstruction of a typical Bronze Age cultic building from the Skeke site in Rasbo parish, Uppland. This particular house was built as part of a burnt mound, used for repeated rituals during hundreds of years. The mound was arranged around a natural boulder, probably an altar – the old Norse *hörgr* – in its original form. Drawing Richard Holmgren, ARCDOC, after Larsson ed. 2014, Figure 7:2, p. 348.

boulder, was built into a complicated structure of spiral-laid stone chains, later supplemented with a cult house. Next to the cult house was a water-well, and after the demolition of the house the well was blocked with a solid boulder. The grave as well as the inner spiral pattern were covered with a thick layer of fire-cracked stone, which was judged to have been added in connection with recurring ritualised cooking in cooking pits in the area (Larsson 2014: 157–160; Artursson, Kaliff & Larsson 2017: 107–109). This type of small cultic building, documented on the Skeke site, is a type of structure that has been found in a number of ritual sites from mainly the Late Bronze Age and most often in connection with funerals (Kaliff 1995; Victor 2002; Mattes 2008; Kaliff & Mattes 2017) (Figure 4.11).

Seen from a 'grave perspective', a fire-cracked stone can be seen as a trace of recurring festivities to remember or honour the dead whose bones (or parts of them) rest in the earth. At the same time, these remains may also be physical traces of sacrifices, which correspond well with the traces of both food and drink sacrifices that were found on sites such as Nibble and Skeke. The difference between these two interpretive perspectives may at first seem larger than it actually is. In fact, they may completely coincide.

Comparative Indo-European studies show that the boundary between grave and cultic place can be very fluid indeed, not least between graves and altars (cf. Kaliff 2007: 75–84). There is a close connection between graves and altars as attested in several ancient Indo-European cultures. In ancient Greece and Rome, as in Vedic India, the altar could take the shape of a burial mound where also sacrifices were performed. Originally, this sacrifice was performed on real graves, but the form of the burial mound was later transferred to what became a pure altar (Edsman 1987: 223). A reasonable interpretation would therefore be that important graves also functioned as places of worship – altar constructions – and that the grave and cult functions reinforced each other. Already the Norwegian historian of religion Emil Birkeli (1938: 56) believed that in pre-Christian Scandinavia the grave was actually the most important cultic site, which also had an important altar function. This seem to have been an enduring tradition. The tradition of making offerings on the farm's burial mound survived in certain parts of Scandinavia well into the 19th century.

When studying different excavated sites, it becomes obvious that most of the remains from the cremated bodies are not at all present in the bone deposits on the prehistoric Scandinavian cemeteries. In other words, most of the cremated bones must have been deposited in other locations and used for other purposes. A tentative explanation would be in lakes and streams, close to the burial grounds and cremation places. There are also a few examples of possible sacred places of this kind, and many prehistoric Scandinavian cemeteries and ritual places are located close to water (e.g. (cf. Kaliff & Oestigaard 2017: 126–131). During the Vedic cremation ritual, the burnt bones and ashes are shovelled into the running water. By performing this ritual, the remaining parts of the body are brought back to one of the original elements – water – after being consumed by fire and air. The death rituals mean that the body is dissolved and returned to its constituent parts.

During early Vedic times, burials of burnt bones also occurred, even in burial mounds, closely resembling Bronze Age practices in Europe. Even burnt mounds as sacrificial altars fit very well into an Indo-European perspective as they begin to appear at this time – the beginning of the Bronze Age – when Indo-European lifestyle and culture are likely to have a major impact in Scandinavia. This puts the emphasis on the links between east and west and how Indo-European ideas spread back and forth across the Eurasia for millennia. It is reasonable to imagine that important rituals and religious beliefs have been closely linked to particular living conditions – not least animal husbandry – as well as basic social institutions, but also having a strong oral tradition, which was at least partly transmitted in bound verse form. The latter case may explain the survivability of the ancient Indo-European elements that we see in the Old Norse poetry of the Late Iron Age. Moving further east, we find other evidences.

# 5

# FIRES FROM HEAVEN

## The links between East and West

### From the steppe to Eastern Europe and back again

The migration of nomadic pastoralists from the Eurasian steppe as a decisive factor behind the early spread of Indo-European language and culture is by now a well-established fact. Ever since the ground-breaking aDNA results of the now already classical papers published in *Nature* less than a decade ago (Allentoft, Sikora & Willerslev 2015; Haak, Lazaridis & Reich 2015), this scenario has received increasing support. Nevertheless, the complexity of what really happened during the 3rd millennium BC has simultaneously been deepened (e.g. Librado, Khan & Fages 2021; Wilkin, Ventresca Miller & Fernandes 2021). A more complex picture has gradually emerged compared to the first decisive studies, although the overall scenario remains. The latter also confirms the basic features of the interpretations made by prominent researchers in the Indo-European field even long before the aDNA studies were made possible (e.g. Mallory 1989; Anthony 2007; Kuzmina 2007, 2008). It is now an accepted fact – but for a long period intensively questioned – that the aDNA studies essentially confirm the interpretation put forward by Marija Gimbutas in her so-called Kurgan theory (Gimbutas 1956, cf. 1970, 1994).

Furthermore, it can now be shown in more detail that the first flow of people from the Yamnaya culture (equivalent to what Gimbutas labelled as the 'Kurgan culture') on the Pontic steppe westwards towards Europe was followed by a reflux from Eastern Europe back to the steppe. This 'return' was discernible in DNA already in one of the studies from 2015 (Allentoft, Sikora & Willerslev 2015), but has later been followed up by more detailed studies of the eastern variant of the Corded Ware Culture designated as Fatyanovo culture and its even more eastern variant, the Balanovo culture (about 2900–2050 BC). This eastern part of the Corded Ware cultural complex has not received much attention in the

DOI: 10.4324/9781003300915-5

**FIGURE 5.1** Grave from the Fatyanovo culture of the typical Corded Ware type, from a Russian museum exhibition. Public domain.

past (Figure 5.1), but is now proving to be of crucial importance for the continued Indo-European development. As Kerkko Nordqvist and Volker Heyd write about the Russian Fatyanovo Culture:

> The Fatyanovo Culture, together with its eastern twin, the Balanovo Culture, forms part of the pan-European Corded Ware Complex … Its immediate roots are to be found in the southern Baltic States, Belarus, and northern Ukraine (the Baltic and Middle-Dnepr Corded Ware Cultures), from where moving people spread the culture further east along the river valleys of the forested flatlands. By doing so, they introduced animal husbandry to these regions … Fatyanovo Culture is formed by the reverse movement to the (north-)east of the Corded Ware Complex … Through its descendants (including Abashevo, Sintashta, and Andronovo Cultures) it becomes a key component in the development of the wider cultural landscape of Bronze Age Eurasia.
>
> *Nordqvist & Heyd 2020: 65*

The Fatyanovo culture, named after the village of Fatyanovo in Yaroslavl district in Russia, had a close interaction with the older, Neolithic European agricultural cultures in the southwest from which both innovations and genes were incorporated: '… the Fatyanovo Culture individuals were genetically similar to other Corded Ware cultures, carrying a mixture of Steppe and European early farmer ancestry and thus likely originating from a fast migration towards the northeast from somewhere in the vicinity of modern-day Ukraine' (Saag, Vasilyev & Varul 2021: 2–9). A crucial role in this process had another cultural group with close ties to the Corded Ware complex, called the Middle Dnieper Culture (c.

2800–1900 BC). As the name shows, it is geographically centred to the middle reach of the Dnieper River, an area located in today's northern Ukraine and Belarus. The people of the Middle Dnieper culture were the first herding and pastoral culture–carrying stockbreeding economies northwards into the Russian forest zone. The passage along the Pripyat tributary of the river Dnieper was a possible 'bridge' between Yamnaya and Corded Ware/Fatyanovo cultures between the proper steppe in the south and the northern forest steppe. In the words of Anthony: 'They followed marshes, open lakes, and riverine floodplains where there were natural openings in the forest. These open places had grass and reeds for the animals, and the rivers supplied plentiful fish. The earliest Middle Dnieper sites are dated about 2800–2600 BCE; the latest ones continued to about 1900–1800 BCE' (Anthony 2007: 377).

The Fatyanovo culture could in itself be seen as an eastern extension of the Middle Dnieper culture. Like the even more easternly variants known as the Balanovo culture, they all make up different variations of the Corded Ware phenomenon. Available dating implies that the development of Fatyanovo was not significantly later than the Corded Ware Culture further west and had a continuation to around 2000 BC. Analyses show that it was through the Fatyanovo culture that animal husbandry and, probably, crop cultivation were first introduced into the forest belt of Eastern Europe. Its distribution area covers a vast geographical region in the zone of deciduous and mixed forests with sites and finds mainly following the major river valleys and watersheds (Nordqvist & Heyd 2020: 68–69) (Figure 5.2).

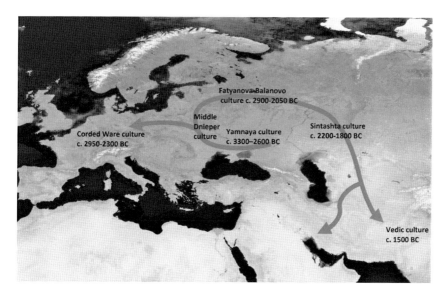

**FIGURE 5.2** Simplified and schematic map of early Indo-European cultures and migrations. Illustration made by Terje Oestigaard and Anders Kaliff (background map by Visible Earth, NASA).

The Fatyanovo culture is likely to play an important role in transferring cultural elements and people from Eastern Europe eastwards and further towards the southeast. In this way, it also functioned as a 'cultural bridge' over to the Abashevo culture – the most eastern of the Corded Ware–related cultures – and then via the subsequent Sintashta culture into the emerging Indo-Iranian cultural sphere. The Fatyanovo culture is interpreted as a chief- and male-oriented society of a kind traditionally associated with Indo-European cultures due to the richly furnished male burials, occasionally accompanied by sacrificed household members or wives. Interestingly, there are also evidences of fire cult or special fireplaces and traces of fire making in and near burials, and evidence of sun-symbolism (Nordqvist & Heyd 2020 with referred literature), which are other typical features that are particularly associated with an Indo-European cultural context. The presence of fire cult and sun symbols in the Fatyanovo and Balanovo cultures – where the latter is also characterised by metallurgy – may have great explanatory value for the early spread of such phenomena. These are cultures that constitute a potential east-west bridge between the Balto-Slavic and Indo-Iranian territories, and thus constitute a key to explaining the existence of similar cultural phenomena in very distant geographical areas where similar Indo-European features are found.

> As Fatyanovo groups spread eastward down the Volga they discovered the copper ores of the western Ural foothills, and in this region, around the lower Kama River, they created long-term settlements. The Volga-Kama region, which became the metallurgical heartland for almost all Fatyanovo metallurgy, has been separated from the rest of Fatyanovo and designated the Balanovo culture. Balanovo seems to be the settled, metal-working aspect of eastern Fatyanovo. At the southern fringe of Balanovo territory, in the forest-steppe zone of the middle Volga and upper Don where the rivers again flowed south, a fourth group emerged (after Middle Dnieper, Fatyanovo and Balanovo). This was the Abashevo, the easternmost of the Russian forest-zone cultures that were descended from Corded Ware ceramic traditions. The Abashevo culture played an important role in the origin of Sintashta.
>
> *Anthony 2007: 382*

The Abashevo culture is dated to approximately 2500/2400–1900 BC, and is thus partly parallel to, but also preceding the closely related Sintashta culture, dated c. 2200–1800 BC.

## Sintashta – an Indo-European key culture

Starting in the Sintashta culture (also known as Sintashta-Petrovka or Sintashta-Arkaim culture), it is possible to trace the continued spread of Indo-European–speaking people towards south and southeast – a migration that constitutes the origin of both the Vedic culture in northern India and the ancient Iranian culture (e.g. Witzel 2019). This may also be in line with linguistic developments and further diversification in the Indo-Iranian region. A few centuries after the final phase of the Sintashta culture, we are confronted with the oldest written evidence for Indo-European languages at a time when the closely related Ancient Indian and Ancient Iranian languages have already been separated: 'The undocumented language that was the parent of both, common Indo-Iranian, must be dated well before 1500 BCE, because, by this date, Old Indic had already appeared in the documents of the Mitanni in North Syria … Common Indo-Iranian probably was spoken during the Sintashta period, 2100–1800 BCE. Archaic Old Indic probably emerged as a separate tongue from archaic Iranian about 1800–1600 BCE' (Anthony 2007: 408).

Through the circumferential movement – the migration from Yamnaya to the west and the return of steppe-related people via the Fatyanovo-Balanovo culture – also now with elements of DNA as well as cultural traits from the Neolithic farmers in Europe, a merged heritage is brought back to the steppe in the east. In this way, the continued Indo-Europeanisation, starting from Sintashta, contains a potential mix of elements from the steppe nomads and from the early European farmers, although, at present, in uncertain proportions. This means that the Vedic people of India, like the ancient Iranians, also carried a genetic heritage from Neolithic Europe, and therefore possibly also cultural features. The genetic traces can still be read today where north Indians, in general, and individuals belonging to Indian Brahmin caste, in particular, carry a well-preserved genetic heritage of the Vedic immigration (Sharma, Rai & Sharma 2009; Debortoli, Abbatangelo & Ceballos 2020; cf. Singh, Sarkar & Nandineni 2018; Shinde, Narasimhan & Reich 2019) (Figure 5.2). As we have also pointed out earlier:

> A particularly interesting aspect of the Sintashta culture is that the genetic heritage can apparently not be traced directly from the Yamnaya culture, but that the ancestors were first part of the Corded Ware culture in Europe – descendants of Yamnaya themselves. DNA analyses have shown clear similarities in genetic heritage, between the Corded Ware culture and the Sintashta culture. In both cases, there was a higher proportion of heritage from the early peasants in Central Europe compared to the population of the Yamnaya culture … This means that part of the eastern movement of the Yamnaya's descendants first took a trip to the west to Eastern and Central Europe, received new genetic additions there from the former peasant population, and only then migrated east. Indo-European migrations, therefore, appear to have taken place in a somewhat complicated way, which highlights the extensive contacts between East and West, even over long distances. This shows that the people of the Sintashta culture are also carriers of a genetic heritage from Europe.
>
> *Kaliff & Oestigaard 2020: 138–139*

As a matter of fact, the development of Sintashta through an influx of cultural impulses from the West was presented as a hypothesis even before aDNA analyses were available on purely archaeological grounds. This was also combined with an insight that the culture in question was Indo-Iranian. In her book *The Prehistory of the Silk Route*, Elena Kuzmina wrote (2008: 40–41): '... we advanced a bold hypothesis of a western influx of people that led to the development ... In conclusion, our opinion was that the founders of the Novy Kumak-type sites were Indo-Iranians, which confirmed the hypothesis we had developed earlier'. This purely archaeological analysis, from the time before the 'aDNA revolution', clearly shows how aDNA and archaeology complement and confirm each other instead of speaking completely different languages as sceptics sometimes argue (cf. Kaliff & Oestigaard 2020: 139).

This reflux movement, with its combined heritage from the steppe and Neolithic Europe, has great potential to be linked to particular problems in comparative linguistics: We may here track a movement of people that likely spread unique features shared between Indo-Iranian and Balto-Slavic languages (Narasimhan, Patterson & Reich 2019). Less discussed, but equally reasonable, is that a broader register of cultural phenomena than just language may have been transferred in a similar way. This northern route, where aDNA together with cultural features have been shown to travel back from west to east, has the potential to explain similarities between geographically remote areas, such as parts of north-eastern Europe and South Asia. Narasimhan, Patterson and Reich (2019: 1) say:

> This special connection between Indo-Iranian and Balto-Slavic languages may seem strange at first glance, at least starting from the simplified picture of a direct spread of Indo-European features, from the steppe to different geographical areas. The alternative scenario, with a first spread to the west and a return to the east via the Fatyanovo culture radically changes this. The fact that there is a direct line from Fatyanovo-Balanovo, via Abashevo over to the Sintashta culture, and from there further towards the early Indo-Iranian culture, has the potential to explain the special, close relationship between Balto-Slavic and Indo-Iranian.

Already 25 years before the first aDNA breakthrough in Indo-European research, the linguist Frederik Kortlandt (1990: 131–140) identified the earliest stages of Balto-Slavic with the Middle Dnieper culture, an interpretation that is now strongly supported by genetics. Kortlandt argued that the early speakers of Balto-Slavic were the people who remained in the Yamnaya area after the migrations of part of the population towards west, east and south. As now shown (e.g. Nordqvist & Heyd 2020), the scenario may be partly different and more complex given that recent research posits a more northern location of the early Balto-Slavs, stretching in a west-east belt of the forest and steppe-forest zone. Importantly, in the south-eastern part of this belt, we meet the area where the Indo-Iranian language and culture seem to have been formed.

Viewed from a strict geographical perspective, Balto-Slavic and Indo-Iranian thus appear to have developed as a continuum from the areas of present-day northern Ukraine, Belarus and parts of today's Baltic States given that they share both satemisation and the so-called Ruki sound law. Indo-European languages are generally classified as either so-called centum languages or satem languages. The difference between these consists in the pronunciation of so-called dorsal consonants, such as 'K' and 'G'. A classic example is the words for 'hundred' (lat. centum and avest. satum), which named the two different branches. In centum languages, the consonant is pronounced 'hard' (k); while in satem languages, it has a 'soft' pronunciation (s). The Ruki sound law in turn refers to a sound change that took place in the satem branches of Indo-European, namely in Balto-Slavic, Indo-Iranian and also in Armenian, with an original $\star$s sound changed to $\star$š after certain consonants, the latter a sound to be pronounced similar to English 'sh'.

Although it has been debated, it seems very likely indeed that the Balto-Slavic–Indo-Iranian link is a result of a common ancestry, closer than between several of the other Indo-European languages. In this context, it is significant that even today's Slavic and Baltic populations in north-eastern Europe share much larger amounts of the R1a haplogroup on the male, Y-chromosome line, with north Indians, than they do, for instance, with most Germanic populations, where instead the R1b haplogroup is most frequent (cf. Underhill, Poznik & Rootsi 2015; Papac, Erneé & Haak 2021). The fact that there are also significant points of contact between Balto-Slavic and Germanic does not have to affect this understanding. Mallory (1989: 108) even writes about 'a continuum of Slavic-Baltic-Germanic that stretched across Northern Europe from east to west'. However, he wrote this long before the knowledge existed about the reflux in the eastern direction via the Fatyanovo-Balanovo cultures.

As archaeologists, however, we do not want to delve further into the purely linguistic conditions, but stick to generally known facts and to emphasise the geographical and archaeological picture. Through the reflux via the Fatyanovo culture, a very probable scenario emerges for how the special relationship between Balto-Slavic and Indo-Iranian may have arisen. In any case, it seems unlikely that these events would have taken place as a completely parallel phenomenon without any connection to the context in which the similarity between the Balto-Slavic and Indo-Iranian languages arose.

Genetics is certainly one thing, culture and language another, something that is often highlighted as a problem when criticism is levelled at the use of aDNA studies in archaeology (e.g. Heyd 2017, cf. Kristiansen, Allentoft & Frei 2017). Nevertheless, there is usually a close connection between genes, language and culture. From an overall perspective, and despite many exceptions in human history – exceptions that rather confirm a rule – genetic kinship, language and culture are, in most cases, inherited together. The closest family and relatives are, in most cases, the context in which language is passed on between generations, which in itself constitutes the most reasonable explanation for the fact that genes and language are so often historically connected. To find genetic kinship, alongside similarities, in languages, myths and rituals, etc., is thus hardly surprising in general, and consequently not in the specific case regarding the Balto-Slavs and the Indo-Iranians. The interesting question is more specific: Are there any particularly significant cultural elements – typical of Indo-Europeans – besides linguistic ones that can be linked to the reflux from Europe to the steppe?

This question is complicated by the fact that the spread of people and ideas from the steppe took place in more than one 'wave'. From Sintashta, there is a second spread, not only southward towards the Indo-Iranian area, but also again westward towards Europe. To the Indo-Iranian territory, this spread included people as well as innovations such as the chariot and equestrian art used for military purposes. The spread from Sintashta to the west may also have included population movements, but may, to an even greater extent, have taken place in the form of the transfer of ideas and innovations, at least in part accompanying a mobile elite with warlike characteristics (e.g. Librado, Khan & Fages 2021: 634–640). It can, therefore, be difficult to distinguish the primary features of the steppe and returned to Sintashta from elements that may have been 'caught along the way' in the forest and forest steppe area of the Fatyanovo and Balanovo cultures.

## The Baltic fire worship

One of the cultural elements that is of special significance in both the Balto-Slavic and the Indo-Iranian area is the sacred fire. Fire as a sacred tool is central to several older Indo-European cultural traditions, to such an extent that it can be highlighted as a particularly significant ritual element, along with, for example, horse sacrifices and initiation rites linked to various societies of young warriors, the so-called Kóryos, often referred to as 'Männerbunde' (e.g. Kaliff & Oestigaard 2020, 2022). A distinctive feature is not least the ritual seasonal fires, linked to beliefs in the protective aspect of fire in combination with its sympathetic magic role to infuse the sun's power into the growing crop, and thus to increase the fertility of the agricultural year. Not least among the Baltic peoples are there such long-standing traditions where fire as a sacred tool also seems to have had a very central significance. These in turn have close parallels in other related cultures, in geographically more or less remote areas in the east and west. Common features can be traced in pre-Christian Scandinavian ritual traditions, on the one hand, as well as in the Vedic and also Ancient Iranian, on the other hand, but also in, for instance, the ancient Greek and Roman traditions (cf. Kaliff 2005, 2007; Kaliff & Oestigaard 2017).

In the Vedic ritual, as in the Ancient Iranian counterpart, the importance of fire is well-documented. In the more than 3000-year-old Vedic tradition (see Chapter 6), still surviving as part of present-day Hinduism, ritual fire is an element of overall importance, both as a sacrificial tool and in funeral rites. In the case of the Balto-Slavic area, the documentation does not go as far back in time. However, the folkloristic material shows a very strong belief in holy flames and a tenacious tradition of ritual fire.

Furthermore, and as indicated above, the Proto-Baltic (or Balto-Slavic) context may actually be a primary area for Indo-European fire rituals. Today, the Baltic States Latvia and Lithuania cover a rather limited geographical area, a region that does not reflect the original distribution of the Baltic language and culture. During the formatting phase of the Balto-Slavic languages, the Proto-Baltic area was considerably larger, with a more eastern distribution than the original Proto-Slavic counterpart. The early Baltic language is thus with great certainty associated with the widespread expansion of the Fatyanovo culture, or at least large parts of it, while the Slavic branch is more probably linked to the south-western part of the cultural corridor formed by the Middle Dnieper culture. This in turn would support an early, close relationship between the Baltic and Indo-Iranian languages and cultures, and hence also with Slavic. Not least linguistic relics in the landscape in the form of names of lakes and rivers support the existence of a vast original Baltic area. It is also worth mentioning that the Balts survived in some areas far east of the modern Baltic linguistic frontier well into Medieval times.

Also, archaeology provides evidence. Pre-Christian Baltic sites have been excavated not only in the territories of modern Lithuania and Latvia, but also in the much larger area towards east and southeast: Belarus, North-Eastern Poland and Russian Kaliningrad Oblast. Several excavations of sites belonging to the Fatyanovo culture provide supportive evidence of this spread (Zaroff 2019: 188).

> The Middle Dnieper and Fatyanovo migrations overlapped the region where river and lake names in Baltic dialects, related to Latvian and Lithuanian, have been mapped by linguists: through the upper and middle Dnieper basin and the upper Volga as far east as the Oka. These names indicate the former extent of Baltic-speaking populations, which once occupied an area much larger than the area they occupy today. The Middle Dnieper and Fatyanovo migrations probably established the populations that spoke pre-Baltic dialects in the Upper Volga basin. Pre-Slavic probably developed between the middle Dnieper and upper Dniester among the populations that stayed behind.
>
> *Anthony 2007: 380*

There are also many signs of particularly close connections in ritual and beliefs between Baltic and Indo-Iranian. The Balts, in their language as well as in their religion, have preserved many elements undoubtedly belonging to the oldest phase of the common Proto-Indo-European religion. In addition to conformities in divine names and ritual practices, not least the sacred nature of fire, there are also other similarities. According to the Latvian-Swedish historian of religion Haralds Biezais, this applies not least to notions of the sun as a deity, called Saule in the Baltic language and Sūrya in Sanskrit. He saw that the similarities between the two deities were so great that had not the Balts and the people of India been separated by several thousand miles and several millennia, direct contact would be considered the probable cause rather than a common origin. Several Baltic divinities, as Indo-Iranian variants, are closely associated with horses, riding or being drawn in chariots across the sky, etc. (Biezais 2021). At the same time, the Baltic culture has a clear geographical touch also with the Germanic area to the west. Not least, the Baltic Sea context may be of interest here, as both early and intense interaction between Baltic and Germanic groups may have taken place in this environment (cf. Ström & Biezais 1975).

The pre-Christian Baltic religion, like the ancient Scandinavian one, clearly represents a religious complex with many original Indo-European elements (e.g. Biezais 1972, 1976). One basic example is the Dievas in Lithuanian, with the Latvian version Dievs and the Old Prussian Deivas, equivalent to the proto-Indo-European *Dyēus. It originally meant the physical sky, but became personified as an anthropomorphic deity. Dievs, the pre-Christian name for God, is actually still used in Baltic language:

> It is worth recalling here that the term Dievas in Lithuanian denotes a Christian God, but in pre-Christian times it was a name for the sky. At the same time the name is cognate to a number of Indo-European sky deities such as the Vedic Dyaus, Greek Dzeus, Latin Dies pitar (Jupiter), and Germanic Tiwaz. Furthermore, it is more than simply coincidence that all Balts concurrently associated the Latin term for the god 'Deus' with their name for the sky. Hence, the only explanation is that the Christian God just replaced the old Baltic sky god Dievas. Otherwise why would all the Balts name the Christian God the Sky? After Christianisation the name survived in Baltic ethnographic sources, mainly denoting only ghosts and spirits.
>
> *Zaroff 2019: 191–192*

The proto-Indo-European name of the central sky-god *Dyēus, etymologically meaning 'the shining one', may therefore refer to the disc of the sun. Similar names referring to this god can be found in all main Indo-European contexts—deus, deivos and dávus – and are thus an original designation for 'god'.

Even though Slavic languages (like Russian) today are spoken in most of the area of the prehistoric Fatyanovo culture, it is probable that at least large parts of this geographical area were originally rather populated by people who spoke an early Baltic language. The fact that the closely related Slavic languages subsequently spread over this area would then be a later development and the relatively western location of the Baltic people today would be misleading. The Fatyanovo culture as Proto-Baltic can therefore provide a reasonable explanation for the close linguistic connection between the Baltic and Indo-Iranian languages.

*Ad Part I Cap Vn III & Cap VII n III*

FIGURE 5.3 Romuva sanctuary in Prussia. After an illustration published by Christoph Hartknoch in 1684, based on an early 16th-century account of the Dominician priest Simon Grunau, digital file: UNESCO PhotoBank (Lithuania - Historical Collections of the Vilnius University Library). Public domain.

The same could then also apply to other cultural elements, not just language, with rituals of fire as one significant example. This would also be in line with preserved traditions. Especially in the historical Baltic cultural area, there are important fire rituals known as *Romuva*. These have a documentation covering the period from the Middle Ages up to modern time (not to be confused with the influential post-Soviet neo-pagan movement that goes by the same name). However, given that a large part of the historical Baltic area, the Lithuanian Empire, was the last major geographical area that was Christianised in Europe (the late 14th century), there is every reason to believe that Lithuanian folk customs have been well preserved, especially in more remote parts of the countryside (Figure 5.3).

> The Balts were the last people in Europe that converted to Christianity. In the case of the Prussians, Christian missionaries reached their lands as early as the late 10th century, however the real, albeit brutal and forceful Christianisation began with the arrival of the Teutonic Knights in the region in the 1230s ... The case of the Lithuanians was different again ... Officially, Lithuania converted in 1387 when their ruler Jogaila married

Polish princess Jadwiga and became a Polish king. Needless to say, the conversion of the Baltic people took many generations and an echo of pagan beliefs and rituals was well preserved in Baltic folklore till modern times.

*Zaroff 2019: 186*

Thus, even late-documented folkloric material has the potential to reflect genuine pre-Christian ideas. Moreover, some older written documentation is also available, which indicates the great importance of the fire cult. Peter of Dusburg's (also spelled Duisburg) Chronicle of Prussian Lands – *Chronicon terrae Prussiae* – from around 1330, is an early written source that provides at least some important information about the Baltic fire cult. The written sources are unfortunately limited and Peter of Dusburg's Chronicle is considered one of the main sources for the early Prussian history. Despite later strong association with the north-eastern part of the German Empire, Prussian is actually a collective term for several Baltic tribes with similar languages and cultures as the others. And according to the chronicle by Peter of Dusburg, some of the information is relevant to the Baltic people in general. The Chronicle describes a sacred place of worship called Romowė (or Romuva) located in one part of the land of the Prussians, a region called Nadrovia. In his paper *Some aspects of pre-Christian Baltic religion*, Roman Zaroff (2019: 196–197) writes:

> According to Peter of Dusburg there was a certain outstanding sacred place in the Prussian lands that he called Romowė (Romuva), located in the Nadrovia region where a priest-like person called Kriwe (Krive) was regarded as a pope-like figure in pagan Prussian religion. He also stated that Krive exercised religious power and authority over all Prussian tribes and people, as well as the Lithuanians and the Latvian tribes, and there was a holy fire kept burning all the time.
>
> *Zaroff 2019: 207*

There is, of course, a reason to look critically at Peter of Dusburg's description in the same way as all older sources of a similar kind, but, at the same time, there is no reason to assume that the basic description is incorrect (cf. Zaroff 2019: 207–208). Around the 12th–13th centuries, such major religious centres as the described Romowė did evidently still exist among the Baltic tribes in Prussia as well as among the different Lithuanian and Latvian tribes. As the northernmost clan, the Nadruvians were last conquered by the Teutonic Knights in their campaign to Christianise the Prussians. The fact that the memory of a pre-Christian place of worship was preserved here, as in the even later Christianised Lithuania, is therefore not surprising.

Another Medieval scholar that gives us information about the fire rituals of the Baltic people was the philosopher Hieronymus Pragensis (1379–1416), also known as Jerome of Prague. He reports that Lithuanians worshiped holy fire and that an eternal flame was kept at an unspecified location. This eternal fire was maintained by priests and local people came to sacrifice and ask the pagan priests for divination. In addition, Jerome of Prague described the Lithuanians' worship of the sun, a religious practice that clearly has strong links to fire rituals, in general, and with parallels also in other Baltic contexts. In addition, there are very close similarities with the ancient Indian tradition, not least to the sun and horses. Again, following Roman Zaroff (2019: 195):

> Similarly in Latvian folklore we encounter frequent references to the Sun and also common association of the Sun with horses. To cite a few, we find phrases like: 'the Sun with two golden horses', 'the Sun drove by two golden horses through the gate', 'the Sun on the mountain holds the reins of the horses', 'the Sun saddles a hundred black horses' or 'the Sun daughters ride horses'.

According to the polish priest and historian Jan Długosz (1415–1480), also known as Longinus Johannes, the Samogitians were also fire worshipers. A holy and much venerated eternal fire was kept and maintained, apparently placed on some tower-like structure on a hill by the river Nevėžis. In 1413, King Jogaila was supposed to have visited the site ordering that the fire be extinguished and the structure demolished. Another written piece of evidence, this dates to the last year of the 16th century, comes from the churchman Mikalojus Daukša (c. 1527–1613) in the Lithuanian translation of a collection of sermons. Here, he advised the Samogitians on what deeds are against the 1st Commandment. In this long list of prohibitions, it also included the worship of fire. There is also some older information on rural folk customs regarding sacred fire, which to an even greater extent indicates its strong and deep cultural roots. They show that holy fire did not only occur in central shrines, but was a fundamental part of the everyday cult. We probably see here the same tradition that survived in the Baltic area until recent times. In 16th-century Prussia, people would still address fires inside homes with the saying 'Ocho moy myte szwante panicke!' meaning 'Oh! my little sacred Fire' (Zaroff 2019: 196–197).

Ritual fires and the belief in fire as particularly sacred were thus unusually long lasting in the Baltic area, in general, and in Lithuania, in particular. This was due both to the late Christianisation process as well as the fact that the Balts, in both their language and religion, apparently preserved many elements belonging to the oldest phase of Indo-European religion:

> Fire and bread had special importance and were taken along to the house of the newly married couple. These rites persisted until quite late and were to be seen even at the end of the 19th century, though in many cases only as games. In this connection, fire in general occupied a central place in Baltic religion. Considered holy, it was worshiped, and sacrifices were offered to it. It seems unbelievable that even as late as 1377 and 1382, respectively,

the Lithuanian king Algirdas and his brother Kęstutis could still be buried according to the old traditions in a Christian Europe; dressed in silver and gold, they were burned in funeral pyres together with their best possessions, horses, hunting dogs, birds, and weapons. In spite of a ban by the church and subsequent persecution, this rite still persisted in the 15th century....

*Biezais 2021: 'Baltic religion', Encyclopaedia Britannica online*

Given the geographical location of the Fatyanovo culture, where by all accounts the Baltic culture developed in its oldest phase, there is great reason to see this as an area of origin for the kind of fire rituals that via Sintashta gained such significance in the Indo-Iranian culture. Although these rituals do not necessarily occur here for the first time – older origins can be traced to the Middle Dnieper culture and perhaps even to the older Neolithic agricultural culture in Europe – it may be in the Fatyanovo culture that they find much of their typical form, which is later evident in both the Baltic and Indo-Iranian contexts. The east-west, elongated range of the Fatyanovo culture was potentially a very effective 'bridge' for the further spread of these rituals, partly to the southeast, but also back to Europe in a renewed and added form, where not least northern Europe and Scandinavia may have been affected.

## The rise and spread of Indo-European sacred fire

A cohesive geographical link in the chain of common Indo-European ritual features, which extends from India in the southeast to Norway in the northwest, is the area where Balto-Slavic originated. As shown above, this is also where steppe ancestry mixed with Neolithic European farmer ancestry as well as with older hunter-gatherer cultures of the Russian forest zone in an Indo-European reflux to the east: to Sintashta on the steppe and from there further into the Indo-Iranian branch of the Indo-European diaspora. Thus, there is a reason to assume that this particular area houses the melting pot for some of the rituals that after being cast together subsequently spread in geographically remote parts of the Indo-European cultural area. As mentioned above, the Sintashta culture is another cornerstone of this process.

The fortified settlements of the Sintashta culture are of a very special design, with a circular, oval or sometimes rectangular plan. The two most well-known sites, Sintashta and Arkaim, are both round in plan, with concentric rows of walls divided by radial streets. However, these are just two examples of many in the Sintashta culture, mainly located in the settlement area called 'the country of towns' (Zdanovich & Zdanovich 2002), located in the Chelyabinsk district of Russia in southern Ural. Many burial grounds have also been discovered and excavated, often separately connected to individual settlements and usually separated from them by a river or a ridge. The burial sites consist of earthen mounds, of which often one or two are large mounds, centrally located on the burial sites, and with the burial made in shape of timber-roofed chambers of wood. A sacrificial altar has also been documented on a burial ground belonging to the Sintashta settlement itself. The graves contain inhumations with the deceased lying in flexed position, usually resting on the left side but sometimes on the right. In the graves are ceramic vessels and also otherwise rich grave gifts, including copper axe-heads, knives, daggers, socketed spears and arrows and parts of the special compound bow of Sintashta type (Kuzmina 2008: 42–43), the latter with many parallels from the warfare of later mounted steppe nomads.

The Sintashta area is the location where Indo-European features from the first migration from Yamnaya, eventually returned to the steppe mixed with features from Neolithic Europe and hunter-gatherer influences from the forest belt, via the Fatyanovo reflux. But not only that, new features are also added in the Sintashta context, which forms an intensively innovative cultural environment that may have constituted an even more decisive source for Indo-European cultural dissemination than the early migration from Yamnaya itself (e.g. Librado et al. 2021). From Sintashta, there is a spread to the extensive cultural group called the Andronovo culture, a collective name for culturally related groups within a large geographical area. Besides southern Russia, it includes parts of Turkmenistan, Tajikistan and Kyrgyzstan. The name Andronovo refers to a site with the same name where the Russian archaeologist Arkadi Tugarinov discovered the first remains in 1914. This culture as a whole, like Sintashta, is often associated with speakers of the early Indo-Iranian languages (e.g. Shnirelman 1998: 35), something that is now also supported by genetic studies. Already in 2009, Keyser et al. (Keyser et al. 2009) published an aDNA-analysis, which included 26 ancient burials of the Krasnoyarsk region of Russia, later confirmed by other studies (e.g. Allentoft, Sikora & Willerslev 2015). The results indicated that the Andronovo men almost entirely carried a variant of the haplogroup R1a on the male Y chromosome. Furthermore, the Andronovo culture, in general, has shown to be genetically closely related to the Sintashta peoples and clearly represents a geographical extension of the Sintashta gene pool (Allentoft et al. 2015; Mathieson, Lazaridis & Rohland 2015; Mathieson, Alpaslan-Roodenberg & Posth 2018).

Several of the variants of the overall Andronovo culture are better known by their specific names, such as Srubnaya, the Alakul and the Fedorovo cultures. All of these are considered to have spoken Indo-Iranian languages. Not least from the Srubnaya part of the Andronovo culture, some renown Iranian-speaking people originates, '… the ancestors of the Sacae, the Scythians, and the Sarmatians' (Diakonoff 1995: 473). The Scythians have, to a remarkably and surprisingly small degree, been used as a starting point for creating insights into the early Indo-European nomadic societies. Yet, it is very clear that the Scythian culture has the same kind of geographical extent as well as the same type of society and way of life that already existed during the early Indo-European spread (Cunliffe 2019: 22–23). Examples from the Scythians show not least the enormous mobility over large areas and how this in turn in a short time can create great cultural – and sometimes but not always genetic – similarities.

From Sintashta and its successors in the Andronovo culture, the migration takes place south into what is to become the Indo-Iranian territory. The Vedic conquest of northern India, in particular, seems to be largely a military one. Not least the two-wheeled chariot was a decisive factor here, with abundant references in the early Vedic texts. But from Sintashta and its successors, there is also once again an intense spread of innovations to the west, an event that is likely to be decisive for much of what will characterise the Bronze Age in Europe. Within the Sintashta culture, we can find the cradle for several important innovations such as the light two-wheeled cart with spokes: the chariot (Lindner 2020: 361–380):

> Traditionally, most scholars have associated the invention of chariots with Near Eastern societies, something that has been disproved in recent decades. The oldest evidence ever found, in the graves of Sintashta, has shown that wheels with spokes and high-speed chariots were invented in this culture. Chariots were invented earliest in the steppes, where they were used in warfare. They were introduced to the Near East through Central Asia, with steppe horses and studded disk cheekpieces. This innovation took place around 2100 BC, and represents an important technological leap for humanity.
>
> *Kaliff & Oestigaard 2020: 141*

Here, we also find an early centre for metal handling and the development of bronze metallurgy. The very centre of 'the country of towns' located between today's cities of Orenburg and Magnitogorsk, nowadays the largest city in the Chelyabinsk district, is an area that probably held important ancient mines. These in turn are located near the well-known large ore field of Kargaly in the southern Ural with many traces of prehistoric copper mining. Even if there are no signs of craft specialisation in Sintashta – instead, it was a very widespread domestic metal production – undoubtedly metallurgy and metalworking were the most important occupations in this society. This is not least indicated by the discovery of an unprecedented amount of copperware in burials and remains of metalworking in almost every household in the settlements (Kuzmina 2008: 43–45; cf. Gening 1979).

In Sintashta, we also see the oldest clear traces of horse sacrifices of the classic Indo-European model (cf. Kaliff & Oestigaard 2020: 140–141) and not least, these sacrifices seem to be associated with cemeteries and funeral rites. The excavated sites show that horses were sacrificed more than any other animal, and horse bones were three times more frequent in funeral sacrifices than in settlement contexts (Anthony 2007: 406). Studies of DNA have now also shown that it is from here that the domesticated horse and the art of riding spread further around the world in parallel with the spread of chariots from around 2000 BC. Thus, recent studies reject the association between horseback riding and the early expansion of Yamnaya steppe pastoralists into Europe soon after 3000 BC (Librado, Khan & Fages 2021: 634–640). The Asian scenario instead showed that Indo-Iranian languages, chariots, domesticated horses and probably horseback riding spread together, starting with the innovations of the Sintashta culture. David W. Anthony (2007: 375) writes:

> The details of the funeral sacrifices at Sintashta showed startling parallels with the sacrificial funeral rituals of the *Rig Veda*. The industrial scale of metallurgical production suggested a new organization of steppe mining and metallurgy and a greatly heightened demand for copper and bronze. The substantial fortifications implied surprisingly large and determined attacking force … Sintashta was just one of more than twenty related fortified settlements located in a compact region of rolling steppes between the upper Ural River on the west and the upper Tobol River on the east, southeast of the Ural Mountains … Did the people who built these strongholds invent chariots? And were they the original Aryans, the ancestors of the people who later composed the *Rig Veda* and the *Avesta*?

At least one of the concluding questions that Anthony asks has now received its answer: Chariots were most likely invented right here and the most ancient archaeological traces of such items have also been found in the graves of the Sintashta site itself. From here, their spread around the world originated, apparently in parallel with both the art of riding and the origins of today's domesticated horses (Librado et al. 2021). Even before DNA studies could trace the origins of today's (and history's) domesticated horses, skilled archaeologists specialising in steppe archaeology could see that Sintashta and Andronovo were, by all accounts, crucial cultural contexts in this development. This applies to the breeding of horses as well as to the development of the spoke wheeled chariot as described by Elena Kuzmina in her book *The Prehistory of the Silk Road* (2008: 49–70). As Kuzmina, also Anthony published his book *The Horse, the Wheel and Language* (2007) almost a decade before the crucial aDNA studies provided massive support for the old ideas about the spread of Indo-Europeans to both Europe and the Indo-Iranian area (Haak, Lazaridis & Reich 2015; Allentoft et al. 2015).

The traces that lead to Sintashta as a key factor in the spread of Indo-European culture do not only apply to technological innovations and domestication, but also to ritual and religion. In fact, both archaeology and linguistics have also previously argued that important components of the ancient Vedic and ancient Iranian religions also originated in archaeological contexts such as Sintashta and Arkaim (Anthony 2007: 409). Metallurgy, the chariot as well as the horse's functional and ritual significance can all be traced back to Sintashta. But, there are more beliefs, symbolism and rituals that can later be found over large parts of the Indo-European diaspora. Some of these can be found in the architecture and construction plan of the fortified settlements of 'the country of towns'. These structures function as physical manifestations of important cosmological beliefs

**FIGURE 5.4** The Arkaim site on the southern Russian steppe, a typical settlement of the Sintashta type, round in plan, with concentric rows of walls divided by radial streets. Public domain.

and symbols, typical of Indo-European Bronze Age societies, and, at the same time, show a well-organised society with a common ideology, ritual customs and religious beliefs (Figure 5.4). A reasonable interpretation of the concentric circle pattern in the settlement plans of the Sintashta-Arkaim type is that it represents a sun-wheel, which is the same way concentric and spiral patterns in Bronze Age iconography are generally interpreted (Kaliff & Oestigaard 2020: 142). Perceiving the sun as a god was also closely connected to the idea of fire being divine, which is a central concept in Indo-Iranian tradition where fire and the sun were believed to be of the same nature. Also, in this respect, it is possible to find traces in the Vedic texts as well as the ancient Iranian, and in *Avesta* – the holy scripture of the ancient Persians:

> In the opinion of many specialists, Arkaim and similar sites could have been established by the earliest Indo-Iranians long before their separation and their migrations along the Eurasian steppe corridor and the southward movement into Persia and India. Some scholars draw parallels between circular fortified settlements of the type of Arkaim and the city of the legendary King Yima, reproducing the model of the universe described in the Avesta.

*Shnirelman 1998: 35*

Fire cult as well as cremation of corpses has been documented in the so-called Fedorovo culture (1900–1400 BC), a cultural group closely related to Sintashta and a part of the overall Andronovo complex, consisting of a number of different closely related archaeological cultural groups, all of which are considered to have spoken Indo-Iranian languages (Diakonoff 1995: 473).

The claim that these features – fire cult and cremation – appear in the Fedorovo culture for the first time in Indo-European contexts is not entirely true. Fire rituals were also prevalent in Sintashta, although this does not involve cremation as a burial practice. What is clear in Sintashta, however, is that rituals that included fire had a clear connection to the grave mounds and cult practised there. Some of these finds have been classified as 'funeral feasts' and not as sacrifices, but the ritual elements are in any case clear (Kuzmina 2008: 44). Nevertheless, cremations documented in the Fedorovo culture are not completely novel in an Indo-European context, although it may represent something distinctively new in the Indo-Iranian branch.

Cremation was actually practised much earlier in the Middle Dnieper culture far to the west, and, perhaps, it was brought from there into the Fatyanovo culture – where it occurs sparingly – and further east to Balanovo, where it again seems more common. From there, it is likely to have in turn been introduced into first Sintashta and then the subsequent Fedorovo cultures.

However, as already discussed above, there is evidence of fire cult or special fireplaces in and near burials, as well as sun symbolism, already in the Fatyanovo culture, although cremation was not common there. Thus, important fire rituals may have been present already in the early stages of Fatyanovo culture. At least in the preceding Middle Dnieper culture, there are signs of significant fire rituals, at least in connection to the burials where cremation occurs in parallel with inhumation: 'Middle Dnieper cemeteries contained both kurgans and flat-graves, both inhumation burials and cremations' (Anthony 2007: 380).

As far as we know, fire rituals did not have this significance as early as the Yamnaya culture and the first western exodus from the steppe. This may indicate a tradition that was originally picked up from the West, from the early Neolithic cultures of Europe, together with other cultural and genetic additions that arrived via the Middle Dnieper culture. This, in turn, could suggest that the origin of this kind of fire cult, which over time developed into a classical and very common feature of Indo-European ritual tradition, not least sophisticatedly developed within its Indo-Iranian variant, was originally one of the cultural features carried east from Europe as part of the genetic and cultural west-eastern reflux. If the ritual fire that constitutes such a fundamental part of the Vedic tradition turns out to have part of its origin in the Pre-Indo-European, Neolithic cultures of Europe, it would undeniably be startling.

The fact that both fire rituals and sun symbolism seem to be closely associated with the Fatyanovo culture is in good agreement with the culture's northern distribution area in the forest belt. The strong cosmological meaning of the sun is closely associated with agriculture, especially in northern latitudes, where the balance between good and bad years is so intimately and clearly connected with the warming power of the sun. We believe this makes the area of Fatyanovo culture – very large in itself – a reasonable starting point for at least some of the cosmological beliefs that underlie the fire rituals that become so significant to Indo-Europeans. That fire rituals, especially seasonal fires, developed a special significance in northern environments with very noticeable changes of seasons and long cold winters, make perfect sense from an ecological perspective. A more southern environment, the steppe included, seems less likely for the development that initiated these perceptions and made it such a fundamental part of cosmology. Fire rituals and especially seasonal fires are often intimately associated with beliefs about the power of the sun, the change of seasons and the fertility of agriculture. It is probable, then, that it constitutes a ritual with its cradle in the same milieu that brought agriculture into the north-eastern European forest zone.

Not unlikely then, one of the more prominent common features of both the Scandinavian Bronze Age and Vedic India – the ritual fire – may actually have its origins in the northern European forest belt rather than in the Eurasian steppe or further south. That the ritual tradition has since lived on and become even more developed in more southern climate zones is another story. At the time of this latter event, the ritual meaning should have already been well established and the tradition can, therefore, be expected to have lived on and also further developed by inner dynamics, more or less independent of the awareness of its original meaning (cf. Staal 1983).

Although many features are further developed and taking new forms within the Sintashta culture, it is quite possible that their basic structure remained relatively intact. Thus, the fire rituals may have their ultimate origins in the northwest in the middle Dnieper or Fatyanovo culture whereby later they were widely spread 'in a second Indo-European wave' via Sintashta. Eventually, together with innovations such as the horse, the chariot and metallurgy, these cultural traits reached back to their area of origin in the northwest and continued to further influence the very tradition they once had arisen from.

Although much of this interpretative reasoning fits well with a DNA analysis and archaeological data, there are still uncertainties, and some of them relate to the origin of early metallurgy and beliefs in the divine powers of the sun. In the Indo-European cosmology and metallurgical technology, the fires from heaven were without doubt fundamental in the shared beliefs and practices from the Ireland to India, and once again, some of the most elaborate and illuminating examples are found on the steppes.

## Meteoric thunderbolts from heaven

Cremation is intimately connected to intensive use of fire where the forces of cosmos are let loose. There is yet another technological and cosmological process where the mastering of fire is even more explicit, and that is the smithy and the making of metals in the furnace. Cross-culturally, the smith and production of metals is a theme that is widely studied, because it entails so many cultural and cosmological processes structured around cosmic forces, sacrifices and different taboos and notions of seclusion and exclusion, among other features (e.g. Eliade 1962; Herbert 1984, 1993; Craddock 1995; Rijal 1998; Barber 2003; Haaland 2004a, 2004b, 2006). While cremation and bronze smelting seem to occur as a pair in the European Bronze Age, and many archaeologists have pointed out this interrelation which seems to be part of an Indo-European package unifying technology and cosmology, cremation as a funerary practice as well as metallurgy appears both earlier and as distinctive processes. Yet, there is no doubt that the master of fire in the Bronze Age knew the secrets of death and metals. Bronze consists of copper and tin and the different sources and mines enabled wide distribution and contact network throughout the European continent and beyond, and some of the richest ores were in the Ural Mountains. While bronze has defined the Bronze Age, we will put emphasis on another less-known technological advancement, which to some extent is even more spectacular and astonishing: iron melting in the Bronze Age.

Terje Gansum was one of the first to forge the idea that the furnace was the means and medium where cosmic forces were united, because in the very process of making steel from iron, one needs bone-coal to carbonise iron (Gansum 2004; Gansum & Hansen 2004). If bone-coal is used in the furnace, the carbon may penetrate as far as 3 mm into the iron and this transforms iron into steel and metal into weapons. As Gansum says, 'we cannot be sure whether they used human bones in the process of making steel, but symbolically and ritually it seems likely. In this way ritual, technology and symbolism is fused together' (Gansum 2004: 44). Swords had names and magical qualities; they were living beings with the possibility to take and protect life, like a double-edged sword, protecting by killing. A striking aspect of many prehistoric cremations is the extreme high temperatures. In modern crematoriums, the process in the oven starts at around 700°C because the flesh on the corpse self-ignites and combusts at this temperature, and the temperature seldom exceeds 1000°C. Based on analysis of 1082 prehistoric cremations in Norway, 20–30% were conducted at higher temperatures than modern cremations, in other words at temperatures between 1200 and 1300°C (Holck 1987: 146–149). These temperatures are very difficult to reach on open pyres (Kaliff & Oestigaard 2013: 73–83). In practice, this is the temperature range used in metal production. While pure iron smelts at 1537°C (carbonised iron smelts at 1145°C), copper smelts at a significant lower temperature – 1083°C – and bronze around 800–1000°C, depending on the proportions of metals in the alloy (Goldhahn 2007; Oestigaard 2007).

The body is an enormous container of energy, and while it is difficult to cremate a thick and heavy person on open-pyre and easier with skinny people,

**FIGURE 5.5**  Picture stone from Ardre Church, Gotland, Sweden. Human and decapitated bodies are lying next to the furnace. Photo: Terje Oestigaard.

it is opposite in a cremation oven or closed furnace (Ottesen 2006). When the flesh of the body starts burning in a closed room, it releases an enormous amount of energy, which directly results in a rapid temperature increase. If two bodies are burnt after each other, the temperature easily reach more than 1000°C. Per Holck says: '... a corpse creates a considerable surplus of heat [...] the measuring begins after the oven have been ignited, and we see that the temperature rises slowly to 700°C. From the moment the corpse is put in a steep rise in temperature occurs (exothermal reaction). This is caused by the ignition of the most combustible parts of the body (and the coffin), despite a constant supply of energy to the oven. After about 40–60 minutes the temperature will decrease during the cremation of the less combustible parts of the body ...' (Holck 1987: 38). Thus, in many cases, it seems not only possible, but very likely, that technology and cosmology merged together in the furnace (Figure 5.5).

> The cremator and the smith became ritual specialists who controlled the fire and the procreative forces transforming death into further lives and existences, which also included material objects. In the Scandinavian Bronze Age there are finds of human remains in furnaces ... Not only humans, but also animals were used in this process. Animals have often been sacrificed in cremations and may symbolize the transcendence of borders between the living and the dead. One reason why humans and animals were cremated in the smithy can be found in the use of the flesh of the deceased as fuel, but more importantly, in the control and power of the deceased's identity. The deceased and his or her powers have literally been incorporated in ancestral cults by smelting them into objects such as swords and brooches.
>
> *Oestigaard 2013: 504*

In the *Satapatha-Brâhmana*, the sacrificial dagger or scimitar is described in this way: 'The slaughtering-knife of the horse is made of gold, those of the "paryang-yas" of copper, and those of the others of iron; for gold is (shining) light, and the Asvamedha is the royal office: he thus bestows light upon the royal office. And by means of the golden light (or, by the light of the gold), the Sacrificer also goes to the heavenly world; and he, moreover, makes it a gleam of light shining after him, for him to reach the heavenly world' (Satapatha-Brâhmana, Book VIII, 1988: 303). The roles of daggers and fires in sacrifices are intimately connected. In fact, as an alternative to fire, women could choose death by a dagger with a wavy blade called kris, with which the widows pierced their breast. In this way, the dagger and fire had the same cosmological role, and if the widow was burnt on the pyre, she suffered only in proportions of the sins committed, which also were the direct causes and consequences of her widowhood (Weinberger-Thomas 1999: 5, 45).

Turning to Central and Northern Eurasia, an area including the steppes, forest steppes and forests from eastern Europe to western Siberia, the chronology of the Bronze Age is as such: Early Bronze Age (3200–2800 BC), Middle Bronze Age (2700–1600 BC), Late Bronze Age (1600–900 BC) and Final Bronze Age or Transitional period (800–700 BC). From the Early and Middle Bronze Age, more than 46 iron objects are found and there are also finds of four bimetallic (alloy) objects documented. The objects are found on sites from the Pit Grave Culture (24 items), the Afanasievo Culture (21 items) and the Catacomb Culture (1 items). As Koryakove, Kuzminkyh & Beltikova say (2008: 114), 'analyses of iron show unambiguous evidence of a meteoritic content. The earliest metallurgist knew how to work meteoritic iron, which was very hard and could be given heat treatment'. Importantly, this very early iron metallurgy seems to be the original invention of iron production. The meteoric processing in Eastern Europe and the Southern Urals in the third millennia BC was an exceptional innovation, but this tradition did not last. 'There are no artefacts indicative of iron working in the Seima-Turbino, Abashevo, Sintashta-Arkaim, or Petrovka Cultures of the early stage of Late Bronze Age. The meteoritic iron technology of the Pit Grave and Afanasievo Cultures seems not to have continued and the tradition had probably been lost' (Koryakove, Kuzminkyh & Beltikova 2008: 115).

The Don-forestry area shows an early evidence of iron production and, from the Srubnaya (Timber Grave) Culture, this is documented in the mid second millennium BC. Iron and bimetallic production was institutionalised and consolidated, and spread throughout the region. By the late 9th century BC, metallurgists in the Trans-Caucasian, North Pontic and Middle Volga areas fully mastered the process of making iron and, in the 8th century BC, they mastered the technology of making bimetallic swords and also steel. 'The eastern European or Pontic tradition was based on the use of pure iron, the quality of which was much better than that of bronze' (Koryakove, Kuzminkyh & Beltikova 2008: 116).

Thus, the earliest iron artefacts found in Russia derive from the Pit Grave and Catacomb cultures of the Bronze Age, and another Catacomb-grave artefact was found in a burial dated to ca. 1750 BC (Terekhova 2008: 129). If the early tradition of using meteoritic iron disappeared before new metallurgic practices were established in, for instance, the Sintashta-Arkaim complexes, it seems nevertheless that these early metallurgic practices were central in all parts of culture and cosmology. In Indo-European mythology, there is an intimate association between thunder and lightning, meteoritic iron and daggers and divinities. In the Norse mythology, Thor is famous and in the oldest Vedic texts these beliefs are associated with Indra. Throughout history, thunder, lightning and divine daggers have been utmost testimonies of divine powers (Figure 5.6).

**FIGURE 5.6** Thor with the mighty hammer. Painting by Mårten Eskil Winge (1872). Creative Commons.

Although chronologically a bit later, but largely carrying on the legacy of the early steppe nomads, the Scythians may give a unique insight into this long-lost world of Indo-European beliefs. In the first millennium BC, the Scythians were great nomadic horsemen and warriors on the Asian steppes, active in an area from Hungary Plain to the Altai Mountains (Cunliffe 2019). In *The Histories*, Herodotus gives an elaborate and vivid description of the Scythian, a description that to a large extent shaped the posterity's view of them. Here, we will only point out one peculiar and probably very important ritual, which possibly illustrates core beliefs and practices that were central parts of their cosmology. Herodotus describes the most important seasonal sacrifice, and he stresses that the very sacrificial dagger or knife is a divinity in itself, and the main recipient of the sacrifice. This dagger or short sword was called *akinakes*. In other words, it was the divine dagger that was the object of sacrifice: Following Herodotus (Book 4.62):

> Each year they add a hundred and fifty cart-loads of sticks, to make up for the subsistence caused by the winter's storms. On top of this structure the inhabitants of each district place an ancient iron *akinakes*, which is taken to represent Ares. This festival takes place once a year, and at it they offer this *akinakes* more domestic animals and horses as sacrificial victims than all the other gods receive. They also sacrifice prisoners of war to this *akinakes*.

Thus, Herodotus says explicitly that the most important sacrifices were the seasonal ones in relation to the winter and the challenges with subsistence and survival. More horses and animals than in any other sacrifices were given to the god, and it was the very dagger or sacrificial sword that *was* the god. Although Herodotus does not describe the actual killing itself, it seems reasonable to assume that the animals and human victims were killed by the very same dagger or *akinakes*, and the sacrificial objects is revered and sanctified by the blood spilled. It makes the object and subject, means and methods, and goal and gods identical, and herein is perhaps an original Indo-European core of sacrificial developments. A fundamentally similar relationship applies to the ritual fire in the Vedic tradition where Agni transfers the sacrificial offerings to the gods, but at the same time also constitutes an important deity in itself.

If the sacrificial objects were also the divinities the sacrifices were made for, it gives new lights on many of the most spectacular ritual and religious bronzes ever found in Europe and beyond. From this perspective, the Rorby swords (c. 1600 BC) or the Kallerup ceremonial axe (c. 1000 BC) from Denmark, for instance, or the enigmatic scimitars found across the continent (Engedal 2002, 2010), are not only sacrificial objects, but the very objects for sacrifices (Figure 5.7). They are the goals and means, and the origin of iron metallurgy with meteors from heaven may explain this cosmology. Moreover, from recent

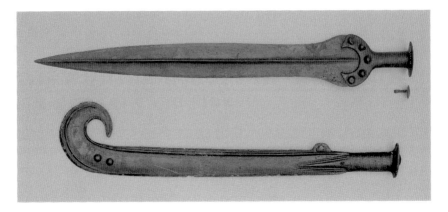

**FIGURE 5.7** Early Bronze Age swords, Denmark. The dagger (above) is from Apa-Hajdusamson horizon (Hungary-Romania). The sword (below) is the famous curved Rørby sword of bronze (c. 1600 BC). The National Museum of Denmark, Creative Commons (CC-BY-SA).

ethnography in Scandinavia, it is documented that the more a weapon has killed, the more powerful it is. If a sword has killed two persons, it contains the life-powers of two men. In other words, killing was a way of sacralising and making objects holy; literally, the murder weapons were filled with life-powers and more-than-human forces, simply because they contained the powers of the added human lives (Oestigaard 2022a: 141).

Returning to the simplified interpretations of an alleged sun cult in Scandinavia and Northern Europe in the Bronze Age, one has to turn the perspective upside down and focus on the bronzes themselves, not only on the circles and the iconography on the metals or the rock art. If the prestigious bronzes are the main divinities because they brought the heat and fire down to earth, including the fire and powers coming from the very production process, then they embody essential parts of the sun's qualities, and as Herodotus said, elaborate sacrifices were made to these holy objects 'to make up for the subsistence caused by the winter's storm'. Iron had a particular role in these Bronze Age cosmologies. As seen, meteors and the melting of them represented earlier technologies than the ones developed in for instance the Sintashta culture. Moreover, across the Indo-European area, this is a prominent feature of the cosmology from Thor in the north to Indra in the south. As some of the mightiest gods, they were controlling wind and weather; they were rain and thunder-gods, but also closely associated with the life-giving powers of the sun.

Not only on the Indian sub-continent, but perhaps even more important in northern ecologies with long winters, keeping these heavenly fires alive was essential for the well-being of humans and animals alike. In cold climates, the perpetual need-fires had to burn throughout the year and, in particular, in the

**FIGURE 5.8** Holy man with fire pot on his head, Shivaratri at Pashupatinath 2002, Nepal. Photo: Anders Kaliff.

long and dark season. This resulted in a specific type of fire rituals, which became such a significant part of the life of the early Indo-Europeans that it lived on even when arriving in completely different geographical environments, and we still find it throughout the Indian continent as an important part of Vedic fire rituals. While many intuitively perceive perpetual fires as burning flames in hearths and homes, this is but one possibility. Among pastoralists and people on the move, the fire had to be portable and transportable. In other words, the fire was not intensively burning, but kept alive in ceramic vessels or containers. In practice, many perpetual fires were glooming charcoal protected in special and sacred pots. These portable fire altars or pots were easily transported and safeguarded by pastoralists constantly moving from one area to another. One finds the same fire rituals and worship among today's holy men of Hinduism, carrying their perpetual fire in a holy pot on their head (Figure 5.8, see Chapter 7).

# 6

# THE INDO-IRANIAN CULTURE AND ITS RITUALS OF FIRE

## Zoroastrianism and its Central Asian origins

The archaeological culture that has primarily been associated with the early Indo-Iranian people and their spread is the so-called Andronovo culture. It is a collective term for a number of similar local Bronze Age cultures that flourished around 2000–900 BC in western Siberia, parts of Central Asia and the Eurasian steppe. The forerunner of the Andronovo culture – the Sintashta culture (2100–1800 BC) – is, as seen, one of the most exciting links between East and West. The traditional image of the Indo-Iranian expansion shows an aggressive movement of warrior people. The transformation from a life as nomadic herdsmen on the steppes of Russia and Central Asia to a successful, expanding warrior people has been closely connected with bronze technology and the introduction of the two-wheeled war chariot. The war chariot was an important technological innovation on the Indo-European steppe by people of the Sintashta with continued development within the Andronovo culture, going hand in hand with intense breeding of domesticated horses impacting on all tame horses even today (Saag, Vasilyev & Varul 2021). The conditions for an expansive, warlike Bronze Age culture increased even more through the fact that the raw materials for bronze were also in plentiful supply in the vicinity.

The theory that warlike people from the north invaded the Indo-Iranian territory and thereby introduced what became the ancient Iranian and the ancient Indian, Vedic culture respectively, has existed since the cradle of comparative Indo-European research. Nevertheless, this view has been controversial, and not least in India, because the interpretation that Indo-Europeans came from outside is still strongly questioned, not least by Hindu nationalist scholars. Still, today the question has finally received a very decisive answer in the form of results from aDNA research. A very significant element of genetic inheritance in India

DOI: 10.4324/9781003300915-6

even today stems from an immigration from the steppes in the north, at the right time in history, is today proven beyond any reasonable doubt (e.g. Narasimhan, Patterson & Reich 2019). Even today, this heritage is particularly evident in northern India and among Brahmin families, in other words, the group that has had the particular role of guarding the Vedic ritual heritage.

'The people who were custodians of the Indo-European language and culture were the ones with relatively more steppe ancestry, and because of the extraordinary strength of the caste system in preserving ancestry and social roles over generations', says David Reich and continues, the 'Indo-European culture as reflected in the religion preserved over thousands of years by Brahmin priests, was likely spread by peoples whose ancestors originated in the steppe' (Reich 2018: 152). The Vedic rituals are one of the best-documented early ritual systems in the world. The documentation covers a tradition lasting more than 3,000 years, which was recorded in writing starting in the second millennium BC and still lives on today. The long continuity back in time applies also to the ancient Iranian tradition as it survived in Zoroastrianism, a religion considered to have its roots in nomadism and pastoral adaptations and mainly associated with today's region of Iran and areas east of the Caspian Sea (Boyce 1977; Hinnells 1981, 2000).

From an Indo-European perspective, this area has historically had a particular role as a bridge between the steppes and India. The development of the ancient Iranian religion into Zoroastrianism corresponds in some respects to the change in the Vedic tradition. Unlike the Vedic religion, this tradition has not resulted in a world religion comparable to what Hinduism became in the due course of history. Despite being the state religion in three mighty Persian empires from 7th century BC to 8th century AD and the dominant religion in Central Asia for more than 1,200 years, Zoroastrianism ceased to be the dominant religious force in Iran with the Islamic conquest. With the spread of Islam from the 7th century onwards, Zoroastrianism was gradually reduced to a small community with a decreasing number of people practising the religion. Zoroastrianism as a living tradition is preserved today by a rather limited group of followers in today's India, chiefly in Mumbai (Bombay), and to a lesser extent also in present-day Iran (and in a diaspora in different countries all over the world) (Boyce 1979: 10–18; Stausberg 2005).

Although Zoroastrianism today is a small religion, practised by devotees mainly in Iran and India, it was once a prophetic religion revolutionising ritual practices and theological ideas (Figure 6.1). Zoroastrianism is named after its prophet – also the reformer of earlier beliefs – who in ancient Greece was known as Zoroaster, but the prophet himself is now more commonly known as Zarathustra (Boyce 1979: 1–2). The Greek believed that he lived around 600 BC, but this date is an artificial calculation among the Hellenistic Greeks. This traditional date was set 258 years before Alexander and was based on a notion that Pythagoras studied with Zarathustra in Babylon. Another improbably Greek construction places Zoroaster 6,000 years ago, while it is now more generally agreed

**FIGURE 6.1**  A Zoroastrian performing a fire ritual, by Bernard Picart (1673–1733). Public domain.

that he lived around 1200 BC (Boyce 2002: 19; Russel 2002: 29), although suggestions for both older and younger dates still exist. Many historians of religion still believe that it would be more reasonable to date him to sometime between 1000 BC and 800 BC. (Stausberg 2005: 31). Despite this, Zoroastrianism is still the oldest religion whose founder is known. But despite Zarathustra as a prophet and founder of the religion, Zoroastrianism is still a religion that is largely based on even earlier Indo-Iranian beliefs.

Mary Boyce (1920–2006), Professor of Iranian Studies at University of London, was one of the foremost scholars of the ancient Iranian beliefs and their development into Zoroastrianism. In the early 1960s, she undertook fieldwork in the Yazd plain in Iran investigating surviving Zoroastrian villages (Boyce 1977). In those days, such villages still remained in some rural areas while Zoroastrians had much earlier been driven out of the urban centres. Despite being officially tolerated by Islam, Zoroastrians were despised as infidels – more precisely as fire-worshipers – and often subjected to harassment. A common notion of relative tolerance towards the Zoroastrians is unfortunately contradicted by both mass murder and mass conversions during historical times. As a consequence, a large proportion immigrated to India, beginning already during medieval times and with a continuation up to the British colonial times. In India, the members of Zoroastrian communities are mainly known as Parsis, referring to their Persian origin.

The Zoroastrian Irani were direct descendants of the Sassanian population existing prior to the Arab invasion in the 7th century AD, and a controversial question has been (and is) where their origins can be found. The source material for the life of Zarathustra is obscure, and mainly represented by legendary material. In Avesta – the holy scripture of ancient Persia – the homeland of Zarathustra is known as *Airiianəm Vaẽjah*. This name also refers to the ancient home of the Indo-Iranian people mentioned in both Avesta and Rigveda, and interpreted as 'the Aryan expanse'. The name is connected to Old Persian *ariya*, and today's country name, Iran, is therefore also related to the word. The historical location of *Airiianəm Vaẽjah* is still uncertain. Different areas in Central Asia and Iran have been suggested by various scholars, while others believe that the place should be considered as a more or less mythical land, although probably reflecting an area known to the authors of the Avesta. Historically though, the Iranian-speaking people were present over large parts of the Eurasian plain from the borders of Rumania in the west to Xinjiang and Afghanistan in the east, and in the south down to the Persian Gulf and the Indian Ocean (Witzel 2000: 9, 2013: 422).

The Avestan language, still in current use in Zoroastrian rituals, is preserved in manuscripts stemming only from the medieval period. However, the texts were composed already in the late Bronze Age and faithfully transmitted orally up to their writing down during the Sassanid Empire, and very similar in language and content to the Vedic texts. Linguists distinguish between Old Avestan, the hymns of Zarathustra and another contemporary texts, dealing with fire worship, and the Later Avestan texts, dealing with other important rituals, including pollution and death as well as the poetic praise and a description of important deities (Witzel 2013: 423–424).

Although the geographical context of *Airiianəm Vaẽjah* thus remains tentative, Mary Boyce favoured the steppe lands of Central Asia, and more precisely the Sintashta context and cultural area, which has been the subject of archaeological research since the 1960s. Sintashta itself was excavated from 1968 onwards, and the importance of this kind of fortified settlements with its symbolic construction plan was even more emphasised with the discovery of the well-preserved site of Arkaim in 1987: 'In general the material remains of the Sintashta people, and the indications which these yield about their social and religious life, accord remarkably well with the relevant facts which can be gleaned from the Gathas' (Boyce 1992: 37). The Gatha songs are written in the ancient Persian, Avestan language and date to around 1200 BC, roughly contemporary with the Indian Rigveda.

Boyce interpreted Zarathustra as a religious reformer, striving to oppose cattle-raiding war bands, a process coinciding with pastoral life of the early Iranians being threatened by the emerging class of warriors. Not least the war chariot became a prominent feature of early Iranian life, as in Vedic India. This may then have coincided with the emergence of a military elite, which in itself matches Sintashta and its successors. More likely, however, we should perhaps seek Zarathustra's time and place somewhat later in history than Sintashta and Arkaim and the other settlements in 'the country of towns'. In fact, archaeology has shed some light here, not least thanks to the excavations carried out by the Russian-Greek archaeologist Viktor Sarianidi (1929–2013) when he explored the archaeological culture traditionally known as the Oxus civilisation, but today more often referred to as the Bactria-Margiana Archaeological Complex (usually abbreviated as BMAC).

The steppe people of the Sintashta-Andronovo culture interacted with the inhabitants of BMAC already before expanding further south. It was a resident, agricultural culture in the oases of Central Asia, areas today located in northern Afghanistan, eastern Turkmenistan, southern Uzbekistan and western Tajikistan. The settlements are centred on the upper course of the Amu Daryas, or Oxus River, hence its traditional name. Much of Sintashta metal production was exported to the settlements of the BMAC, and this trade, for the first time, connected the people of the steppe with the urban civilisations to the south, which provided an almost bottomless market for metals. The same trade routes became the first channel through which horses and chariots entered these areas (Anthony 2007: 391–397).

It was a civilisation that erected large and often monumental buildings in the form of palaces, defences and, notably, temple structures. In addition to horse sacrifices, another typical feature of the Indo-European ritual tradition we find here are clear and partly monumental evidences for advanced fire rituals. Among the finds and building structures that Sarianidi was able to document were fire altars and utensils for libation sacrifices as well as traces of ingredients – ephedra – for the traditional sacred drink of the Indo-Iranians, known in Vedic as *Soma* and in Old Persian (Avesta) as *Haoma*. Here, we can see elements from – and probably a direct forerunner of – the cult that shaped Vedic religion in India and formed the background to the ancient Persian religion, which eventually developed into Zoroastrianism (e.g. Sarianidi 1990, 2005; cf. Dubova 2019).

The most famous BMAC settlement is Gonur Depe, one of the sites discovered by Viktor Sarianidi. It consists of a large, city-like early Bronze Age settlement, dated from 2400 BC to 1600 BC. The urban area within Gonur Depe had a centrally located palace complex, protected by fortified walls that also included the earliest documented fire temple of a type that has direct equivalents in later Iranian and Indian tradition. There were also other temple buildings and two large adjacent water pools, which were interpreted as that the inhabitants of Gonur may have had a cult including not only worship of fire, but also water. The latter, together with the presence of several fire altars, is a particularly interesting feature pointing to important common Indo-European conceptions.

The same patterns and traces of fire cult in combination with water were repeated on other investigated BMAC settlement sites with ritual complexes. Another striking site in the same area as Gonur Depe, also excavated by Sarianidi, is a place called Togolok 21:

If Togolok 21 was a temple connected with cultic libations and a fire cult, we can assume a connection with the milieu from which Zoroastrianism might have sprung ... In Zoroastrianism, we see continuations not only of the fire cult but of the haoma [a divine plant] cult. The evidence from Togolok 21 indicates that during his reform of old Indo-Iranian religious practices, Zoroaster could not ignore the traditions connected with cultic libation.

*Sarianidi 1990: 165*

The primary BMAC population largely derived from earlier local Copper-Age people who were, in turn, closely related to people from the Iranian plateau and had little of the steppe ancestry that is ubiquitous in South Asia today. The main population of the BMAC carried no ancestry from steppe pastoralists and did not contribute substantially to later South Asians. In this case, it has rather been a transfer of ideology, technology and religious beliefs, but with limited immigration of people. However, steppe pastoralist ancestry appeared in outlier individuals at BMAC sites by the turn of the second millennium BC around the same time as it appeared on the southern steppe (Narasimhan, Patterson & Reich 2019).

The migration from Andronovo to the BMAC was filtered through a membrane of agricultural, resident civilisation, which in turn absorbed cultural traits of the steppe people. The mixed culture that first emerged in Central Asia is called the Tazabagyab culture, and within it has been found, among other things, clear traces of fire altars and burnt offerings, typical elements of the Indo-European ritual tradition. The Tazabagyab culture develops into yet another archaeological find group called the Khwarezm culture, named after one of the great oases in the Amu-Darja River delta. The Khwarezm culture is of particular interest for the further development of what becomes the ancient Iranian tradition, since this context with time becomes the centre of several great kingdoms, which eventually formed the basis of the Persian Empire (Mallory & Adams 1997: 73; West 2007: 402–405).

However, the connection between the people in the BMAC area and the ancient Iranian culture – and thus Zoroastrianism – can be closer, and also more directly genetically related compared to the Vedic scenario. After the split from a common origin that takes place between the forerunners of the Vedic culture in northern India and those who form the ancient Iranian variant, each group incorporates both cultural and genetic traits independently of each other. Viktor Sarianidi observed close similarities between the ritual expressions in Togolok 21 and Gonur Depe that may actually shed light on the real environment of Zarathustra and his time. Maybe, then it is the BMAC rather than Sintashta, but perhaps even more likely the Tazabagyab culture or the Khwarezm culture – which are direct predecessors to the Persian empires – that form the real background to Zarathustra's reforms and Zoroastrianism as we know it.

## The Zoroastrian fire rituals

Zoroastrianism can rightly claim to be the oldest of the world's prophetic and revealed religions, although intimately based on a common Indo-European background. With this as a starting point, however, within Zoroastrianism a completely separate variant is formed with special features, not least with regard to the view of fire (Figure 6.2). In Zoroastrianism, the only god is Ahura Mazda, who is represented by fire: 'The fire, according to its nature, is pure and purifying; it is, therefore, a sin, on which the punishment of death is set, to bring to it anything at all impure, to blow it out with the breath of the mouth, or to bring it at all in contact with the dead, to burn a corpse with it' (Cama 1968: 127–128).

**FIGURE 6.2** The Eternal Fire in the Zoroastrian Yazd Fire Temple, Iran. Photo: Soheil Callage. Creative Commons.

While fire has a prominent role in all Indo-European traditions, not least evident in the Hindu-Vedic tradition (e.g. Datta 1936; Knipe 1975) – clearly expressed not least in the *Agni Puranas* (*The Agni Purana* Parts I, II, III, IV 1984, 1985, 1986, 1987) – the perceptions and uses of fire differ, and in particular the Zoroastrian rites and conceptions represent a unique development, which includes their world-famous air-burials taking place in 'towers of silence' (dakhma) where vultures devour the corpses. This funerary practice directly relates to the core concepts and understanding of ritual purity and tenets of the religion (Wadia 2002).

In Zoroastrianism, Ahura Mazda is the supreme god. The name means 'Wise Lord' and just as he is associated with fire, so is he *the* Lord Wisdom. While the popular presentation of Zoroastrianism presents the religion as worship of fire and Ahura Mazda as a fire god, this is a simplification. Compared to most other belief systems and religious practices, Zoroastrianism has an extreme emphasis on purity, and in particular the purity of the elements like fire and water and the sacredness of the earth (Boyce 1979; Choksy 1989). The core of the religion and the rites are that elaborate precautions are required to prevent the good creations of Ahura Mazda from being contaminated. From this perspective, the religious fire is the son of Ahura Mazda and thus he is the 'enlightened one'. Following Zoroastrianism, the good creations are the seven holy immortals (Hinnells 1981: 13): (1) The Wise Lord (Ahura Mazda) – Man, (2) Good mind – Cattle, (3) Righteousness – Fire, (4) Kingdom – Sky, (5) Devotion – Earth, (6) Health – Waters and (7) Immortality – Plants. Thus, the religion is not simply structured around fire, but rather around all the good creations, which in a pastoral world was the relation between humans and cattle, and this symbiosis and interrelation was characterised by specific qualities creating a good life (Boyce 1984, 1992; Clark 2001).

Thus, Zoroastrianism is mainly concerned with protecting the life-giving elements, and quite logically water and fire are the two most vulnerable and venerated elements. Herodotus description is famous: 'Because rivers are objects of particular reverence for them, they do not urinate or spit into them, nor do they wash their hands there or allow anyone else to do either' (Herodotus 1998: 138). Fire and water are distinctive and separate creations that cannot be mixed. The sacredness of water is a consequence of the protection of the Good Creations. The earth was holy because humans owned to it their whole corporeal existence. Extreme purity is one of the cores in the Zoroastrian teaching and practices, and there were special rules concerning water and fire with particular relation to the faith. Most often people use water for everything that is impure, but for the Zoroastrians the cleanliness of water in itself had to be protected.

Whereas other religions use water as the primary purificatory and cleansing agent, Zoroastrianism sees water as a secondary purifying agent. It is possible to use only after ablutions have been performed with un-consecrated bull's urine. This particular belief in cattle urine as a prime purifying agent must have developed among pastoral groups at a very early age and it gives a unique insight into the era when the Iranian and Indian ancestors were nomads herding cattle on the Asian steppes (Boyce 1977: 92). The use of water to wash away dirt and impurities is seen as a heinous sin because then water is exposed to demonic impurities (Choksy 1989: 11). Consequently, nothing impure is allowed to be in contact with a natural source of water such as a lake, stream or river. 'If anything ritually unclean was to be washed, water should be drawn off for this purpose, and even then, this was not to be used directly, but the impure objects should first be cleaned with cattle-urine, and then dried with sand or in sunlight before water was allowed to touch it for the final washing' (Boyce 1979: 44), because water 'promotes the well-being of mankind and animals, refreshes them in the heat, and influences the growth of plants, the fertility of the fields and the luxurious green of the meadows' (Cama 1968: 129).

In practice, water was not much inferior in beliefs and rituals than the fire, and it gives an historic glimpse into the pastoral life on the steppe and the ecological reality constituting economy, culture and cosmology. The water-world defines the life of humans and animals alike, in particular during the harsh and challenging winter season, which puts emphasis on fire and the purity of this ultimate life-giving force. Interestingly, this close connection between fire and water, as well as the fact that both were the subject of sacred rites, was also evident in the archaeological remains documented by Viktor Sarianidi's investigations of the BMAC sites of Gonur Depe and Togolok 21 (Sarianidi 1990: 165), which is an important indicator that the beliefs expressed in these sites really constitute a significant precursor to Zoroastrianism.

Although many fire rituals and associated altars are elaborate and large physical structures, among pastoral groups the perpetual fires were of a different kind, given that their lives were mobile and the fires need to be portable and transportable. In other words, this puts emphasis on the ceramic pots containing charcoal and ever-burning flames, often only visible as glooming lights of heat and smoke; an ever-lasting source of fire possible to ignite and activate – it is latent life and a creator of prosperity. From this perspective, the ceramic pot as a container was a portable chapel or holy container (Figure 6.3). This puts a particular emphasis on the holy and divine fires, and how this process of sanctification and purification takes place. Zoroastrianism gives a unique insight into this process.

In Iran there have been about 20 active fire temples into modern times, and in India about one hundred, of which eight are so-called cathedral fire temples. In Mumbai alone, there are 44 fire temples, and four of these contain cathedral fires (Figure 6.4). The cathedral fire temples are the most holy fires and the utmost divine manifestations of Ahura Mazda. The different fires are illuminating and instructive with regards to ritual practice and the ways purification processes constitute complex cosmologies. There are three levels of consecrating fires for worship and ritual practice. The first and most simple fire is the household fire, which does not necessitate five prayers a day. The two other and purer fires require continuous worship, and the next fire is agiary fire or the chapel fire, which consists of four different fires. These fires represent priests,

**FIGURE 6.3**  A Hindu portable fire pot. Shivaratri, Pashupatinath, 2003. Photo: Terje Oestigaard.

warriors, traders and farmers, and in the sanctuary, it takes three weeks to consecrate this particular sacred fire. The last and the most sacred fire – the cathedral fire – is of a different kind altogether. It consists of 16 different fires and it takes 14,000 hours of prayers to initiate and consecrate this utmost pure and holy fire (see also Chapter 7). Intriguingly, given the prohibition of cremation in Zoroastrianism, one of the 16 fires is from a Brahman being cremated. This fire is actually believed to be the fire of Ahriman – the Devil – but in the cathedral fire all malignant forces and powers are included and overpowered. Hence, the ultimate fire ritual consecrates, purifies and encompasses everything: it is perfect.

Importantly, the cathedral fires cannot be moved or separated and the fire has changed from being mere flames to actually consist of a corporeal identity – a spiritual and metaphysical body made by the meticulous rituals. The fire is built layer by layer through prayers, and one cannot create a new cathedral fire by taking a part of the holiest of the holy. It is only possible to make a new one by physically and spiritually building it by prayers and consecrations. Once it has been created, the perpetual fire may live on and gain strength and holiness throughout the ages, and the oldest still existing cathedral fire is situated in a fire temple in Udvada on the Indian west coast north of Mumbai. Following the orthodoxy, this fire has been continuously burning for 1000 years and five times each day prayers have been uttered (Boyce 1979; Hinnells 1981; Choksy 1989,

**FIGURE 6.4** The Zoroastrian Maneckji Seti Agiary in Mumbai, 2003. Photo: Terje Oestigaard.

2000; Clark 2001). While this is today an example of the almighty, omnipotent and omnipresent fire rituals at an unprecedented scale, it directs the attention to the ancient Vedic fire rituals and fire altars that also have continuity up to today.

Despite the many similarities between the Zorastric and Vedic fire rituals, there is a particularly noticeable difference. This applies to the use of fire in connection with death and funeral. According to Zoroastrianism, existence was dualistic, divided into good/pure and evil/impure. The body was considered impure by nature, and this applied especially to a dead body, which was not allowed to defile either fire or earth. The body was instead supposed to be consumed by vultures and beasts of prey. Funeral rituals in Zoroastrianism were intended to dispose of the corpse in such a way that the living was not harmed by its impurity, and to ease the passage of the soul from this world to the next (Stausberg 2005: 111). The Zoroastrian tradition gradually developed into a refined mortuary method, which culminated in the construction of a special type of building usually referred to as 'the tower of silence' (Figure 6.5). On a platform in the tower, the body was eaten by birds and the remains were left to dry. The bones were thrown into the interior of the tower where slaked lime completed the disintegration of the bones to powder, which rainwater carried through a cleansing filter of sand and charcoal. After this process, the impurity of the body was finally gone and the soul liberated (Thomas 1987: 455–456).

While the Vedic rite of passage for the dead gradually developed into cremation becoming the dominant ritual, fire did not acquire this role at all in Zoroastrianism. The relationship to death and the bodily remains has many similarities, but the rituals for dealing with this were nevertheless developed in very different ways. Although fire was a sacred, divine tool in both traditions, it was given such a sacrosanct role in Zoroastrianism that it was not even allowed to come into contact with the unclean elements of life, like the bodies of the dead.

## The Vedic culture and its origins

The other branch of the Indo-Iranian tree is, of course, the Vedic tradition, with close common roots in the Sintashta culture and its immediate successors. These two Indo-European traditions – Vedic and ancient Iranian – together with Germanic and Celtic as well as ancient Greek and Roman religions, are variations of a theme developed on the basis of a common proto-Indo-European background. Although the common origin within the Vedic and the ancient Iranian religion is particularly clear on a general level, the similarities between all these Indo-European religions that can be traced in terms of cosmology, conception of death, deities and even ritual, are in some cases striking (e.g. Dumézil 1941; de Vries 1956–1957; Eliade 1958; Biezais 1972; Lincoln 1986).

However, while the existence of common Indo-European features in both the ancient Iranian and the Vedic traditions are clear indeed, the latter also shows features that do not occur in any other Indo-European context, the Iranian included. These features are most likely connected to the very long cultural history on the Indian peninsula that preceded the arrival of the Vedic migrants from the north. 'The culture of the Rigveda shares features with other Indo-European cultures, but it also possesses features in common only with the Iranians, and other features not found elsewhere in the Indo-European family' (Staal 1983: 91). The fact that different branches of the Indo-European diaspora incorporated beliefs and traditions from earlier indigenous people with which they gradually

**FIGURE 6.5** Inside a tower of silence and a Parsi burial, 1912. Author unknown. Public domain.

merged, has probably been a common pattern in different geographical areas. Scenarios like these may partly lie behind variations in different Indo-European cultures – differences in both linguistic, religious and social nature, in addition to an internal development within cultures that naturally takes place over time. That this is particularly evident in Vedic culture is probably largely due to the fact that this tradition is so richly documented, but perhaps also to the fact that the earlier culture of the Indian Peninsula was markedly advanced.

The Vedic ritual tradition is one of the oldest documented religious traditions in the world. In addition, it is still alive today, within one of the truly great world religions, with hundreds of millions of practitioners – Hinduism (Figure 6.6). Early scholars working on comparative Indo-European mythology emphasised the importance of Vedic mythology to such an extent that it was practically equated with an original proto-Indo-European tradition. Later on, most scholars have been more cautious, but the vast majority have also later regarded Vedic religion as central to the understanding of the oldest history of the Indo-Europeans (Puhvel 1987: 14).

The traditional picture of how Vedic culture and religion emerged is that it was born in the encounter between Indo-European conquerors and earlier indigenous cultures in north-west India, or rather in areas located in today's Pakistan or eastern Afghanistan, sometimes in its oldest phase before 1500 BC. Genetic studies as well as ancient texts indicate that this traditional scenario is very accurate. The ancient texts speak of a military conquest, in which horses and chariots play a major role. DNA also strongly suggests that it was men who were mainly responsible for the expansion in present India, as shown by the still-living male Y chromosome DNA lines – variants of the R1a haplogroup, typical also of the Corded Ware culture of Europe and subsequently the Fatyanovo culture as well as Sintashta and other closely related ethnic groups. These all show a male dominance where especially some male individuals have become the ancestors of many children in a way that is also repeated in early Bronze Age Europe. Still, today the R1a haplogroup – showing the steppe ancestry – is very common in South Asia, not least among men belonging to the higher castes in India, especially the Brahmins. R1a is also generally more prevalent in modern-day populations in northern India – the area primarily affected by the Vedic migration – than in southern India. A study of ancient DNA from over 500 individuals from Central and South Asia has shed new light on this issue (Narasimhan, Patterson & Reich 2019), revealing a very clear southward spread of genetic ancestry from the Eurasian Steppe correlating with the archaeologically known expansion of steppe pastoralists, down on the Indian peninsula.

Recent data from ancient individuals from the Swat Valley (Pakistan) in the northernmost part of South Asia have shown that steppe ancestry was integrated further and further south in the first half of the second millennium BC, and still today contributed up to 30% of the ancestry of modern groups in South Asia. The steppe ancestry in South Asia has the same profile as that in Bronze Age Eastern Europe – characterised by the R1a variant in the male Y chromosome line – thus tracking a movement of people that affected both regions in the same context as the arrival of unique Indo-European features. Of special interest is, as discussed more in detail in Chapter 5, the close links between Indo-Iranian and Balto-Slavic where genetic data now support a particularly close relationship (Narasimhan et al. 2019; cf. Nordqvist & Heyd 2020).

When Indo-European people penetrated north-west India, the earlier high cultures of the Indus valley, Harappā and Mohenjo-daro, were in decline,

**FIGURE 6.6** Triangular fire altar. Dakshinkali Temple, Nepal, 2002. Photo: Anders Kaliff.

probably for other, more complex reasons, including changes in the rivers' courses (Possehl 1999, 2002). Here, the Indo-Europeans encountered the remains of a high culture that was more advanced than their own. It is natural that they brought their language to the new area where they settled. There are strong indications that it was a military conquest, not least shown by the Vedic texts. The Indo-European – Aryan – immigrants may have had a highly developed linguistic culture with advanced poetry and narrative technique, especially connected to myth and ritual. In addition to the military strength of the Vedic people, this would have given them a prominent ritual and religious position vis-à-vis other people, despite the fact that the people who previously lived in northern India definitely represented themselves as a both developed and sophisticated culture (Staal 1983: 92–95).

What is normally called the Vedic period in India, c. 1500–500 BC (the dating varies), should not be immediately interpreted in images of today's Hinduism, which would give a misleading picture. Of course, Hinduism is a descendant of Vedic religion, but one with many added features both from the earlier Indian high cultures and later influences and through change over time (cf. Flood 1998: 23–50; Staal 1983: 60). An aspect that can illustrate this is that anthropomorphic images of the Hindu gods – so closely associated with the religious expressions of Hinduism today – did not occur at all before the start of the Common Era. Poetic and symbolic descriptions of the gods are, however, well represented in the early Vedic tradition; Agni as fire and the sun, Indra as the thunderbolt, etc. (Eck 1983). However, the large share of the 'exotic' iconographic representations of gods which are so intimately associated in the West with Hinduism did not exist in Vedic times.

Part of the origins of Hinduism can probably be traced back to the oldest high culture in India, the Indus Valley civilisation, with its mature phase c. 2600–1900 BC, documented archaeologically within a large geographical area that stretches from the border of present-day Iran in the west to the Himalayas in the northeast and to the coast of Gujarat in the south. The cities of the Indus culture were characterised by advanced urban planning, with brick buildings of different function and shape, metallurgy with copper, bronze and lead, drainage systems and even water supply systems (Possehl 1999, 2002; Wright 2010). Not surprisingly, from the Indus culture we have features that can be traced as direct predecessors of ritual elements and ideas in Hinduism. But still, apart from these, the origin and the major part is primarily found in the Vedic context.

Nevertheless, it has long been debated whether the Vedic culture and its ritual tradition developed on Indian soil or was brought to India through immigration or other external influences as part of Indo-European migrations. Despite overwhelming evidence for the latter scenario, this is not yet accepted by all scholars. As mentioned, this is particularly true for the Indian ritualists who are strongly coloured by Hindu nationalist values in today's India. Their ambition is to see as many links as possible between the Indus Valley Civilisation and the Vedic culture, sometimes leading to statements that might at first sight seem solid enough. After more close inspection, though, much of this can be revealed as empty ideology, principally similar to the old exaggerations of Western scholars searching for the homeland of the Aryans in Europe. As a reaction to older and outdated interpretations of Western scholars about the 'Aryan invasion', the reaction of Indian researchers is understandable, but this does not necessarily make the interpretations any truer.

One example is claims of having deciphered the pre-Vedic Indus Script, which is presented in the book *The Deciphered Indus Script* by Jha and Rajaram (2000). They were not the first scholars to claim to deciphering the script, it has also been done by others before, but another dimension was added. Jha and Rajaram argued that the texts not only included clear references to the Rigveda, but also that the language was indeed Vedic Sanskrit and they came to an astounding conclusion: The Vedic culture actually consisted of the Indus culture being between five and six thousand years old and therefore an indigenous Indian development. Critical analyses, presented by for instance Michael Witzel, show that such claims are completely without substance (Widmalm 2003 with cited works).

Another feature of greater concern to us here has also appeared in this controversy: fire altars (Figure 6.7). There are in fact archaeological evidences that altars for burnt offerings occurred already in the Indus Valley culture (e.g. Chakrabarti 2001: 44–45), although documented only in a few places and dated to a relatively late phase. However, these finds have been used as an argument that typical Vedic ritual practices have an indigenous origin. Examples of such

**FIGURE 6.7** Square fire altar. Pashupatinath Temple, Nepal, 2022. Photo: Terje Oestigaard.

finds occur in the North Indian site Kalibangan, where several fire altars have been discovered, with similar finds at another site, Lothal. Not unexpectedly, these finds have been presented as proof for the existence of Vedic rituals within the Indus culture, but more likely these finds rather show signs of a diversity in religious traditions (Bryant 2001; Lal 2003).

There are obvious nationalist undertones to this discussion in India today. The only relevant argument that could possibly be put forward in support of the hypothesis that Vedic culture originated (at least in part) in the Indus culture would be that the archaeological record shows no clear signs of any cultural break. The Grey Painted Ware pottery associated with Vedic culture, for example, seems to have an earlier local background. However, explanations other than direct continuity can be sought for this and be at least as convincing. The horse-borne immigrants of Indo-European descent who invaded the area may have had a relatively limited material culture. Pottery was probably not their main form of expression, given their semi-nomadic origins. The takeover of older ceramic traditions – and much more – may then have taken place as part of a cultural pattern where men from the immigrant group entered into alliances with local women, who continued to produce ceramics in the traditional style, which gradually and eventually formed a mixture of old and new. As another example, the process when the Corded Ware culture developed in Europe, shortly after 3000 BC, seems to have followed a similar pattern (e.g. Kristiansen, Allentoft & Frei 2017).

However, the bearers of the Vedic traditions created a collection of holy texts, hymns and ritual rules, known as Veda, a collection that gradually expanded with even more texts and comments. Many of the earliest texts are preserved in the so-called *Rigveda*, the most well-known of the Vedas. It consists of 1,028 hymns to recite during votive acts, the majority in honour of the Vedic gods, such as Indra, Agni and Soma. The texts are in Sanskrit, the Indo-European language spoken at the time, and the origin of several modern Indian languages. Sanskrit developed through time into Hindi, Punjabi, Bengali and the other Indo-European languages of northern India. Sanskrit survived only as a religious language, known only to learned persons and ritual specialists, a somewhat similar role as Latin in the Western tradition. Great effort was expended on memorising and preserving the texts for future generations, and correct recitation has always been regarded as necessary for the rituals to have the desired effect. In the Vedic tradition, the knowledge was passed on orally and writing a manual for the rituals as well as even reciting from written texts have always been considered inauspicious.

'For a long time, however, writing was continued to be considered impure and even offensive. A later Vedic text, the *Aitareya Āraṇyaka* (5.5.3), states that a pupil should not recite the Veda after he had eaten meat, seen blood or a dead body, had intercourse, or engaged in writing' (Staal 1983: 31). Thus, there is a traditional, built-in aversion to writing which goes far back in history. This aversion can partly be explained by the fact that oral tradition could be reserved for ritual specialists as exclusive knowledge. For the 'right' learning, the knowledge had to be conveyed by a teacher, who could also give supplementary explanations.

Another possible explanation for the reluctance to writing is that the people and society creating the first Vedic texts actually did not have a written language (Staal 1983: 29–40),

> The Vedic texts were orally composed and transmitted, without the use of script, in an unbroken line of transmission from teacher to student that was formalized early on. This ensured an impeccable textual transmission superior to the classical texts of other cultures; it is, in fact, something like a tape-recording of ca. 1500–500 BC. Not just the actual words, but even the long-lost musical (tonal) accent (as in old Greek or in Japanese) has been preserved up to the present.
>
> *Witzel 2003: 68–69*

Today, there is no agreement among practising Hindus (or scholars for that matter) as to what many of the hymns in the *Rigveda* mean. The exact rendering of the sound has been of greater ritual significance than the actual meaning of the words. Merely hearing Sanskrit – especially the *Rigveda* – has a sacred meaning for many Hindus. Even ritual specialists often recite the words with the right pronunciation, but without reflecting on their meaning. The recitation thus becomes a ritual in itself.

## The Vedic fire-sacrifice and its meaning

The worship of fire as a god – Agni – is central to Vedic religion, a being that originally had a much more prominent role than is reflected in the later Hindu pantheon (Figure 6.8). According to the Vedic as well as the ancient Iranian view, fire is a substance that is active everywhere in cosmos. Fire is the fertile element in the cosmos; in the sky, in the storm and in the soil, as also in man and woman (Edsman 1987: 343–344).

Fire as a giver of life and a destroyer of evil can hardly be expressed in more powerful images than the description of the Vedic god Agni, a divinity who not only represents fire, but also *is* the fire itself. As a god himself, Agni is also the one who transmits the votive gifts to the gods. The name Agni is clearly Indo-European with close parallels in other Indo-European languages, as the appellatives *ignis* in Latin, *ogon'* in Russian and *ugnis* in Lithuanian. Agni is thought to have been born out of the sticks in the fire drill, and he is also present in the sky in lightning and in the sun, but in water too. He is also believed to be intimately connected with the domesticated sphere of life, with the home, the family and the tribe, with a special relation to the clearance of land for pasture and cultivation. 'The burning of forests creates pastures and paves the way for agriculture. The Vedas swarm with cattle and often mention agriculture' (Staal 1983: 99). As a means of this, fire is closely related to the survival of the tribe and the household, but also shows its ability to 'eat' up the forest. The land on which the fire altar is to be built is initially ploughed as a

**FIGURE 6.8** Three holy men in front of their hearth with fire. Pashupatinath, 2022. Photo: Terje Oestigaard.

symbol of agriculture and a ritual to evoke fertility. The connection between fire rituals, clearing, grazing land as well as agricultural land and ploughing has parallels in several other Indo-European traditions (Staal 1983: 73, 99; Parmeshwaranand 2000: 40–48).

Soma, like Agni, is a central divinity in Vedic religion. In a manner similar in principle to Agni, Soma is also at once a god and a part of creation, in this case a plant, and especially the liquid extracted from that plant. Also, in this case there is a direct parallel in the ancient Iranian tradition, and the equivalent is named with the equally closely related word Haoma. This word – Soma or Haoma – was the name of both the plant and the ritual drink that were of such importance among the early Vedic Indo-Aryans. However, today nobody knows for certain which plant it refers to, and the identity has for long been debated among scholars. It has often been suggested that it originally referred to a hallucinogenic plant which led to ecstasy. However, the description of the effect of soma/haoma in the old ritual texts does not agree with a hallucinogenic substance from which the drink is made, and it is also clear that it is not an alcohol-related drink. Instead, it is clear that it contains a substance that rather increases the clarity of thought. Several proposals have been presented, but the most likely candidate for the original plant was ephedra with the active substance ephedrine, an active substance whose effect is well consistent with the description of the ancient texts (e.g. Falk 1989; Houben 2003). Vedic ritualists have for a long time used substitutes for the real plant. In the Iranian tradition however, ephedra has been 'used by the Parsis to this day for their Haoma rituals' (Falk 1989: 79). The consumption of soma is well attested in Vedic ritual and a part of the *Rigveda* is completely dedicated to it. It focuses on the ritual when the soma is pressed, strained and mixed with water and milk. Soma is regarded as the elixir of life – a drink of immortality – and indispensable for both people and gods (Flood 1998: 43; Parmeshwaranand 2000: 611–614).

According to Bruce Lincoln (1986), the cosmological creation myth with its fundamental common Indo-European background is crucial to the design of both sacrificial and burial rites, something that is clearly expressed in the Vedic tradition. It is fundamental to the design of sacrifices as well as to the burning of the dead on the funeral pyre. In the Vedic version, as in the Old Norse, for example, a primordial being is killed and dismembered by the gods. In the well-known and often referenced hymn *Purusasūkta* ('The Hymn of Purusa') from the *Rigveda* (10.90), the world is created when the gods cut up a cosmic giant, Purusa. It is this narrative that is the archetype for the Vedic offering. Purusa acquired a companion in Manu ('man'), the first being to invent sacrifice. The first sacrificial victim is Purusa himself, who then becomes lord of the dead.

The homology found in the creation myths, the identification of different elements in the cosmos with the body parts of the sacrificed primordial being is a fundamental cosmological idea. One entity is created from the matter in another as alternative guises of each other. Moreover, one entity can change into the other like meat and earth, for example, believed to be of the same material substance. In a similar way, the bones are equated with the mountains and the stones in the earth while plants are associated with hair. Connected to the alloform meat–earth, there is often another, namely stone–bone. Just as bones are the harder substance inside the flesh of the body, stones are the harder counterpart in the earth. The identification of different elements corresponding to different parts of the human body made up, according to Bruce Lincoln, is a mythology of deep impact embraced by virtually all Indo-European speaking people. An important element that also derives from the original cosmological sacrifice is fire itself, as well as Agni, who personifies it (Figure 6.9). In the Vedic tradition, fire is very important as a cosmological, divine element and consequently as a ritual tool. Roughly 200 of the 1,028 hymns in the *Rigveda* are dedicated to Agni, which puts him in second place after Indra, both gods who are central in the Vedic religion but who in time have been given a more obscure role in Hinduism. Agni is also significant throughout the rituals. Fire was regarded not just as a god in itself, but simultaneously as a divine messenger. Himself a god, Agni is also the one who conveys the sacrificial gifts to the other gods (Lincoln 1986: 5–40).

As creation proceeds from the cosmological, primordial body of the first sacrificial victim, this process can also be reversed. One of the Upanishads, *Aitrareya Upanishad* (1.4), not only describes how the cosmos is shaped from the parts of Purusa's body, but also depicts an anthropogony and how the different parts of creation can take shape in a human body:

**FIGURE 6.9**    Agni – the sacrificial fire. Pashupatinath, Nepal, 2022. Photo: Terje Oestigaard.

Fire, having become speech, entered into the mouth. Wind, having become the breath, entered into the nostrils. The sun, having become vision, entered into the eyes. The four quarters, having become hearing, entered into the ears. Plants and trees, having become bodily hair, entered into the skin. The moon, having become the mind, entered into the heart.

> Death, having become the downward (anal) breath, entered into the navel.
> The waters, having become semen, entered into the penis.
>
> *transl. by Lincoln 1986: 33*

In the inverted cosmogony, the body becomes an alloform for the cosmos as a whole. Just as creation is composed of the body parts from the primordial being, this process can be repeated and strengthened through sacrifice where a body is cut up or burned to add new power to creation. This is a fundamental meaning behind the Indo-European sacrifice and, furthermore, also for funeral rituals. For animal sacrifices, this link is particularly obvious, where the ritual reproduces a very clear image of the primordial sacrifice. Accompanying the hymns of the *Rigveda* are ritual manuals to ensure that the rites can be performed properly with exact descriptions of how the sacrificial victim is cut up, corresponding directly to the homology in the creation myth. Through sacrifices and funeral rituals, the creation process can be repeated or humans can help to maintain creation by repeating it (Lincoln 1986: 5–40).

Vedic rituals are performed at different levels of complexity and in different contexts from more mundane to highly elaborate ceremonies taking a long time to prepare and several days to complete. The rituals have developed in two different directions and can be divided into two main categories. The first is the *gṛhya* or household rituals, which are *rites de passage* accompanying events such as birth, initiation, marriage and death. The second is the *śrauta*, that is, solemn public rites of much greater complexity. The difference between these two categories is seen in the role of the fire and its rituals: śrauta requires three fire altars with several officiating priests, while gṛhya needs only one, namely the household fire, and only one priest. While the function of gṛhya is quite concrete, the meaning of śrauta is less clear, with a complex form and framing (Staal 1983: 4–6, 35).

The śrauta rituals are the oldest and a number of them are documented already in Vedic texts. *Agnistoma* is an example of a simple sacrificial ritual performed in one day while *agnicayana*, as described in Chapter 1, is a complex ritual that requires several days. The divinities involved in śrauta are Agni and Soma, fire and sacred fluid, and the offerings are sacrificed through fire, Agni. Although Soma, as we have seen, originally constituted a mind-raising elixir, its ritual role is also twofold and seemingly contradictory. From a cosmological point of view, it does not have to be the effect of the plant or drug that is decisive, but rather that it represents a part of creation. In some sense, it can simply be perceived as the watery element inside matter and thus constitute an important ritual complement to fire as a central element. 'This contradiction becomes explicable if one assumes that Soma is a secondary element in what formed Vedic mythology ... Soma as a complementary element to Agni is by no means indispensable. In the dualistic mythology too Soma can be replaced simply by water' (Falk 1989: 77–78).

The śrauta rituals are performed in an order of increasing complexity and must be done in this order. The simplest ritual consists of a fire sacrifice to Agni (*agnihotra*), which is performed by a priest in a ritual enclosure in the home of the person who wishes to make the offering. Three fires are needed: *gārhaptya*, the household fire, *āhavanīya*, the sacrificial fire, and *daksiṇāgni*, which is believed to give protection from evil. The fires are installed on altars made of clay, a cosmological material in itself, where clay and water were transformed by fire. The altar for the household fire is round and is placed in the western part of the enclosure while the sacrificial altar is square and placed in the eastern part. The southern altar is semi-circular (Staal 1983: 40–41; cf. Tachikawa, Bahulkar & Kolhatkar 2001).

The functions of the different altars are connected to the elements: *gārhaptya*, symbolising the earth and its fire, *āhavanīya* representing the sky and its four directions and *daksiṇāgni* symbolising the atmosphere as a medium between heaven and earth. Between *gārhaptya* and *āhavanīya,* there is a structure called *vedi*, which usually consists of a shallow pit where the sacrificial fires were lit (Edsman 1987: 223). The Iranian fire ritual is in many respects like the Vedic one, particularly when it comes to the design of the altars. But interestingly enough, these altar forms have parallels in a number of Indo-European contexts. Also, in ancient Rome there was a circular altar for Vesta (*aedes rotunda*), but also *templa quadrata*. The Greeks had a round household altar on which they offered milk and honey, and a bigger square one which was used for animal sacrifices (Staal 1983: 93).

Agni is believed to be present in both the sacrificial fire and the cremation fire, and it is he who divides the votive gifts and the dead body into their original elements. The actual cremation can be regarded as a sacrificial ritual (Figure 6.10). During Vedic times in India, when the custom of sacrificing generally increased in frequency, the cremation ritual was viewed as a person's last sacrifice in which his own body was offered to the flames. It was believed that the deceased would be reborn out of this sacrifice in a new existence together with his ancestors. In Vedic texts, this is called a person's third birth. The cremation was therefore regarded as a transition from earthly existence to the world beyond (Olivelle 1987: 389). The earliest textual evidence of the belief in death being associated with the division of a person into the different elements – alloforms of the body parts of the primordial victim of the creation myth is found in an important hymn in the *Rigveda* (10.16.3), which pays tribute to the cremation fire and its effect with an explicit link to the elements:

> Your eye must go to the sun, and your self (must go) to the wind. You must go to heaven and earth, according to what is right – Or you must go to the waters, if that is fated for you; you must stand in the plants with your flesh.
>
> *transl. by Lincoln 1986: 124*

This theme has a clearly documented counterpart also in ancient Iran where one text, *Zad Spram* (34:7), gives a detailed and intact picture of the destiny of the

**FIGURE 6.10** Honourable cremation at Arya Ghat, Pashupatinath, Nepal, 2022. Photo: Terje Oestigaard.

body after death, according to the same underlying Indo-European eschatology. The passage cited here comes also in Bruce Lincoln's (1986: 122) translation:

> There are five collectors, receptacles of the corporeal substance of those who have died. One is the earth, which is the keeper of flesh and bone and sinew (or: fat) of men. The second is water, which is the keeper of blood.

The third is the plants, preservers of bodily hair and hair of the head. The fourth is light, recipient of fire. Last is the wind, which is the life-breath of my own creatures at the time of the Renovation.

Here are three of the traditional homologies present; blood/water, breath/wind and hair/plants. Added to these is a fourth one, fire/light. The basic feature, however, is that death and the disintegration of the body restore matter from the microcosm to the macrocosm and from the body to the surrounding world. The Vedic sources reveal a similar perception of the fate of the body after death. In the early Upanishads, we find the first reference to the idea of cyclic rebirth, depending on a person's deeds in life, a familiar concept also in present-day Hinduism. However, the view of death as a kind of sacrifice is older, occurring already in the earliest Indian texts. Here, we find the idea that death is only a temporary end, from which new life can arise. This is in the same way that a fire is absorbed by the wind when it has gone out and is aroused to a new life when the wind sweeps over glowing coals (Lincoln 1986: 121–126).

As presented in Chapter 1, agnicayana is one of the most advanced Vedic fire rituals, which, among other things, requires the building of a large bird-shaped altar of more than a thousand fired clay bricks representing Purusa. Although the exact meaning of the different elements is partly obscure, it is clear that these burnt clay bricks, as well as several central elements in the performance of the ritual, have a deep cosmological meaning. A large part of this meaning refers to the transformation of the elements in accordance with the creation myth. Thus, the strengthening effect of fire on materials such as clay is noticeable when for instance converted into bricks and pottery. To quote Frits Staal in a proverb translated by him from Hindi says a lot about the impression burning of clay gives: 'It was born right in the water, but seeing the water it dies. Brother, let's go and cremate it; then it will be immortal' (Staal 1983: 133). In cremation, however, the process seems to look completely different, and the result is instead a dissolution. This is the reversed cosmological process where the elements of existence are separated and released.

The cremation ritual agrees well with the outlook on death that is found in Vedism with close parallels in other early Indo-European traditions, not least the Iranian. Death is portrayed as a dismemberment of a whole, a fragmentation and decomposition. Viewing ageing and death as a process like any other disintegration in the cosmos is fundamental for an understanding of this, where death and cremation is regarded as the final dissolution of a complex whole (Lincoln 1986: 119). But there are other aspects to this as well, reminding of the strength given by fire to the clay. The parts of the body that do not dissolve during cremation – the burnt bones – seem to have turned into indestructible stones, which they are also considered by today's Hindus. The burnt bone fragments that are passed down into the river water after a cremation carried out on the shoreline no longer represent the remains of the deceased. Most noticeably, they are now considered only as pebbles and gravel at the bottom of the river (cf. Kaliff & Oestigaard 2008).

The cremation of the dead, in addition to fire sacrifices, is actually one of the ritual traditions still performed, which has the clearest roots back to its Vedic origins. Not only do Brahmins recite verses from the Vedic texts, in a more than 3000-year-old tradition, but the cremation bonfire itself and the rituals when the dead are taken and burned are also performed according to rules that can largely be traced in the Vedic texts.

# 7

# CREMATION, SACRIFICE AND COSMOGONY IN HINDUISM

## Agni, fire offerings and cremation as 'the last sacrifice'

The Sanskrit word *antyeshṭi* means 'final sacrifice' (Barrett 2008: 52–53). Agni is the god of fire and cremation is a fire offering. Cremation is seen as *dah sanskar* or the 'sacrament of fire', or more precisely as *antyeshṭi* – the 'last sacrifice' where the dead are offered to the gods (Parry 1994: 178), or in the words of Stevenson (1920: 145), 'From this point of view the body is looked on as an offering to Agni'. Veena Das writes in *Structure and Cognition* (Das 1990: 122–123):

> Thus the site of cremation is prepared in exactly the same manner as in fire-sacrifice, i.e. the prescriptive use of ritually pure wood, the purification of the site, its consecration with holy water, and the establishment of Agni with the use of proper *mantras*. The time chosen for cremation has to be an auspicious one. The dead body is prepared in the same manner as the victim of a sacrifice and attributed with divinity … As in other sacrifices, the sacrificer, who is the son in this case, achieves religious merit through having performed the sacrificial rituals in accordance with pre-scribed procedures.

The final sacrifice is ultimately of fundamental importance since it is the last opportunity for ritual purification of the living and the dead. 'Cremation is a sacrifice. It is not just a destruction but simultaneously an act of creation … cremation and sacrifice are the same' (Ghimre & Ghimre 1998: 64–65). The fire is not only a god and 'The first word in the Rig Veda, the most ancient of the Vedas, is *agni*, fire. The Vedic religion is basically a religion of fire worship … Always remember this: fire is a living being. Once you bring it to life you are responsible for it' (Svoboda 1993: 33, 47). Thus, fire is at the origin and end of cosmos,

DOI: 10.4324/9781003300915-7

as Jonathan Parry says: 'an equivalence between cremation which destroys the microcosm of the physical body, and the general conflagration which consumes the macrocosm at pralaya. Cosmic dissolution, however, is not only an end of the universe, it is also a beginning, a necessary prelude to a new world cycle and hence a renewal of time. Similarly, cremation is not just a destruction but simultaneously an act of creation' (Parry 1982: 340).

Mary Levin studied early funerary practices based on *The Satapatha Brahmana*, an early Indian commentary on Vedic rituals. The point of departure is the Fire Altar and the fact that the sacrificial fire is not only representing dissolution, but more importantly, reconstruction and reconstitution (Levin 1930a). The sacrifice is 'becoming Agni' – 'the fire, being the early representative of the sun, could endow with life things burnt in it … Although Agni was a life-giving power, and could make immortal whatever was burnt in the sacrificial flame, he possessed also the power of destruction …those who were not sacrificially pure were hurt by the flames …' (Levin 1930b: 45–46). Mary Levin concludes: 'Thus, both the initiation through the sacrificial offerings or the building of the Fire Altar, and the cremation of the dead are considered as rebirth, or obtaining a new body…The object of the Fire Altar ritual and the funeral ceremonies was to obtain as much "life" as possible for the sacrifice, or, in the case of the dead, to restore "life" that had been lost … These funeral customs were closely associated with the ceremony of building the Fire Altar, for they formed part of this great ritual … This explains the purpose of cremation. The pyre represented the Fire Altar' (Figure 7.1) (Levin 1930c: 64–65).

**FIGURE 7.1** The construction of the funeral pyre with five layers of wood. Pashupatinath, Nepal, 2002. Photo: Anders Kaliff.

Agni is seen as the greatest protector against illness, demons and hostile spirits and he is propitiated and recognised in all major rituals since he wards off evil influences. Thus, Agni is the first and most permanent constituent in all life-cycle rituals and fire is lightened in the beginning of these rituals (Pandey 1969: 36–37). As Frits Staal says: 'Vedic ritual is not only the oldest surviving of mankind; it also provides the best source material for a theory of ritual. This is not because it is close to any alleged "original" ritual ... But it is the largest, most elaborate and (on account of the Sanskrit manuals) best documented among the rituals of man' (Staal 1996: 69). In the *Agni Purana* (Vol. II, p. 612), the fire god himself describes cremation as a funerary rite:

> Brahmans should carry the remains of a Brahmana to the cremation ground and there having washed the body and decorated it with flowers and garlands, should commit it to the flames. The entire body must not be reduced to ashes, but a remnant should be preserved; and it should be held positively sinful to burn a dead body entirely naked. The Grotajas or persons belonging to the same family with the deceased, should place the body on the funeral pile, which should be lighted with the three fires known as Ahitagni, Anahitagni and the Loulikagni. The son of the deceased, should three times touch the face of the deceased on the pier with a bundle of burning fagots and by repeating the Mantra which runs as "you have sprung from the energy which is also manifest in the fire. You be and return to the original (spiritual) fire which brought you into being. May fire lead you to pleasure and paradise". Then the friends and relations ... should sprinkle water over the dead body.

In the *Atharva-Veda-samhitā* (Whitney & Lanham 1905: 874), it is explicitly stated that the cremation fire should consist of three specific fires; the eastern fire, the householder's fire and the southern fire with distinctive qualities. The funeral pyre is separately but simultaneously lit by these fires: 'Let the eastern fire burn ... thee happily ... in front; let the householder's fire burn happily behind; let the southern fire burn refuge, defense for thee; from the north, from the midst, from the atmosphere, from each quarter, O Agni, protect him round about from what is terrible'. The householder's fire is the western fire, the eastern fire is the domestic fire and the southern fire is the fire of Fathers (Firth 1994: 206).

There is yet more to this constellation of fires, which has roots back to the Indo-Iranian heritage as discussed in Chapter 6. Not only do the fires constitute culture and cosmology, but also the caste system. The cooking or household fire, the *gārhapatya*, corresponds to the *vaisya* class or varna, who produces the earth. The southern fire is the *dakṣiṇagni* or the prophylactic fire, which works as a defence against the quarter of death and demons. This is also the realm of the *ksatriya* caste or the warriors protecting the worldly realms. The last fire, which is the most important, corresponds to the Brahmans or the priestly class and caste. This eastern fire is the *āhavanīya* or the offering fire belonging to the heavenly region

(Knipe 1975: 23). Thus, the fire constitutes not only culture and cosmology, but also Man and the cosmic body from where also the caste system has its origin.

David Knipe cites the ways the Indo-Iranian fire was built: 'The Bahrâm fire is composed of a thousand and one fire belonging to sixteen different classes (ninety-one corpse-burning fires, eighty dyers' fires, &c). As the earthly representative of the heavenly fire, it is the sacred centre to which every earthly fire longs to return, in order to be united again, as much as possible, with its native abode' (Daremesteter 1895: 112. fn. 2).

The complexity and sanctity of these fires becomes clear when we understand how they are built up and how different fires constitute the holy bodies of the flames. If a specific fire consists of 91 fires from various cremation pyres, this is a highly complex fire taking long time to consecrate. Each of these fires have to be carried in pots and taken meticulously care of – may be for weeks, months and years – before united with other fires in elaborate fire rituals on altars. From this perspective, it also seems reasonable that not all cremation fires were auspicious, but that some fires from pyres of priests or kings were highly esteemed and seen as more powerful compared to the fires cremating ordinary people. In practice, such sacred fires have the possibilities to be built in an endless number of ways where some fires being purer, more auspicious and holier than others.

David Knipe (1975: 25) exemplifies how an earthly fire of the world contained all the fires unified in one flame. Building on the Zend-Avesta, the consecrated flame consisted of 16 fires. These were one natural fire, 1) lightning fire; three ritual fires, 2) the royal or official fire, 3), the cremation fire, 4) the ascetic's fire, and 12 productive fires, including fires from craftsmen; 5) the fire of the dyer, 6) the fire of the potter, 7) the fire of the brick maker, 8) the fire of the goldsmith, 9) the fire of the mint master, 10) the fire of the ironsmith, 11) the fire of the armorer, 12) the fire of the baker, 13) the fire of the brewer, 14) the fire of the soldier or traveller, 15) the fire of the shepherd and 16) the fire of the household (Figure 7.2). Although this fire of 16 fires is complex, it is much simpler than, for instance, the Bahrâm fire where the fire was seen as 'king'. Thus, the fire rituals literally build up a whole cosmos where everything can be untied, and the ordinary cremation fire consisting of three different fires is, from this perspective, an important fire, but yet quite simple.

When the household fire is taken from the deceased's home, as one of three fires, it is carried in an earthen pot along with the corpse. The number three is important in Vedic rituals and Hindu traditions, and in eras long gone, there are scriptural indications that the body should burn for three days. Nowadays, a cremation takes some few hours whereupon the ashes are immediately immersed in the river; but in the past, the *asthisancaya* rite (collecting of bones) was usually performed on the third day after a cremation. The chief mourner collected the bones after the pyre was extinguished and placed them in an urn (Kaushik 1976: 270, 272). Among the Brahmans, A. J. A. Dubois reports about the rites carried out on the third day after the cremation: The chief mourner then returns to the

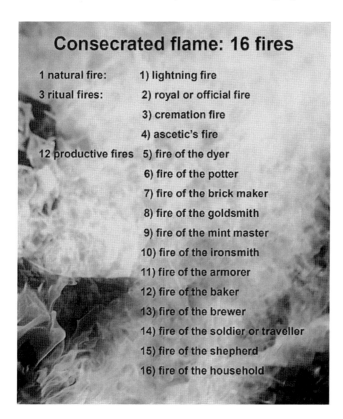

**Consecrated flame: 16 fires**

| | |
|---|---|
| 1 natural fire: | 1) lightning fire |
| 3 ritual fires: | 2) royal or official fire |
| | 3) cremation fire |
| | 4) ascetic's fire |
| 12 productive fires | 5) fire of the dyer |
| | 6) fire of the potter |
| | 7) fire of the brick maker |
| | 8) fire of the goldsmith |
| | 9) fire of the mint master |
| | 10) fire of the ironsmith |
| | 11) fire of the armorer |
| | 12) fire of the baker |
| | 13) fire of the brewer |
| | 14) fire of the soldier or traveller |
| | 15) fire of the shepherd |
| | 16) fire of the household |

**FIGURE 7.2** Model of a consecrated flame consisting of 16 fires. Illustration by Terje Oestigaard.

burning-ground and 'fills a new earthen pot with water, which he sprinkles over the ashes of the deceased. After that he sprinkles them with milk. He ... stirs the ashes with [a] small stick ... looking for any bones that may have escaped the flames, and these he puts into an earthen pot ... Gathering up a portion of the ashes, he throws them into water. The remainder he collects into a heap, to which he gives the rough resemblance of a human figure, supposed to represent the deceased ... He then raises a mound of earth twelve inches high on the exact spot where the dead body has been burnt' (Dubois 1899: 496). Among the Sudra caste, too, the rituals on the third day are called the *day of milk offering*. The chief mourner 'collects the bones which have escaped the flame ... He calls the deceased by name and pours milk over the bones ... [and] then piles up the ashes over the bones' (Dubois 1899: 504). This practice of pouring milk over the pyre to 'cool' it is still used today in cremations (Parry 1985a: 616).

Thus, after this introduction to Agni in some of the ancient Vedic texts and cremations in Hinduism, we will follow the holy rivers from the High Himalayas and the holiest place and cremation ground in Nepal, Pashupatinath in Kathmandu, to India and the cosmic origin and end in Varanasi.

## *Dagbatti,* cooking and conception of a child

The lighting ceremony of the cremation pyre is called *dagbatti* in Nepali funerals (Figure 7.3), and this rite is central in cremations. It is the deceased's eldest son lightning the pyre and he carries the fire three times around the pyre, symbolising the course of the sun and the holy trinity in Hinduism: Brahma, Vishnu and Siva (Figure 7.4). A small piece of sandalwood is usually placed below the deceased's mouth, and the sandalwood symbolises that the whole pyre is built of this precious and aromatic wood. The fire is placed either on the sandalwood of put directly in the deceased's mouth. The deceased's last breath left the body

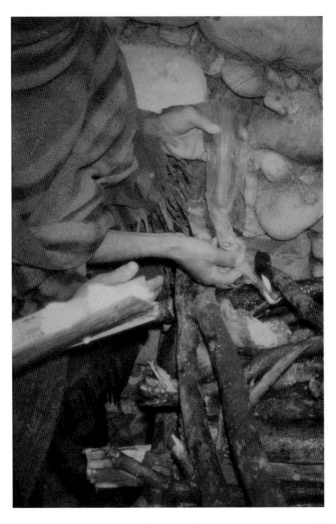

**FIGURE 7.3** The *dagbatti* rite, Nire Ghat, Baglung District, Western Nepal, 1997. Photo: Terje Oestigaard.

from the mouth and it is here the next life and reincarnation will start when the 'vital breath' renters into a new body. A cremation is a procreative funeral giving birth to new life, and raw rice is given in the deceased's mouth as a grave gift (Oestigaard 2005: 11, 167).

**FIGURE 7.4** The deceased's son carrying the cremation fire three times around the pyre. Pashupatinath, 2022. Photo: Terje Oestigaard.

Beliefs and practices of cremation are pervaded with symbols of embryology (Parry 1985b: 52). Being reincarnated means being reborn, and humans are born as babies and, therefore, funerals are intimately related to marriage, fertility and sexual relations. A funeral of an old person is in fact often referred to as the 'second wedding'. In theory, when a son as a Householder cremates his father, the soul leaves the pyre with the smoke from the flames to be reborn as part of the cosmic cycles. Theoretically, the father's soul may reincarnate in his son's forthcoming child so that the grandfather and the grandson, in fact, are the same soul in two different bodies. While some learnt and laymen present this as a hypothetical option, in practice the connections and conceptions are more complicated and less straightforward. This probes to the heart of the funerals and the cremation fire: depending upon karma, the deceased's soul will eventually be reborn as a human, and that links the human reproduction to cosmic recreation – uniting micro- and macrocosm in the human embryo.

'Do not burn him entirely, Agni, or engulf him in your flames. Do not consume his skin or flesh. When you have cooked him perfectly, O knower of creatures, only then send him forth to the father' (*Rigveda* 10.16.1). Agni – the Vedic God of Fire – is not burning the corpse during a cremation, but cooking it. Cooking is regarded as the opposite of eating and raises the corpse to a higher state (to heaven) whereas eating reduces the dead body to a lower state (to animals). Thus, Agni prepares the corpse for the gods by cooking it (O'Flaherty 1994: 49) and the souls become food of the gods (Brahma-Sutras 3.1.7). Regarding the elements of sacrifice, according to *Rigveda*, 'The same water travels up and down day after day. While the rain-clouds enliven the earth, the flames enliven the sky' (*Rigveda* 1.164.51). In some texts, the deceased is referred to as a person who enters the smoke of the cremation pyre, becomes clouds and rain, then vegetables (O'Flaherty 1994:42). When a person dies, the cremation fire releases the soul on the pyre and the fire from the sacrifice goes to heaven. Here, it becomes clouds turning into rain giving the life-giving waters to the fields creating grains and seeds. Thus, the hydrological cycle produces the sperm that metaphorically is 'planted in the fields', eventually creating new humans. The hydrological and cosmological cycles are identical and symbolised by the process of cooking rice, which creates human life physically and spiritually (Oestigaard 2005):

> In the cooking vessel the rice and water remain separate. Water is above fire. The rice is above water. The wind slowly blows against the fire beneath the water. The fire kindled by the wind makes the water boil. The rice with hot-boiling water all around it becomes cooked. When cooked it becomes separated into sediment and juice. (More or less a similar process takes place in the body).
>
> *Siva-Purana III, 22.3–5, p. 1541*

Cremation is thus a procreative process, creating new life by representing microcosms of the cosmic processes working at large. Being a Householder is a fundamental duty and part of the social, moral and metaphysical orders of the world, and, from a practical point of view, a man may fulfil his moral duties by maintaining his purity, accumulating good merits, being devoted to gods and producing a male offspring (Bennett 1983: 50). The importance of having a son to conduct your own funeral is explicitly stated in the Garuda Puranas: 'There is no salvation for a man without a son. He can never attain heaven without a son' (Garuda Purana II, II.13.18 & III, II.29.4). 'A man is released from his debt to the manes on seeing his son's face. A man is released from three types of debts (to the sages, gods and manes) on seeing his grandson. On seeing his son, grand-son, and great grandson he attains eternal or celestial worlds' (Garuda Purana III, II.25.33–34). 'Even a man having sons, dying without the performance of these rites, does not attain salvation. A man without son by doing these rites beforehand shall have a happy journey on the Great Highway' (Garuda Purana II, II.14.14).

Being a Householder and having a son put emphasis on marriage and, in particular, the fire from the wedding ceremony. While Agnicayana was the cosmic grand fire ritual, there is a smaller and more common fire ritual, and that is the Agnihotra. The sacrifier performing the Agnicayana has to perform the Agnihotra rite each morning and evening on his home altar for the rest of his life, and some Brahmins 'declare that the rising and the setting of the sun is caused by the performances of the morning and the evening Agnihotra' (Staal 1996: 77, 457). After a wedding, the husband may choose whether he would be an ordinary householder content with the full 16 rites or an Agnihotri observing 48 rites. If a Householder is an Agnihotri, he brings the fire from his father-in-law's house when he marries and this fire is not allowed to extinguish as long as his wife lives (Stevenson 1920: 107). In ordinary weddings, a special fire was made:

> Whilst they are looking at each other, the priest puts a fire of burning char-coal into the square fenced in with the string and earthen pots … During all the remaining wedding ceremonies this fire must never be allowed to go out, or some misfortunes will happen. The Scriptures ordain that this fire should be kindled by rubbing sticks together, but as a matter of con-venience it is actually just brought from the bride's house. In the old days some of this fire was taken to the young people's new home, and from it the fire on their domestic hearth was kindled; but this is done nowadays only by Brāhmans who are *Agnihotrī*.
>
> *Stevenson 1920: 79*

Thus, in the old days, this wedding fire was made like a need-fire, and among orthodox Hindus this fire should be kept burning continuously throughout the marriage. In death, this fire could be used to light the funeral pyre. 'Just as the renouncer must abandon the fire of his domestic hearth at the time of his initia-tion, so at death the domestic hearth is extinguished so that the deceased can be consumed by the fire of cremation (represented by the fire of ascetic austerity)', says Parry and continues: 'In other words, both the renouncer and the deceased leave the fire of their domestic hearth behind them in order to offer themselves up into the fire of their asceticism' (Parry 1994: 189). From this perspective, it is said that among the ascetic sect Aghoris, their most profound expression of love is 'You will cremate me' (Svoboda 1986: 34). Still, not all are cremated, and this depends upon the deceased's initiation rituals and to what extent and in which ways the dead had entered into samsara, 'the round of birth and death'.

In Hinduism, there are five main or orthodox life-cycle rituals or *samskaras* (Pandey 1969; Bennett 1983). First, birth or the name-giving ceremony whereby the child becomes member of its father's patriline and the family's caste. Second, *pasne*, the first rice ceremony or the rice-feeding ceremony when the child receives its first rice meal and thereby enters the world of rice and the sphere of purity and pollution. This rite is conducted at the age of five months for girls and six months for boys. Third, *bartamande*, which also includes 'the second birth' for Brahmans and Chhetris, is not only a transition from boys to men, but it also involves personal responsibility for his own ritual purity, *karma caleko*, or 'activated karma'. 'The second birth is a religious event occurring when a boy reaches a level of maturity that enables him to "understand the Vedas". Because he is able to appreciate and read the sacred texts, the boy's actions become morally significant in that they affect his future re-birth (karma)' (Gray 1995: 32). Fourth, marriage where men become responsible Householders, and finally, the death ceremonies. In the *Satapatha Brahmana* (S.B., XI, 2, 1, 1.), it is said that a man is born thrice: 'Verily, a man is born thrice, namely in this way: first, he is born from his mother and father; and when he to whom the sacrifice inclines performs offerings he is born a second time; and when he dies, and they place him on the fire, and when he thereupon comes into existence again, he is born a third time'.

The social and religious status of the deceased also determines the funerary rites. The first is the presence or absence of grave goods. Since rice is the main food item in the funerals, deceased without the *pasne* ceremony cannot receive rice as a grave gift. The second is cremation or burial. The *karma caleko* state, which boys reach as part of the *bartamande* initiation, demands cremation as a funerary rite. Women achieve this social and moral stage only through wedding; so, unmarried women and boys not initiated into manhood are not cremated, but given a burial. Nevertheless, many older women, if unmarried, are cremated. Holy men, on the other hand, are buried and not given a cremation because a cremation promises a rebirth and sadhus have transcended this round of life, death and rebirth. Finally, the widow's jewellery are included in her husband's funeral as a grave gift. If a man dies before his wife, the widow disposes of all the jewellery and symbols her husband was responsible for and obliged to give to her, in particular gifts from the wedding. As a widow, she breaks her bracelets marking her new and stigmatised social status and her husband is cremated with her jewellery. The widow's former social status as a wife burns together with the body of her deceased's husband on the pyre (Oestigaard 2000, 2005).

## Sacrifices on the cremation pyres

The Hindu cremation is commonly seen as a sacrifice, but a cremation is not a simple or single sacrifice; it represents numerous sacrificial rites involving different transformations and rebirths of all participants, living or dead. Sadhus may not make any distinctions between a funeral pyre and a sacrificial fire (Svoboda 1993: 45) and sacrifices 'feed and satisfy deities and other ethereal beings with *prana* (life-force) transported to them via fragrance of the smoke from the burnt offerings of consecrated plants and animals' (Svoboda 1998: 30). While the lightning ceremony – *mukhagni* or *dagbatti* – puts emphasis on the vital breath through the mouth, there are yet other rites and perceptions that are even more explicit, and given the long Vedic history and development in rites and beliefs, there will always be numerous concepts, partly overlapping and sometimes contradicting each other. Following tradition, the deceased on the pyre is not properly dead before the cremation is conducted and the soul released from the body. The deceased is only dead after being killed on the pyre and this is the ritual obligation of the son. Thus, by cremating his father, the son commits a symbolical homicide and the death pollution starts when the soul is released from the body. The mourning period and death pollution is a period of purification because of the sin of burning human flesh and killing the father, and this ritual affects the whole family (Figure 7.5).

In death, funeral priests and the transaction and flows of pollution not only defined and challenged caste structures (e.g. Parry 1980, 1982, 1986, 1987), gifts were poisonous and dangerous (Raheja 1988) and following the 'coded substance theory' (Marriott & Inden 1974, Marriott & Inden 1977, Inden & Nicholas 1977), stressing the non-duality of South Asian social thought: 'South Asians do not insist on drawing a line between what Westerners call "natural" and what they call "moral" things; the Hindu moral code books are thus filled with discussions of bodily things, while the medical books at many points deal with moral qualities' (Marriott & Inden 1977: 228). Bodies and human flesh are a bio-moral substance, and when the Chief Minister of Bihar was cremated in 1983, the corpse burnt with greatest difficulties despite the size of the pyre and the alleged reason was apparently the burden of sins accumulated in his flesh due to corrupt earnings (Parry 1994: 127). In Varanasi, it was said that it could take up to six hours to cremate a sinner (Oestigaard 2000: 30) whereas an ordinary cremation is possible to complete within one to two hours by skilled funeral priests. Not all bodies and humans are fit or optimal as sacrifices and being sacrificed.

Thus, 'before the cremation the corpse is not a corpse but an animate oblation to the fire' (Parry 1994: 182). This puts emphasis on the cremation pyre. A proper pyre consists of five layers of wood, each layer symbolising one of the primeval elements, and built by professionals, the weight is around 300 kilos, but up to 500 kilos of wood may occasionally be used (Oestigaard 2005: 15–17). In rural areas, in particular if the deceased has to be carried over long distances to a particular cemetery, firewood for the pyre is a limitation. Also, if the deceased

**FIGURE 7.5** Death pollution and hair shaving ceremony, Pashupatinath. Photo: Terje Oestigaard.

is poor, the wood is a considerable expense for the family. Still, if the dead was an honourable and respected man in his village, all villagers in the procession might carry one piece of firewood to the pyre as the last honour (Oestigaard 2000: 34). One of the greatest gift is to be able to enjoy a proper and auspicious funeral, since the exit of this life determines the entrance to the next, both individually, socially and cosmologically.

Through Agni as the god and mediator, all the elements are dissolved and returned to their cosmic origins from where they are taking new forms again; fire goes to fire, ether goes to ether and air to air. When the ashes and the burnt remains are immersed into the river, not only are the male bones inserted in the female river, but the water element is returned to its origin from where life arise again (Figure 7.6). The *Vishnu Dharma Sutra* (19.11.12) gives a religious explanation for extreme fragmentation of cremated bones in water after the funeral: '[...] the collected bones should be cast in Ganges water, since as many particles of the bones a man remain in Ganges water for so many thousands of years he dwells in heaven' (Kane 1973: 243).

As an analogy, this is a fit for heaven, so to speak, but given the established Indo-European links in time and space, a relevant question is if such perceptions also existed in Bronze Age Europe, in general, and ancient Scandinavia, in particular. As a small detour, one may have a look at some particular cases and contexts. In many contexts, there is a very high degree of fragmentation of the cremated bones, which is not only a result of crushing, but also grinding (e.g. Kaliff 2007; Kaliff & Oestigaard 2017; Oestigaard 2021a, 2022a). From Norway, Per Holck analysed 1,082 contexts from the Bronze Age and Iron Age. The average weight of a cremated adult was 3,075 grams (3,375 grams for men and 2,625 grams for women); but in the archaeological contexts, only 10–20% of the cremated cremains were left, on average 269.7 grams (Holck 1987). From the

**FIGURE 7.6**   The ashes after the cremation are washed and immersed into Bagmati River, Pashupatinath. Photo: Terje Oestigaard.

Late Bronze Age and the Early Iron Age cemetery Ringeby in Östergötland, Sweden, the results were the same and the cremated bones varied from 0.2 grams to 983 grams as the maximum, with an average of 159 grams (Kaliff 1997: 90).

As another example of extreme fragmentation of cremated bones, Broby in Börje parish in Uppland, also Sweden, is a representative case. From seven mortuary contexts on this site, including four burnt mounds, there were found cremated human remains with a weight of 4,189 grams, approximately equal to the total weight of bone remains after only one large adult individual; but in this context, the bones came from several individuals. The total number of bone fragments were no less than 15,064, and this was based on a total mass of just over 4 kilos! (Sjöling 2016). If we consider the Hindu notion that each piece of bone fragment in water represented a thousand year in heaven, this may explain reasons and beliefs behind the very high degree of fragmentation and crushing of burnt bones in Scandinavian prehistory.

An interpretation that may be somewhat a reminiscent of this has been put forward regarding the fact that ancient Scandinavian graves not only contain small fragments of cremated bones, but that the amount of bones found at the same time is very limited. Without referring to comparative Indo-European research, it has been suggested that 'findless graves' – stone settings containing not only extremely few but actually no bones at all – show striking similarities to Zoroastrian mortuary practices. A central element in these practices is the annihilation of the bones as a symbol of the inherent evil of the material world (Ericsson & Runcis 1995: 31–40; cf. Kaliff 2007: 93–94).

Warm, fresh-cremated bones turn into fragments in an almost explosive process when they are immersed in cold water and rivers. This is a very powerful symbol for dissolution, reunion and transformation of elements. In Bronze Age Scandinavia, there are also clear contexts were cremated remains have been deposited in water (Kaliff & Oestigaard 2013: 118). Similarly, the physical presence of cremated bones in various archaeological contexts should also reflect particular perceptions of the human body and how the bodily remains – blood, bone marrow, meat and burnt bones – have been included and perceived in ancestral cults.

Returning to Hinduism and current cremations, there is yet a last element, and that is earth, and occasionally in some rare cremations a last rite is performed, which is called *astu*. Astu literally means 'the dead man's skull bone' and it is supposed to consist of a part of the deceased's brain, but, in practice, any body part or flesh of the deceased may be used in the rite. Traditionally, it is said that it should be a part of the heart or the brain where the 'third eye' – the soul – is located. It has mainly been a practice among orthodox Hindus and high-status people, and this piece of the deceased's body may be buried in the riverbed close to the very cremation or the body part may be carried to other holy rivers far away, like Varanasi. In Nepal, this practice has been conducted among kings and commoners along the cremation platforms at Pashupatinath. On one occasion, the astu-ritual concluded the cremation after all the other ashes had been given to the Bagmati River. An elderly relative supervised the cremation and looked

**FIGURE 7.7**  The *astu* is collected from the pyre and wrapped in a piece of cloth, Pashupatinath. Photo: Terje Oestigaard.

through the ashes to ensure that no flesh was left unburnt, but as part of the cremation, a small piece of the dead's body had been kept a part (Figure 7.7). When the cremation was completed, this little piece of charcoaled flesh was wrapped in a white cloth and two sons dug a hole in the riverbed and buried the astu in the middle of the river (Figure 7.8). Earth was buried in earth and the water eventually dissolved everything and the ritual was complete (Kaliff & Oestigaard 2004, 2017; Oestigaard 2005).

As a sacrifice, cremation is not only polluting and destructive, but also procreative and constituting the new social and cosmological order. The dead father is reborn and gains a new reincarnation through the rite and the son attains his father's social place in the family and becomes the lineage's Householder. Thus, cremation as a sacrifice is a double birth of both father and son, and in funerals, it is men who gives birth. The father repays his debt to the ancestors by giving the lineage a son, and the son repays his debt by giving his father a new birth (Parry 1994: 151–12). The birth symbolism may also take explicit forms, although some rites are highly unusual. In theory, only the corpse of man should lie on the back with the face up on the pyre whereas a woman should lie with the face down, since this is the way the sexes are believed to enter the world. In Varanasi, although rarely practised, if a husband and wife die at the same time, they could be cremated together with the man on top of the woman with his face down on her in the same position as in copulation (Parry 1994: 176).

The human sacrifice on the cremation pyre is also very literal and physical. Apart from the life-force coming with the sperm, another theory postulates that the vital breath (*pran*) enters the embryo during the fifth month of pregnancy

**FIGURE 7.8** The two sons buried the *astu* in the riverbed of Bagmati River, Pashupatinath. Photo: Terje Oestigaard.

through the suture at top of the skull. Herein, in the skull is the vital breath or soul residing until it is released during the creation in a special rite called *kapal kriya*. This vital breath is generally seen as the 'soul', and during the cremation, the soul will eventually be released by itself when the skull cracks open because of the heat. After some time, the internal pressure of the boiling brain is so high that the skull explodes and it sounds like a gun-shot, and at the moment the skull explodes, the soul is released and it is first now that the deceased is properly dead and the next incarnation may start. However, although this is a natural process that happens by itself, ritually it should be conducted by the son. *Kapal kriya* or 'the rite of the skull breaking' is the act whereby the son cracks open his father's skull on the pyre and thereby releases the soul. Obviously, this takes a heavy mental toll on already mourning sons and it rarely happens, but it may explain the severe death pollution and why cremation is a sacrifice of the dead (Parry 1994: 181–184). However, as we have already discussed, the reason for the role of cremation as a person's last sacrifice also has even deeper roots in the fact that both cremation and sacrifice take place according to patterns from the common Indo-European creation myth.

There are, however, also other practices that closely resemble to this part of the cremation ritual. A chief mourner may lift a large earthenware pot with water from Ganges onto his left shoulder. While standing with his back to the funeral pyre, he let the pot fall to the ground so it smashes. A saying goes, 'pot broken, relationship finished', and some mourners describe the pot-breaking as *kapal kriya* (Parry 1994: 177). Breaking the pot is also seen as identical to breaking the skull, and, in Varanasi, the chief mourner may break a pot instead of the skull. Breaking a pot has also been seen as comparable to the burning of the body, since the broken pot releases space inside to become part of the outside in the same way as fire releases the soul (atman) to take part of universe again. Importantly, *kapāla* means both skull and pot, and hence the pot may work as a surrogate for the skull enabling the soul to leave from the head rather than the anus (Firth 1994: 226–227). As Dubois writes: 'The chief mourner walks round the funeral pyre three times, and pours upon it some water that is allowed to trickle from an earthen vessel which he carries on his shoulder, and which he afterwards breaks on the head of the deceased' (Dubois 1899: 492).

From an archaeological and comparative Indo-European perspective, it seems likely that there is a close relation between urns and the ceramic pots containing the cremation fire. If the skulls of the deceased is symbolised by the pot from the household whereby the relatives and chief mourners carry the fire lightning the pyre, cremations not only mark a transition of householders from fathers to sons, but also recreated new households on a societal scale, thus not only combining micro- and macro cosmos, but also meso-cosmos and daily life in villages with fertile fields and bountiful harvests. Interestingly, ceramic vessels have also played a very prominent role in the ancient Scandinavian funeral ritual. On the one hand, they often appear as containers for the burnt bones on the burial grounds, but also in the form of scattered sherds or only as single fragments of pots which have been deposited in connection with deposits of burnt bones or cremation sites.

As we have pointed out, a central feature of the success of the Indo-European worldview is the integration of ecology and cosmology of the sun and water in an agricultural perspective. Importantly,

> Agni lurks behind other images: he is, like the sun, the first-born child of Order or Truth and he is born of the waters. The interaction of the sun and the waters make sense of a number of obscure references to Vedic theory of the rain cycle: the rays of the sun (cows) drink up earthly waters with the lowest point of the ray (the foot) and then give back rain (milk) from their top (head) after they carry the moisture back up to the sun. The sun is thus clothed in the waters.
>
> *O'Flaherty 1994: 75*

By the turn of the millennia, there were annually about 5,000-6,000 cremations on the ghats or cremation platform along the Bagmati River in front of the Pashupatinath temple in Kathmandu (Figure 7.9). Twenty years later, in 2022, it was estimated that approximately 10,000 cremations took place each year. After the cremations, the ashes were given to the river and thus ensuring a new incarnation. In India and Nepal in total, more than 7 million human bodies are burned annually, according to data from 2010 to 2011 by the Indian Ministry of Home Affairs (Chakrabarty et al. 2014).

Myologically, the Bagmati River is the holiest river in Nepal constituting culture and cosmology and the cremations are part of cosmogonic processes

**FIGURE 7.9** Cremation at Pashupatinath by the turn of the millennia. Photo: Terje Oestigaard.

whereby the individual is part of the grand cosmic and procreative forces structured around water and the life-giving fire. The world of the living is also the hydrological world of rivers and rain and the procreative forces enabling rich and bountiful harvests. This water world is the world of rice, which has such a prominent role not only as food, but also in funerals and is a symbol of both purity and pollution. However, despite the mythological grandeurs and aura of the Bagmati River, the river has often been severely polluted, not only from the remains of the thousands of cremations each year, but more importantly from sewage and carpet factories upstream. The holiness of the holy has been highly contaminated and polluted, which is a major concern among scholars and laymen, since the cosmic consequences of a deteriorated river affect the devotees and the deceased's future reincarnation (Oestigaard 2005, 2017). This question of purity and pollution also relates to the extensive literature on the caste system and notions of purity and pollution (see e.g. Dumont 1970; Quigley 1995), which has direct consequences for understanding the last Hindu cremation of a king on the Indian sub-continent (Shrestha 2001; Raj 2001).

## Kings, katto and royal funerals

Year 2001 was a tragedy for Nepal and its royal family. In the so-called Narayanhity Palace massacre on 1 June 2001, nine members of the royal family died, and while the truth of what happened may or may not have been revealed, within the next three days, Nepal experienced the funerals of two kings: King

Birendra on 2 June and his son Dipendra, who was crowned as a king while lying unconscious in coma in a hospital whereupon he died, on 4 June. The astu ritual was part of the royal funeral, but the most unique and also controversial rite was the 'katto-ritual'.

'*Katto*' means literally 'something not worth eating' (Shrestha 2001: 131). The katto-ceremony (Saiyya Daan) takes place the 11th day after death. The king is believed to be an incarnation of Lord Vishnu and, after death, he joins the heavenly abode of Vishnu. On earth, the king is a living deity embodying the kingdom, but in the process of being transformed and transferred to heaven, it involves a scapegoat and sin-eater cleansing the king from all earthly imperfections and impurities. This is where the katto-ritual and its priest are important. In the 2001 royal funeral, it was the 75-year old priest Durga Prasad Sapkota who performed the katto-ritual for King Birendra. For 11 days, the priest lives as the king in his palace, he sleeps in the king's bed, wears his clothes and eats like a king. On the final day, he consumes a special meal that traditionally is believed to consist of 84 ingredients and delicacies. But, one piece of this meal is the 'uneatable' and indeed the unthinkable to eat: a piece of the king's dead body, and, in particular, the part of the brain where the 'third eye' is located. By this ritual, the priest becomes temporarily at one with the king and he can convey all the precious gifts to the king in heaven, like gold, horses and elephants. Consequently, and importantly, the katto-priest becomes a sin-eater. By conducing this ritual, the priest sacrificed his social status and indeed his caste status, and even low-caste people detested the former Brahman priest after the conclusion of the ceremony. They threw stones and rotten tomatoes at him and chased him away while he was riding on an elephant. Symbolically, the katto-priest was expelled from the old kingdom in Kathmandu. The priest himself, however, objected strongly to not only the notion that he had become a low caste and lost his Brahman caste status, but also to the very idea that he had eaten a bodily part of the king (Figure 7.10). Following him, the katto-meal did not consist of 84 ingredients, but it was an ordinary meal of daal baat (rice, vegetables and lentils) and goat meat, and certainly no human flesh of the king. Still, one of the funeral priests cremating the king could tell that some security guards came and collected some of the ashes from the king's funeral pyre, which they would insert in the katto-priest's meal without his knowing. And as common people rhetorically asked, how could he lose his caste status and become so polluted if he did not fulfil the katto-ritual? (Oestigaard 2005: 17–25).

Obviously, the amount of sin embodied in the king as it was expressed in this ritual cannot be the king's personal sin, accumulated by his own deeds and doings as an incarnation of Vishnu on earth. On the other hand, since the king embodied the kingdom and the commoners, it seems more likely that the amount of sin represented the sins in the kingdom. In other words, by taking on the sins of the commoners in the kingdom, the priest purified the king who was incarnated in the heavenly abode of Vishnu. Since this ritual has long historical roots, it may also shed lights on some of the ancient practices, beliefs and the ways the caste

**FIGURE 7.10** Durga Prasad Sapkota and his wife in the backyard of their house showing some of the late king's personal items. Pashupatinath, 2002. Photo: Anders Kaliff.

system was organised. Arthur M. Hocart is the scholar who developed a particular theory of not only the caste system as a ritual organisation, but in essence that all societies are communities organised for ritual purposes aiming to secure and procure life in its broadest sense (Hocart 1954, 1970a). The divine king was both god and human, and this creates structural ways of organising society where the purity of the kings has to be protected (Hocart 1969). 'The object of the ritual is to make the macrocosm abound in the objects of men's desires. But the spirit of macrocosm resides in the king, and so prosperity is to be attained by making microcosm prosperous and bountiful. A poor king is a contradiction in terms. All nations like their kings to live in splendour, and to be liberal' (Hocart 1970b: 202). The caste system was a particular way of organising society around the royal sacrifice and the king as sacrificer needs priests and serfs. In an organisation where everything is structured around the king and his sacrifices, different groups have different obligations in relation to the sacrifices. The Brahmans' role in this system is to assist in the sacrifice, even at the expanse of their own purity and the essential thing is that those who rule must be pure (Hocart 1950).

   When Declan Quigley rephrases Hocart's theory, he says: 'there are two kinds of families: those who rule and those who are ruled. It is the ritual task of the ruled to keep their rulers free from pollution and the ritual task of the rulers to ensure that they do' (Quigley 1995: 122). He continues: 'The function of brahman and sudra alike is to ensure that the rulers are kept pure – free from the dangerous and polluting forces of nature – particularly at the moment of sacrifice when order is ritually re-established … It is not that the priests must be kept pure but that kings (patrons) must be kept pure. The priest is essentially a vessel and as such is a liminal, ambivalent character – at once necessary but dangerous' (Quigley 1995: 139). This seems to be the most accurate explanation for the katto-ritual, which was a cosmic rite constituting not only the king, but more importantly the kingdom and cosmos. And while it represented the utmost pollution for the katto-priest, the king's bones immersed in the river had turned into their original element and as such part of the cosmos (Kaliff & Oestigaard 2008).

Not only priests and people, but also gods and goods may become temporarily polluted and contaminated in death. Although the main ritual function of Agni is to purify, even the fire god may become impure, and this makes cremation different from ordinary sacrifices, as a devotee in Varanasi once pointed out: 'Agni is the mouth of the god so that even the polluted dead body can become purified. Agni has such power that it can purify everything. Agni is the witness of a marriage. The same Agni is used for cremation. At the marriage you should keep the same fire, Dev Agni, so that every time food is prepared it is offered to Agni. The same fire is used for the cremation, so the whole house becomes impure and the fire becomes impure, so guests will not take food until the thirteenth day when a special haven is lit with sandal paste and herbs' (Firth 1994: 225). In other words, the god's impurity is transferred to the deceased's household and it is the relatives' moral obligation to purify themselves and the ritual fire.

In Hinduism, there are many sacred and holy places, but nothing compares with Benares or Varanasi – or Kashi – 'the city of light'. 'Kashi is the pious Hindu's name for Benares, the sacred city of Siva – the Great Ascetic and Destroyer of the Universe. It is here – at the city's main cremation ground – that Siva and Parvati created the universe at the beginning of time; and here that the corpse of the universe burns at the end of time. Only Kashi survives' (Parry 1980: 89). If the dead are cremated on the banks of Ganges whereupon the ashes are immersed in the holy river, they may attain salvation and be liberated from the eternal round of life and death.

## Varanasi – Fires at the origin and end of this cosmic era

If there is one city in the world without origin or end where mythology and cosmology are interwoven since time immemorial to the new cosmic time era, it is the 'City of Light'. Kashi literally means 'luminous'. In Varanasi, Vishnu, with his burning fire of asceticism, performed austerities for 50,000 year, and one of the most holy places is the spot where he meditated. Here, his footsteps are still visible (Figure 7.11). Manikarnika ghat is located next to Vishnu's footsteps, and hence the cremations take place as part of cosmogony (Parry 1982: 339). There are many mythologies surrounding Varanasi. It is said that Sati herself sat ablaze after her father humiliated Lord Siva. He carried her around cosmos in grief and

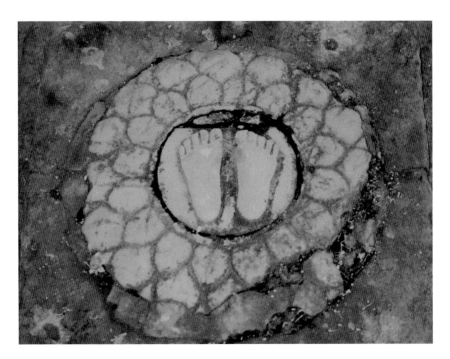

**FIGURE 7.11** Vishnu's footsteps. Varanasi. Photo: Terje Oestigaard.

parts of her ended up falling at many places, and her earring or an eye fell at what became the Manikarnika ghat. Sati was then reborn as Parvati, Siva's new wife (Eck 1983: 173). Following other cosmogonic myths, the earring belonged to Siva himself (Parry 1994: 14).

One of the jyotirlingas – the linga of light – is residing in Varanasi, and it gives the city the luminosity that reveals untruth and darkness. All of the 330 million gods in Hinduism reside in the city and all the tirthas – passages between this world and the sacred – are there. Varanasi lives in a constant stage of purity whereas the rest of the world is decaying. The city stays in Krita Yuga or the Age of Perfection whereas everyone else live in Kali Yuga. Following the faith of the sacred city, 'Kashi is the whole world ... Everything on earth that is powerful and auspicious is here, in this microcosm. All of the sacred places of India and all of her sacred waters are here. All of the gods reside here ... and all of time is here' (Eck 1983: 23). Fire and water are not only mediators between humans and gods: the elements can be gods themselves. This is particularly seen in Hinduism where Ganges is the most holy river stemming mythologically from Kailash (Darian 1978: 1), the holy mountain of Tibet, in Hinduism traditionally recognised as the abode of Siva. This river is eternally pure and cleanses sins, and as the holiest river in Hinduism concentrates the sanctity of all rivers (Figure 7.12): 'Not only is the Ganges said to be present in other rivers, but other rivers are present in her' and Ganges is the 'nectar of

**FIGURE 7.12**   The holy Ganga in Varanasi with the palace of the Dom Raja (head of the cremation group) to the left overlooking the river. Photo: Terje Oestigaard.

immortality', which brings life to the dead cremated on the banks of the River of Heaven (Eck 1983: 214–215).

Hydrologically, Ganges is a river with five headstreams and all of them having their origins in the Himalayas of the Uttar Pradesh state. The length is about 2,510 kilometres and one of the major tributaries is the Yamuna River, which passes today's capital New Delhi. While flowing in a south-easterly direction from the Himalayas to the Bay of Bengal, the river suddenly turns northward a short distance, and as if that was not special enough, this northern course is demarcated by the Assi River flowing into the Ganges in the south and the Varuna in the North. Varanasi is located on the west bank of Ganges and encircled by these rivers, the name 'Varanasi' actually originating from the combined names of the rivers, Varuna and Assi. Stepped ghats link the city to the river's lowest water level. Living in cosmic symbiosis with the river, the water level rises by 5–10 meters every year after the monsoon and exceptional floods have been 20-meter high. During the lowest water levels, the river is 300 to 500 meter wide; but after the monsoon, the width might be more than 1 km (Jalais 2014).

'Varanasi is called the Mahatirtha—the great passage or pilgrimage—and Hindu devotees usually embark on a pilgrimage to the city at least once in their lifetime, or are brought here at death to be cremated on the riverbank. It is thought to be auspicious to come to die in the city, because by dying or being cremated in Varanasi, one supposedly gains liberation from rebirth', says Savitri

Jalais and continues, 'In Varanasi, five ghats, named Panchtirth ("the five pilgrimages"), are acknowledged as being more sacred than the others. Mythical Kashi is symbolically identified with a divine body where these five important ghats correspond to the five elements of which the body is constituted, or, in a more popular version, to the five parts of the human body' (Jalais 2014: 285). These five parts are representing Siva's body with his navel or centre as Manikarnika *ghat*; the most important cremation ground in Varanasi, the other being Harischandra *ghat* (Jalais 2014: 291). From this perspective, the cremations at Manikarnika *ghat* are not only taking place at the footsteps of Vishnu, but in Siva's navel as well – the very centre of cosmos. As David M. Knipe says in *In the Image of Fire: Vedic Experience of Heat*, 'since a fire is located in the belly the action of withdrawing the navel to the spinal column kindles and increases this purificatory blaze' (Knipe 1975: 130). The five ghats correspond to the five elements constituting the body.

Manikarnika ghat is perceived as the most holy place for a Hindu to be cremated, and if a person dies in Kashi, then he or she may cross the river of samsara, and be freed from further rebirths (Figure 7.13). The holiness of Ganges is so powerful that even the smallest drop of her water in Kashi cleanses and purifies the living and liberates the dead, devotees say. Thus, this is cosmogony whereby cosmos is recreated every moment and minute by a close ritual and sacrificial

**FIGURE 7.13** Manikarnika ghat and the river of samsara in Varanasi. Photo: Terje Oestigaard.

co-existence by humans and divinities, and human failures or misdeeds will impact not only the divine realms, but the very cosmos itself (Oestigaard 2011). Cosmogony, as a term, comes from the two Greek words *kosmos* and *genesis*. *Kosmos* refers to the order of the universe (and/or the universe as the order) whereas *genesis* refers to the process of coming into being and thereby the origin and the creation of the gods and cosmos as well as how the world came into existence (Long 1993: 94). And in Kashi, it is Siva himself whispering the 'ferryboat mantra' or the 'mantra of the crossing' in the deceased's ear (Eck 1983: 331).

In Varanasi, there is a special group of undertakers known as Dom and their leader is the Dom Raja, raja means king – and he is the king of the cremation ground (see Parry 1994). 'In brief, their main role in the death ritual of all castes is to arrange the funeral pyre, provide the wood and sacred fire, which is kept alive perennially', writes Meena Kaushik and continues: 'The sacred fire is seen to symbolise the fire of the ascetic Śiva. It is auspicious and kept alight perennially. It is believed that if it were not kept alight, misfortunes would strike the Doms' (Kaushik 1976: 269). There are numerous stories about this perpetual fire, and its flames must never die. This eternal flame is said to be more than 3,500 years old and this sacred fire is protected and kept alive by the Doms in a temple in front of the Manikarnika ghat. It is kept refuelled by logs used in cremations and thus the cosmogonic act is constantly repeated, but the Dom Raja and his family also use these burning logs from cremations when they cook their daily food. Originally lit by Lord Siva, some say, this eternal flame is kept in a holy hearth and shrine in the temple on the cremation ground. It is believed that this flame enables moksha – release from samsara and the round of birth and death. Each funeral should be lit by this fire (mukhagni), and according to traditions, the Dom Raja should also provide and place the first five logs of wood necessary to build the funeral pyre.

The cremations burn continuously all day and night without interruption, and it is believed that if the cremation fires extinguish at Manikarnika ghat and there is an abruption in the cremations, then the current world is disrupted. 'Since cremation is sacrifice, since sacrifice regenerates the cosmos, and since the funeral pyres burn without interruption throughout day and night at Manikarnikā ghāt, creation is here continually replayed. As a result, it is always satya yuga – the first and best of the four world ages – in Kashi, for in this way it is always the beginning of time when the world was new' (Parry 1982: 340). As long as the cremations burn, Kashi is in the golden age of the original time, and left-over logs from the cremations fuel the original fire from where all new cremations start. This is cosmogony: cremations recreate cosmos, and the fires have to burn continuously to maintain Kashi is its golden age.

## A comparative Indo-European approach

The Hindu cremation on open pyres along the holy rivers is the classical image of not only Hindu mortuary practices, in general, but also cremations, in particular. While today's funerals are direct continuities of their Vedic predecessors, it is important to keep in mind that there have also been more than two millennia long theological and ritual development from its early origins, and thus the ancient religious texts describe rituals from another era. From a comparative Indo-European perspective, this provides genuine insights into prehistoric cremation beyond the Vedic influence. The Vedic texts and the successive sacred books describe religious practices that belong to a particular eastern Indo-European tradition, but as seen, influxes and refluxes went in different directions in Eurasia, and hence the similarities because of direct contact shaped prehistoric beliefs and rituals to a greater extent than hitherto known. In practice, many of the ancient Vedic texts seem almost like ritual guides and descriptions of prehistoric funeral practices also in other Indo-European areas in the Bronze Age, such as Scandinavia (Figure 7.14).

Thus, there are significant similarities seen from a common Indo-European perspective, but not surprisingly also differences across time and space. The specific European developments from the Bronze Age onwards are partly due to a not-yet-explored degree of influence from the former indigenous Neolithic population, not least agrarian fertility rites, and partly related to particular ecological adaptations. Of course, internal development over time leads in itself to a development and 'dialectification' of both beliefs and rituals, which in principle is analogous to how language develops.

As Frazer elaborated in depth in *Spirits of the Corn and the Wild* (Frazer 1912a, 1912b), in Europe north of the Alps the fundamental importance of winter sacrifices was to create continuity in between the agricultural seasons. Fire, and not least keeping the yule-log fire alive throughout the coldest period of the year securing life and livelihoods, was the centre of the hearths and homes. Also, using cremated ashes and bones in bread made by the grain of the last sheaf and scattering this on the barren fields during sowing in the spring were active ways of not only fertilising the fields, but also investing them with ancestral powers uniting fire and water. In European pastoral societies, the seasonality and the pastures of cattle were also largely structured around rituals and practices that focused on fire and water in particular (Frazer 1913a, 1913b). While these examples build on European ethnography primarily documented in the 19th century, moving eastwards and back in time, the pastoral adaptations on the Eurasian steppe give important clues not only to the spread and migration of Indo-European groups, but also why ritual traditions and religious ideas institutionalised in similar ways in so many different and distant geographical areas.

The role of fire in cult, culture and cosmology is unrivalled because it enables innumerable rituals, but it also enables an unprecedented flexibility and mobility. Since time immemorial fires, or more precisely pots with burning or glooming charcoal, have been the core of homes and hearths. The latent fires were always kept as the most precious treasures. They were the sources of warmth and wealth, and there is no wonder why these powers were seen as ancestors and divinities. The ways and the means by which holy fires were made illustrate the complexity of the elaborate fire rituals, and a unique aspect of these Indo-European rites lies

**FIGURE 7.14**   The Indo-European fires burn as they have done since time immemorial. Pashupatinath, Nepal, 2022. Photo: Terje Oestigaard.

precisely in the fact that everyone – whether rich or poor, wealthy or unhealthy – could partake in making and maintain these cosmological fires (Figure 7.15).

A central feature of all these Indo-European fires – from the Beltane fires of the Celtic world to the cremation fire in Varanasi in India – is that they comprise of several fires. Not only may fires be moved from one hearth to another, but the very household fire may be taken from the hearth to the seasonal bonfires

**FIGURE 7.15** Fire offering at family altar, photographed in the Baglung District, Nepal in 1997. Photo: Terje Oestigaard.

or even used to light cremation pyres. In the same vein, fires and woods from pyres may be brought back to reignite or rebuild the household fire and thereby give renewed life to the deity living in the hearth. This fire can be built and purified in innumerable and endless ways, where the Vedic or Indo-Iranian fire, comprising of 16 flames, is but one example. There are many other fires that are even more complex consisting of very distinct end exclusive fires. This way of building up a unique fire with specific qualities and powers, ancestral or divine capacities one may say, also illustrates parts of the reasons why fire rituals and sacrifices have such a long continuity in Indo-European traditions.

If we, for a last time, return to 'the Age of Burning', following Snorri, one may get a better understanding of cremation in prehistoric Scandinavia. The common Indo-European background makes analogies from Nepal and India relevant as a way of highlighting general features of this funerary practice, but the most important aspects are probably found in the very distinct and differing characteristic of fire itself. Based on comparative Indo-European ethnography, life-giving fires were moved from the hearths to bonfires and back. It is therefore reasonable to assume that also cremation fires constituted the ancestral fires residing in and coming from the hearths, and that these fires were used to lighten the cremation pyres. As seen, specific fires were built up of fires from the bonfire, pyre, smithy, pottery makers, etc., and objects like pottery, metal tools and weapons were invested with powers because of the heat and transformation, and the ancestors living in the fires. Specific fires and objects could therefore be used as prophylactic and fertilising means on agricultural fields and for the welfare of cattle. This, we believe, is at least part of Snorri's 'Age of Burning' – the north-western part of this Indo-European tradition.

The fire rituals were not only for the devotees, but also for the deities, since fire was a mediator between humans and gods. But, the fire was also an ancestor or a god in itself in numerous ways – from Eldbjørg and Domovoy to the more famous Vedic fire god Agni.

# REFERENCES

Ackerman, R. 1987. *J.G. Frazer. His Life and Works*. Cambridge University Press. Cambridge.

*The Agni Purana Part I*. (n.d.). Translated and annotated by Gangadharan, N. In Shastri, J.L. (ed.). *Ancient Indian Tradition & Mythology*, Vol. 27. Motilal Banarsidass. Delhi, 1984.

*The Agni Purana Part II*. (n.d.). Translated and annotated by Gangadharan, N. In Shastri, J.L. (ed.). *Ancient Indian Tradition & Mythology*, Vol. 28. Motilal Banarsidass. Delhi, 1985.

*The Agni Purana Part III*. (n.d.). Translated and annotated by Gangadharan, N. In Shastri, J.L. (ed.). *Ancient Indian Tradition & Mythology*, Vol. 29. Motilal Banarsidass. Delhi, 1986.

*The Agni Purana Part IV*. (n.d.). Translated and annotated by Gangadharan, N. In Shastri, J.L. (ed.). *Ancient Indian Tradition & Mythology*, Vol. 30. Motilal Banarsidass. Delhi, 1987.

Allen, J.P. 1892. Prehistoric Art in the North. *Saga Book of the Viking Club*, Vol. I: 54–74.

Allen, R.E. (ed.). 1966. *Greek Philosophy: Thales to Aristotle*. The Free Press. New York.

Allentoft, M.E., Sikora, M. & Willerslev, E. et al. 2015. Population Genomics of Bronze Age Eurasia. *Nature*, Vol. 522. doi:10.1038/nature14507

Amaldi, G. 1966. *The Nature of Matter. Physical Theory from Thales to Fermi*. The University of Chicago Press. Chicago.

Andersen, S.T. 1993. History of Vegetation and Agriculture at Hassing Huse Mose, Thy, Northwest Denmark, Since the Ice Age. *Journal of Danish Archaeology*, Vol. 11: 57–79.

Anthony, D.W. 2007. *The Horse, the Wheel, and Language: How Bronze Age Riders from the Eurasian Steppes Shaped the Modern World*. Princeton University Press. Princeton.

Arcini, C. 2007. Elden Utplånar Inte Allt. Brandgravar Och Bålplatser i Gualöv. In Artursson, M. (ed.). *Vägar till Vætland. En Bronsåldersbygd i Nordöstra Skåne 2300–500 f.Kr*: 169–186. Riksantikvarieämbetet. Lund.

Arcini, C., Höst, E. & Svanberg, F. 2007. Gravar, Bålplatser Och Två Bronsåldersfamiljer i Gualöv. Studier Av En Gravmiljö. In Artursson, M. (ed.). *Vägar till Vætland. En Bronsåldersbygd i Nordöstra Skåne 2300–500 f.Kr*: 107–168. Riksantikvarieämbetet. Lund.

Armit, I., Swindles, G.T., Becker, K., Plunkett, G. & Blaauw, M. 2014. Rapid Climate Change Did Not Cause Population Collapse at the End of the European Bronze Age. *PNAS*, Vol. 111, No. 48: 17045–17049.

Artursson, M., Björck, N., Grandin, L., Hjärthner Holdar, E., Larsson, F. & Lindberg, C.-F. 2017. Vardagsliv Och Fest i Gård Och by – Ekonomi Och Hantverk 1100–0 BC. In Artursson, M., Kaliff, A. & Larsson, F. (eds.). *Rasbobygden i Ett Långtidsperspektiv 1100 BC till 1100 AD – Kontinuitet Och Förändring*: 65–95. OPIA 62. Uppsala.

Artursson, M., Kaliff, A. & Larsson, F. (eds.). 2017. *Rasbobygden i Ett Långtidsperspektiv 1100 BC till 1100 AD – Kontinuitet Och Förändring.* OPIA 62. Uppsala.

Artursson, M., Karlenby, L. & Larsson, F. (eds.). 2011. *Nibble. En Bronsåldersmiljö I Uppland. Särskild Undersökning, 2007. E18 Sträckan Sagån-Enköping. Uppland, Tillinge Socken, Tillinge-Nibble 1:9 & TillingeMälby 5:1.* Riksantikvarieämbetet. UV Rapport 2011:111. Stockholm.

*Atharva-Veda-samhitā*. Translated by Whitney, W.D. and Lanham, C.R. 1905. Cambridge University Press. Cambridge.

Aveela, R. 2018. *A Study of Household Spirits of Eastern Europe.* Bendideia Publishing. Bridgend.

Bachelard, G. 1968. *The Psychoanalysis of Fire.* Beacon Press. Boston.

Bachelard, G. 1988. *The Flame of a Candle.* The Bachelard Translations. The Dallas Institute Publications. The Dallas Institute of Humanities and Culture. Dallas.

Bachelard, G. 1990. *Fragments of a Poetics of Fire.* The Bachelard Translations. The Dallas Institute Publications. The Dallas Institute of Humanities and Culture. Dallas.

Bachelard, G. 1994. *Water and Dreams. An Essay on the Imagination of Matter.* The Dallas Institute of Humanities and Culture. Dallas.

Barber, M. 2003. *Bronze and the Bronze Age. Metalwork and Society in Britain c. 2500 – 800 BC.* Tempus. Stroud.

Barber, J. & Russel-White, C. 1990. Preface. Scottish Contributions. *Burnt Offerings. International Contributions to Burnt Mound Archaeology.* Compiled by Victor Buckley. Dublin.

Barrett, R. 2008. *Aghor Medicine: Pollution, Death, and Healing in Northern India.* University of California Press. Berkeley & London.

Beard, M., North, J.A. & Price, S.R.F. 1998. *Religions of Rome: A History,* Vol. 1. Cambridge University Press. Cambridge.

Behringer, W. 2004. *Witches and Witch-Hunts.* Polity Press. Oxford.

Bellander, E., 1938. Bålrösen - Offerrösen. *Kulturhistoriska Studier Tillägnade Nils Åberg*: 91–100. Stockholm.

Bennett, L. 1983. *Dangerous Wives and Sacred Sisters.* Columbia University Press. New York.

Bernstein, A.E. 1982. Esoteric Theology: William of Auvergne on the Fires of Hell and Purgatory. *Speculum,* Vol. 57: 509–531.

Bernstein, A.E. 1993. *The Formation of Hell. Death and Retribution in the Ancient and Early Christian Worlds.* Cornell University Press. Ithaka & London.

Bhandar, U.R. 1988. *Pashupatinath. Holy of the Hindu Holiest.* Pashupati Deopatan. Kathmandu.

Biezais, H. 1972. *Die Himmlische Götterfamilie Der Alten Letten.* Acta Universitatis Upsaliensis, Historia Religionum 5. Uppsala.

Biezais, H. 1976. *Der Lichtgott Der Alten Letten.* Scripta Instituti Donneriani Aboensis, 8, Almqvist & Wiksell. Uppsala.

Biezais, H. 2021. 'Baltic religion'. *Encyclopedia Britannica.* https://www.britannica.com/facts/Baltic-religion. Accessed 29 November 2021.

Birkeli, E., 1938. *Fedrekult i Norge. Et forsok på en systematisk-deskriptiv fremstilling.* Skrifter utg. av det Norske Videnskaps-Akademi i Oslo. II. Hist. -Filos. Klasse. 1938. No 5. Oslo.

Björck, N. 2014. Osteologiskt Material – Liv Och Död På Björkgärdet. In Björck, N. (ed.). *Björkgärdet – Aspekter På Vikingarna Och Deras Förfäder. Gårdar Och Rituella Komplex Från Yngre Bronsålder Och Järnålder. Arkeologisk Undersökning. Utbyggnad Av Väg 288, Sträckan Jälla–Hov. Uppsala Län, Uppland, Uppsala Kommun, Rasbo Socken. Älby 2:1 Och Örby 4:2. Raso661 (Björkgärdet) Och Rasbo 658 (Älby).* Riksantikvarieämbetet. UV Rapport 2014:125.

Bourke, A. 2001. *The Burning of Bridget Cleary: A True Story.* Penguin Group. New York.

Boyce, M. 1977. *A Persian Stronghold of Zoroastrianism.* Oxford at the Clarendon Press. Oxford.

Boyce, M. 1979. *Zoroastrians. Their Religious Beliefs and Practices.* Routledge & Kegan Paul. London.

Boyce, M. 1984. *Textual Sources for the Study of Zoroastrianism.* The University of Chicago Press. Chicago.

Boyce, M. 1992. *Zoroastrianism. Its Antiquity and Constant Vigour.* Mazda Publishers. California.

Boyce, M. 2002. The Teachings of Zoroaster. In Godrej, P.J. & Mistree, F.P. (eds.). *A Zoroastrian Tapestry. Art, Religion & Culture*: 18–27. Mapin Publishing. Ahmedabad.

Brahma-Sutra (n.d.). Published by Swami Mumukshananda. Advaita Ashrama. Calcutta.

Braudel, F. 1980. *On History.* Weidenfeld and Nicolson. London.

Bryant, E. 2001. *The Quest for the Origins of Vedic Culture: The Indo-Aryan Migration Debate.* Oxford University Press. New York.

Buchet, B. 2019. Beyond Rome. The Cult of Vesta in Latium 1. In Bispham, E. & Miano, D. (eds.). *Gods and Goddesses in Ancient Italy*: 63–70. Routledge. London.

Cama, K.R. 1968. *The Collected Works of K. R. Cama*, Vol. I. The K. R. Cama Oriental Institute. Bombay.

Caplan, P. 1994. *Feasts, Fasts, Famine: Food for Thought.* Berg Occasional Papers in Anthropology. Oxford.

Carroll, M.P. 1985. Some Third Thoughts on Max Müller and Solar Mythology. *European Journal of Sociology/Archives Européennes De Sociologie/Europäisches Archiv Für Soziologie, 1985*, Vol. 26, No. 2: 263–281.

Celander, H. 1920. Sädesanden Och Den Sista Kärven i Svenska Skördebruk. *Folkminnen Och Folktankar*, Vol. 7: 97–108.

Celander, H. 1928. *Nordisk Jul. 1, Julen i Gammaldags Bondesed.* Geber. Stockholm.

Celander, H. 1936. Lucia Och Lussebrud i Värmland. *Svenska Kulturbilder Ny Följd*, häfte, Vol. 5.

Celander, H. 1955. *Förkristen Jul. Enligt Norröna Källor.* Göteborgs Universitets Årsskrift No. LXI:1955:3. Stockholm.

Chakrabarti, D. 2001. The Archaeology of Hinduism. In Insoll, T. (ed.). *Archaeology and World Religion.* Routledge. London & New York.

Chakrabarty, R.K., Pervez, S., Chow, J.C., Watson, J.G. & Dewangan, S. 2014. Funeral Pyres in South Asia: Brown Carbon Aerosol Emissions and Climate Impacts. *Environmental Science & Technology Letters*, Vol. 1: 44–48.

Charpentier Ljungqvist, F. 2015. *Den Långa Medeltiden. De Nordiska Ländernas Historia Från Folkvandringstid till Reformation.* Dialogos. Stockholm.

Charpentier Ljungqvist, F. 2017. *Klimatet Och Människan Under 12000 år.* Dialogos. Stockholm.

Choksy, J.K. 1989. *Purity and Pollution in Zoroastrianism. Triumph Over Evil.* University of Texas Press. Austin.

Clark, P. 2001. *Zoroastrianism. An Introduction to an Ancient Faith.* Sussex Academic Press. Brighton.

Craddock, P.T. 1995. *Early Metal Mining and Production*. Edinburgh University Press. Edinburgh.

Cunliffe, B. 2019. *The Scythians. Nomad Warriors of the Steppe*. Oxford University Press. Oxford.

Curtin, D.W. & Heldke, L.M. (eds.). 1992. *Cooking, Eating, Thinking. Transformative Philosophies of Food*. Indiana University Press. Bloomington and Indianapolis.

Daremesteter, J. 1895. *The Zend-Avesta. Part 1. The Vendidad*. Oxford at the Clarendon Press. Oxford.

Darian, S.G. 1978. *The Ganges in Myth and History*. The University Press of Hawaii. Honolulu.

Das, V. 1990. *Structure and Cognition. Aspects of Hindu Caste and Ritual*. Oxford University Press. Delhi.

Datta, B.N. 1936. Vedic Funeral Customs and Indus Valley Culture. *Man in India, Vol.* XVI: 221–307.

Davies, J.C. 1911. *Folklore of West and Mid-Wales*. Welsh Gazette Office. Aberystwyth.

Debortoli, G., Abbatangelo, C. & Ceballos, F. et al. 2020. Novel Insights on Demographic History of Tribal and Caste Groups from West Maharashtra (India) Using Genome-Wide Data. *Scientific Reports, Vol.* 10: 10075. doi:10.1038/s41598-020-66953-3

Diakonoff, I.M. 1995. Two Recent Studies of Indo-Iranian Origins. *Journal of the American Oriental Society*, Vol. 115, No. 3: 473–477. doi:10.2307/606224

Domenico, R.P. 2002. *The Regions of Italy: a Reference Guide to History and Culture*. Greenwood Publishing Group. London.

Doniger, W. 1981. *Siva: The Erotic Ascetic*. Oxford University Press. London and New York.

Doniger, W. 1987. *Tales of Sex and Violence. Folklore, Sacrifice, and Danger in the Jaiminiya Brahmana*. Motilal Banarsidass. Delhi.

Dorson, R.M. 1955. The Eclipse of Solar Mythology. *The Journal of American Folklore*, Vol. 68: 393–416.

Dubois, A.J.A. 1899. *Hindu Manners, Customs and Ceremonies*. Oxford at the Clarendon Press. Oxford.

Dubova, N.A. 2019. Gonur Depe – City of Kings and Gods, and the Capital of Margush Country (Modern Turkmenistan) Its Discovery by Professor Victor Sarianidi and Recent Finds. In Baumer, C. & Novák, M. (eds.). *Urban Cultures of Central Asia from the Bronze Age to the Karakhanids Learnings and Conclusions from New Archaeological Investigations and Discoveries. Proceedings of the First International Congress on Central Asian Archaeology Held at the University of Bern*, 4–6 February 2016: 30–53. Harrassowitz Verlag. Wiesbaden.

Dumézil, G. 1941. *Jupiter, Mars, Quirinus: Essai Sur La Conception Indo-Europennes De La Societe Et Sur Les Origines De Rome*. Gallimard. Paris.

Dumont, L. 1970. *Homo Hierarchicus*. The University of Chicago Press. Chicago.

Eck, D.E. 1983. *Banaras – City of Light*. Penguin Books. New Delhi.

Edsman, C.M. 1987. Fire. In Eliade, M. (ed.). *The Encyklopedia of Religion*, Vol. 14. MacMillan & Co. New York.

Elfstrand, B. 1995. Läderproduktion - Kanske En Binäring Och Handelsvara i Södermanland Och Östergötland Och Skärvstensrösenas Roll i Sammanhanget. In Larsson, M. & Toll, A. (eds.). *Samhällsstruktur Och Förändring Under Bronsålder. Rapport Från Ett Seminarium 29–30 September 1994 På Norrköpings Stadsmuseum i Samarbete Med RAÄ UV Linköping. Riksantikvarieämbetet*: 24–33. Arkeologiska undersökningar, Skrifter nr 11. Norrköping.

Eliade, M. 1958. *Patterns in Comparative Religion*. Sheed and Ward. New York.

Eliade, M. 1962. *The Forge and the Crucible*. University of Chicago Press. Chicago.

Engedal, O 2002. *The Nordic Scimitar. External Relations and the Creation of Elite Ideology*. BAR International Series 1050. Oxford.

Engedal, O 2010. *The Bronze Age of Northwestern Scandinavia*. Dissertation for the degree doctor philosophiae (dr.philos.). University of Bergen. Bergen.

Ericsson, A. 2002. *Liv, Död Och Jordbruk i Ett Bronsålderslandskap*. Kulturell mångfald i Södermanland del, Vol. 1: 58–66. Stockholm.

Ericsson, A. & Runcis, J. 1995. Gravar utan Begravningar. Teoretisk Diskussion Påkallad Av En Arkeologisk Undersökning Inom RAÄ 40 Vid Skalunda i Sköldinge Socken, Södermanland. In Ericsson, A. & Runcis, J. (eds.). *Teoretiska Perspektiv På Gravundersökningar i Södermanland*: 31–40. Riksantikvarieämbetet, Arkeologiska undersökningar, Skrifter nr 8. Stockholm.

Eriksen, B.V. & Andersen, H.C.H. 2016. Hammelev. An Early Mesolithic Cremation Grave from Southern Jutland, Denmark. In Grünberg, J. M. et al. (eds.). *Mesolithic Burials – Rites, Symbols and Social Organisation of Early Postglacial Communities. Int. Conference Halle (Saale), Germany*, 18th–21st September 2013: 13–24. Tagungen des Landesmuseums für Vorgeschichte. Halle.

Fagerlund, D. 1998. *Skärvstenshögar i Sneden. En Långvarig Historia – På Sidan Om. Arkeologisk Undersökning För Järnvägen Mälarbanan. Delen Grillby-Enköping. RAÄ 328, Snedens Allmänning, Litslena Socken, Uppland*. Riksantikvarieämbetet UV Uppsala Rapport 1997:48. Uppsala.

Falk, H. 1989. Soma I and II. *Bulletin of the School of Oriental and African Studies*, Vol. 52, No. 1: 77–90. doi:10.1017/S0041977X00023077

Feilberg, H.F. 1904. *Jul. Allesjæletiden, Hedensk, Kristen Julefest*. Første bind. København.

Firth, S. 1994. *Death, Dying and Bereavement in a British Hindu Community*. SOAS. London.

Flood, G. 1998. *An Introduction to Hinduism*. Cambridge University Press. New Delhi.

Forsman, C. & Victor, H. 2007. *Sommaränge Skog. Begravningar, Ritualer Och Bebyggelse Från Senneolitikum, Bronsålder Och Folkvandringstid*. Arkeologi E4. Societas Archaeologica Upsaliensis. SAU Skrifter 18. Stockholm.

Forsyth, N. 2003. *The Satanic Epic*. Princeton University Press. Princeton and Oxford.

Fortes, M. 1959. *Oedipus and Job in West African Religion*. Cambridge University Press. Cambridge.

Frazer, J.G. 1890a. *The Golden Bough. A Study in Comparative Religion*, Vol. 1. Macmillan and Co. London.

Frazer, J.G. 1890b. *The Golden Bough. A Study in Comparative Religion*, Vol. 2. Macmillan and Co. London.

Frazer, J.G. 1911a. *The Golden Bough. A Study in Magic and Religion. Third Edition. Part. I. The Magic Art and the Evolution of Kings*, Vol. II. Macmillan and Co. London.

Frazer, J.G. 1911b. *The Golden Bough. A Study in Magic and Religion. Third Edition. The Dying God*. Macmillan and Co. London.

Frazer, J.G. 1912a. *The Golden Bough. A Study in Magic and Religion. Third Edition. Spirits of the Corn and the Wild*, Vol. 1. Macmillan and Co. London.

Frazer, J.G. 1912b. *The Golden Bough. A Study in Magic and Religion. Third Edition. Spirits of the Corn and the Wild*, Vol. 2. Macmillan and Co. London.

Frazer, J.G. 1913a. *The Golden Bough. A Study in Magic and Religion. Third Edition. Balder the Beautiful*, Vol. 1. Macmillan and Co. London.

Frazer, J.G. 1913b. *The Golden Bough. A Study in Magic and Religion. Third Edition. Balder the Beautiful*, Vol. 2. Macmillan and Co. London.

Frazer, J.G. 1913c. *The Golden Bough. A Study in Magic and Religion. Third Edition. The Scapegoat*. Macmillan and Co. London.

Frazer, J.G. 1922. *The Golden Bough. A Study in Magic and Religion.* Macmillan & Co. London.

Frazer, J.G. 1930. *Myths of the Origin of Fire. An Essay.* Macmillan & Co. London.

Frazer, J.G. 1936. *Aftermath. A Supplement to the Golden Bough.* The Macmillan Press Ltd. London.

Gansum, T. 2004. Role the Bones – from Iron to Steel. *Norwegian Archaeological Review,* Vol. 37, No. 1: 41–57.

Gansum, T. & Hansen, J. 2004. Fra Jern Til Stål. In Melheim, L., Hedeager, L. & Oma, K. (eds.). *Mellom Himmel Og Jord. Oslo Arkeologiske Serie,* Vol. 2: 344–376. University of Oslo. Oslo.

*Garuda Purana Part II* (n.d.). Translated by a boards of scholars and edited by Shastri, J.L. Volume 13 in *Ancient Indian Tradition & Mythology.* First Edition: Delhi, 1979. Reprinted: Delhi, 1996. Motilal Banarsidass Publishers. Delhi.

*Garuda Purana Part III* (n.d.). Translated by a boards of scholars and edited by Shastri, J.L. Volume 14 in *Ancient Indian Tradition & Mythology.* First Edition: Delhi, 1980. Reprinted: Delhi, 1996. Motilal Banarsidass Publishers. Delhi.

Gray, J.N. 1995. *The Householder's World.* Oxford University Press. Delhi.

Gening, V.F. 1979. The Cemetery at Sintashta and the Early Indo-Iranian Peoples. *Journal of Indo-European Studies,* Vol. 7: 1–29.

Ghimre, B. & Ghimre, B. 1998. *Hindu Death Rites (Antyeshti Samskar).* Nepal Lithographic Co. Pvt. Ltd. Kathmandu.

Gimbutas, M. 1956. *The Prehistory of Eastern Europe. Part I: Mesolithic, Neolithic and Copper Age Cultures in Russia and the Baltic Area.* American School of Prehistoric Research, Harvard University Bulletin No. 20. Cambridge, MA.

Gimbutas, M. 1970. Proto-Indo-European Culture: The Kurgan Culture During the Fifth, Fourth, and Third Millennia B.C. In Cardona, G., Hoenigswald, H.M. & Senn, A. (eds.). *Indo-European and Indo-Europeans. Papers Presented at the Third Indo-European Conference at the University of Pennsylvania.* University of Pennsylvania Press. Philadelphia.

Gimbutas, M. 1994. *Das Ende Alt-Europas. Der Einfall Von Steppennomaden Aus Südrussland Und Die Indogermanisierung Mitteleuropas.* Institut für Sprachwissenschaft. Innsbruck.

Ginzburg, C. 1983. *The Night Battles: Witchcraft and Agrarian Cults in the Sixteenth and Seventeenth Centuries.* Routledge. London.

Goldhahn, J. 2007. *Dödens Hand. En Essä Om Brons- Och Hällsmed.* Göteborgs Universitet. Göteborg.

Goldhahn, J. 2019. *Birds in the Bronze Age: A North European Perspective.* Cambridge University Press. Cambridge.

Goody, J. 1982. *Cooking, Cuisine and Class.* Cambridge University Press. Cambridge.

Goudsblom, J. 1992. The Civilizing Process and the Domestication of Fire. *Journal of World History,* Vol. 3, No. 1: 1–12.

Goudsblom, J. 2015. Fire and Fuel in Human History. In Christian, D. (ed.). *The Cambridge World History (The Cambridge World History):* 185–207. Cambridge University Press. Cambridge.

Gustawsson, K.-A. 1949. *Kokstenshögar.* Fornvännen, Vol. 44: 152–165.

Guthrie, W.K.C. 1967. *The Greek Philosophers from Thales to Aristotles.* Methuen & Co Ltd. London.

Haak, W., Lazaridis, I. & Reich, D. et al. 2015. Massive Migration from the Steppe Is a Source for Indo-European Languages in Europe. *Nature,* Vol. 522 (11 June 2015). doi:10.1038/nature14317

Heyd, V., 2017. Kossinna's Smile. *Antiquity*, Vol. 91, No. 356 (2017): 348–359. doi:org/10.15184/aqy.2017.21

Haaland, R. 2004a. Technology, Transformation and Symbolism: Ethnographic Perspectives on European Iron Working. *Norwegian Archaeological Review*, Vol. 37, No. 1: 1–19.

Haaland, R. 2004b. Iron Smelting – a Vanishing Tradition: Ethnographic Study of This Craft in Ethiopia. *Journal of African Archaeology*, Vol. 2: 65–80.

Haaland, R. 2006. Iron in the Making: Technology and Symbolism. Ethnographic Perspectives on European Iron-Working. In Andren, A., Jennbert, K. & Raudvere, C. (eds.). *Old Norse Religion in Long-Term Perspectives. Origins, Changes, and Interactions. An International Conference in Lund, Sweden*, June 3–7, 2004. Nordic Academic Press. Lund.

Hachlili, R. 2001. The Archaeology of Judaism. In Insoll, T. (ed.). *Archaeology and World Religion*: 96–122. Routledge. London.

Hagberg, L. 2016. [1937]. *När Döden Gästar. Svenska Folkseder Och Svensk Folktro i Samband Med Död Och Begravning*. Ersatz. Stockholm.

Hauge, H.-E. 1965. *Levande Begravd Eller Bränd i Nordisk Folkmedisin. En Studie i Offer Och Magi*. Almqvist & Wiksell. Stockholm.

Heath, T. 1921. *A History of Greek Mathematics*, Vol. 1. From Thales to Euclid. The Clarendon Press. Oxford.

Herbert, E.W. 1984. *Red Gold of Africa. Copper in Precolonial History and Culture*. University of Wisconsin Press. Wisconsin.

Herbert, E.W. 1993. *Iron, Gender and Power. Rituals of Transformation in African Societies*. Indiana University Press. Indianapolis.

Herodotus. *The Histories*. A new translation by Robin Waterfield. Oxford World's Classic. Oxford University Press. Oxford, 1998.

Hinnells, J. 1981. *Zoroastrianism and the Parsis*. Ward Lock Educational. London.

Hinnells, J. 2000. *Zoroastrian and Parsi Studies. Selected Works of John R. Hinnells*. Ashgate. Aldershot.

Hjärthner-Holdar, E. 1993. *Järnets Och Järnmetallurgins Introduktion i Sverige*. Aun 16. Uppsala.

Hjärthner-Holdar, E., Eriksson, T. & Östling, A., (eds.). 2008. *Mellan Himmel Och Jord. Ryssgärdet, En Guldskimrande Bronsåldersmiljö i Centrala Uppland*. Arkeologi E4 Uppland – Studier, Vol. 5. RAÄ. Stockholm.

Hocart, A.M. 1950. *Caste. A Comparative Study*. Methuen & Co. Ltd. London.

Hocart, A.M. 1954. *Social Origins*. Watts & Co. London.

Hocart, A.M. 1969. *Kingship*. Oxford University Press. Oxford.

Hocart, A.M. 1970a. *The Life-Giving Myth and Other Essays*. Methuen & Co Ltd. London.

Hocart, A.M. 1970b. *Kings and Concillors. An Essay in the Comparative Anatomy of Human Society*. The University of Chicago Press. Chicago.

Holck, P. 1987. *Cremated Bones. A Medical-Anthropological Study of Archaeological Material on Cremated Burials*. Antropologiske skrifter nr. 1, Anatomisk Institutt, Universitetet i Oslo. Oslo.

Houben, J.E.M. 2003. The Soma-Haoma Problem: Introductory Overview and Observations on the Discussion. *Electronic Journal of Vedic Studies*, Vol. 9, No. 1. doi:10.11588/ejvs.2003.1.783

Hubert, H. & Mauss, M. 1964. *Sacrifice: Its Nature and Function*. University of Chicago Press. Chicago.

Huhtamaa, H. 2018. Combining Written and Tree-Ring Evidences to Trace Past Food Crises: A Case Study from Finland. In Collet, D. & Schuh, M. (eds.). *Famines During the "Little Ice Age" (1300–1800). Socionatural Entanglements in Premodern Societies*: 43–66. Springer. Leiden.

Huhtamaa, H. & Helama, S. 2017. Reconstructing Crop Yield Variability in Finland: Long-Term Perspective of the Cultivation History on the Agricultural Periphery since AD 760. *The Holocene*, Vol. 27, No. 1: 3–11.

Hultgård, A. 1996. Fornskandinavisk Kult – Finns Det Skriftliga Källor? In Engdahl, K. & Kaliff, A. (eds.). *Religion Från Stenålder till Medeltid*: 25–57. Riksantikvarieämbetet. Arkeologiskaundersökningar. Skrifter nr 19. Linköping.

Hunt, R. 1997. Frazer, Sir James (1854–1941. In Barfield, T. (ed.). *The Dictionary of Anthropology*: 206–208. Blackwell Publishing. Oxford.

Hyenstrand, Å., 1968. Skärvstenshögar Och Bronsåldersmiljöer. *Tor*, Vol. 12: 61–80.

Hyltén-Cavallius, G.O. 1863–68. *Wärend Och Wirdarne. Ett Försök i Svensk Ethnologi.* Band 1 och 2. Stockholm.

Inden, R. & Nicholas, R. 1977. *Kinship in Bengali Culture.* University of Chicago Press. Chicago.

Jalais, S. 2014. An Urban Structure along the Sacred Waters of the Ganges in Varanasi. In Tvedt, T. & Oestigaard, T. (eds.). *A History of Water. Series 3, Vol. 1. Water and Urbanization*: 283–304. I.B. Tauris. London.

James, E.O. 2017. *The Beginnings of Religion. An Introductory and Scientific Study.* Routledge. London.

Jeppsson, A. 2019. *Skärvstenshögen i tid och rum. En landskapsanalys av Upplands skärvstenshögars geografiska och kronologiska placeringsmönster.* Master thesis in Archaeology. Uppsala University.

Jensen, R. 1989. The Bronze Age in Eastern Central Sweden – Heaps of Fire Cracked Stones and the Settlement Pattern. In Ambrosiani, B. (ed.). *Die Bronzezeit Im Ostseegebiet. Ein Rapport Der Kgl. Schwedischen Akademie Der Literatur Geschichte Und Altertumsforschung über Das JulitaSymposium 1986.* KVHAA Konferenser 22. Stockholm.

Jha, N. & Rajaram, N.S. 2000. *The Deciphered Indus Script. Methodology, Readings, Interpretation.* Aditya Prakashan. New Delhi.

Kahn, C.H. 1993. *The Art and Thought of Heraclitus. An Edition on the Fragments with Translation and Commentary.* Cambridge University Press. Cambridge.

Kaliff, A. 1992. *Brandgravskick Och Föreställningsvärld. En Religionsarkeologisk Diskussion.* Occasional papers in archaeology 4. Uppsala.

Kaliff, A. 1994. Skärvstenshögar och kremeringsplatser. Exempel och experiment med utgångspunkt från en utgrävning i Ringeby, Kvillinge sn, Östergötland. *Tor 26.* Uppsala.

Kaliff, A. 1996. *Ringeby. En grav- och kultplats från yngre bronsåldern. Arkeologisk undersökning, RAÄ 6, Kvillinge sn, Norrköpings kommun, Östergötland.* Riksantikvarieämbetet, Avdelningen för arkeologiska undersökningar, UV Linköping 1995:51. Linköping.

Kaliff, A. 1997. Grav Och Kultplats. Eskatologiska Föreställningar Under Yngre Bronsålder Och äldre Järnålder i Östergötland. Aun 24. Uppsala.

Kaliff, A. 2005. The Vedic Agni and Scandinavian Fire Rituals A Possible Connection. *Current Swedish Archaeology*, Vol. 13, No. 2005: 77–98.

Kaliff, A. 2007. *Fire, Water, Heaven and Earth. Ritual Practice and Cosmology in Ancient Scandinavia: An Indo-European Perspective.* National Heritage Board. Stockholm.

Kaliff, A. & Mattes, J. 2017. *Tempel Och Kulthus i Det Forna Skandinavien. Myter Och Arkeologiska Fakta.* Carlsson Bokförlag. Stockholm.

Kaliff, A. & Oestigaard, T. 2004. Cultivating Corpses – A Comparative Approach to Disembodied Mortuary Remains. *Current Swedish Archaeology*, Vol. 12, No. 2004: 83–104.

Kaliff, A. & Oestigaard, T. 2008. Excavating the King's Bones: The Materiality of Death in Practice and Ethics Today. In Fahlander, F. & Oestigaard, T. (eds.). *The Materiality of Death. Bodies, Burials, Beliefs*: 47–57. BAR International Series 1768. Oxford.

Kaliff, A. & Oestigaard, T. 2017. *Cremation, Corpses and Cannibalism. Comparative Cosmologies and Centuries of Cosmic Consumption.* Cambridge Scholars Publishing. Newcastle.

Kaliff, A. & Oestigaard, T. 2020. *The Great Indo-European Horse Sacrifice: 4000 Years of Cosmological Continuity from Sintashta and the Steppe to Scandinavian Skeid.* OPIA 72. Uppsala.

Kaliff, A. & Oestigaard, T. 2022. *Werewolves, Warriors and Winter Sacrifices. Unmasking Kivik and Indo-European Cosmology in Bronze Age Scandinavia.* OPIA 75. Uppsala.

Kaliff, A. & Østigård, T. 2013. *Kremation Och Kosmologi - En Komparativ Arkeologisk Introduktion.* OPIA 56. Uppsala.

Kane, P.V. 1973. *History of Dharmaśāstra: Ancient and Mediaeval Religious and Civil Law in India,* Vol. 4. Bhandarkar Oriental Research Institute. Poona.

Karlenby, L. 2011. *Stenbärarna. Kult Och Rituell Praktik i Skandinavisk Bronsålder.* OPIA 55. Uppsala.

Kaufmann, Y. 1960. *The Religion of Israel.* University of Chicago Press. Chicago.

Kaul, F. 1998. *Ship on Bronzes. A Study in Bronze Age Religion and Iconography.* PNM Studies in Archaeology and History 3:1/2. Copenhagen.

Kaul, F. 2004. *Bronzealderens Religion.* Nordiske Fortidsminder Serie B 22. København.

Kaul, F. 2005. Hvad Skete Med Den Dodes Sjæl? Sjælsforestillinger i Bronzealder. In Goldhahn, J. (ed.). *Mellan Sten Och Järn:* 263–278. Gotarc Serie C. Arkeologiska Skrifter 59. Göteborg.

Kaushik, M. 1976. The Symbolic Representation of Death. *Contributions to Indian Sociology (NS),* Vol. 10, No. 2: 265–292.

Keyser, C., Bouakaze, C., Crubézy, E., Nikolaev, V.G., Montagnon, D., Reis, T. & Ludes, B. 2009. Ancient DNA Provides New Insights into the History of South Siberian Kurgan People. *Human Genetics,* Vol. 126, No. 3: 395–410.

Kirk, G.S. 1949. Heraclitus and Death in Battle. *The American Journal of Philology,* Vol. 70, No. 4: 384–393.

Knipe, D.M. 1975. *In the Image of Fire.* Motilal Banarsidass. Delhi, India.

Kortlandt, F. 1990. The Spread of the Indo-Europeans. *Journal of Indo-European Studies,* Vol. 18: 131–140.

Koryakove, L., Kuzminkyh, S. & Beltikova, G. 2008. The Introduction of Iron Technology into Central-Northern Eurasia. In Forenius, S., Hjärthner-Holdar, E. & Risberg, C. (eds.). *The Introduction of Iron in Eurasia:* 112–127. The National Heritage Board & Department of Archaeology and Ancient History. Uppsala.

Kramrisch, S. 1981. *The Presence of Shiva.* Princeton University Press. Princeton.

Kristiansen, K. 2007. Eurasian Transformations: Mobility, Ecological Change and the Transmission of Social Institutions in the Third Millennium and Early Second Millennium BCE. In Hornborg, A. & Crumley, C.E. (eds.). *The World System and the Earth System: Global Socioenvironmental Change and Sustainability Since the Neolithic:* 149–162. Left Coast press. Walnut Creek.

Kristiansen, K., Allentoft, M.E. & Frei, K.M. et. al. 2017. Re-Theorising Mobility and the Formation of Culture and Language Among the Corded Ware Culture in Europe. *Antiquity,* Vol. 91, No. 356: 334–347. doi:10.15184/aqy.2017.17

Kuzmina, E.E. 2007. *The Origin of the Indo-Iranians. Leiden Indo-European Etymological Dictionary Series,* Vol. 3. Brill. Leiden.

Kuzmina, E.E. 2008. *The Prehistory of the Silk Road.* University of Pennsylvania Press. Philadelphia.

Kvanvig, J.L. 1993. *The Problem of Hell.* Oxford University Press. Oxford.

Lal, B.B. 2003. *Excavations at Kalibangan, the Early Harappans, 1960–1969.* Memoirs of the Archaeological Survey of India 98. New Delhi.

Larsson, B.M.P., Morell, M. & Myrdal, J. (eds.). 1997. *Agrarhistoria*. LT. Stockholm.

Larsson, F. 2014. Människor, djur och handlingar i benmaterialet. In Larsson, F. (ed.). *Skeke – gudar, människor och gjutare. Rituella komplex från bronsålder och äldre järnålder samt en höjdbosättning från yngre järnålder med gjuteriverkstad. Utbyggnad av väg 288, sträckan Jälla–Hov. Arkeologisk undersökning. Uppsala län; Uppland; Uppsala kommun; Rasbo socken; Skeke 1:3, 2:6, Rasbo 55:1–2, 654, 655, 889, 695, 696, 697, 626:1, 627:1, 682–688 samt delar av Rasbo 628:1 och 629:1*. Riksantikvarieämbetet. UV Rapport 2014:53.

Le Goff, J. 1984. *The Birth of Purgatory*. Scholar Press. London.

Leach, E. 1961. Golden Bough or Gilded Twig? *Daedalus*, Vol. 90, No. 2: 371–387.

Leach, E. 1966. Frazer and Malinowski. A CA Discussion. *Current Anthropology*, Vol. 7, No. 5: 560–567.

Leach, E. 1985. Reflections on a Visit to Nemi. Did Frazer Get It Wrong? *Anthropology Today*, Apr., 1985, Vol. 1, No. 2: 2–3.

Levack, B.P. 2006. *The Witch-Hunt in Early Modern Europe*. 3rd ed., Longman. London.

Lévi-Strauss, C. 1981. *Introduction to a Science of Mythology, Vol. 4. The Naked Man*. Cape. London.

Lévi-Strauss, C. 1983. *Introduction to a Science of Mythology, Vol. 2. From Honey to Ashes*. Cape. London.

Lévi-Strauss, C. 1990. *Introduction to a Science of Mythology, Vol. 3. The Origin of Table Manners*. The University of Chicago Press. Chicago.

Lévi-Strauss, C. 1994. *Introduction to a Science of Mythology, Vol. 1. The Origin of Table Manners*. Pimlico. London.

Levin, M. 1930a. Mummification and Cremation in India – Parts I & II. *Man*, Vol. XXX: 29–34.

Levin, M. 1930b. Mummification and Cremation in India – Part III. *Man*, Vol. XXX: 44–48.

Levin, M. 1930c. Mummification and Cremation in India – Part IV. *Man*, Vol. XXX: 64–66.

Librado, P., Khan, N. & Fages, A. et al. 2021. The Origins and Spread of Domestic Horses from the Western Eurasian Steppes. *Nature*, Vol. 598: 634–640.

Lid, N. 1923. Norske Slakteskikkar. *Skrifter Utgitt Av Det Norske Videnskaps-Akademi i Oslo. II. Historisk-Filosofisk Klasse*. I kommisjon hos Jacob Dybwad. Oslo.

Lid, N. 1928. *Joleband Og Vegetasjonsguddom Skrifter utgitt av Det norske videnskaps-akademi i Oslo. II. Hist.-filos. Klasse. 1932*. No. 4. I kommisjon hos Jacob Dybwad. Oslo.

Lid, N. 1933. *Jolesveinar Og Grøderiksdomsgudar. Skrifter utgitt av Det norske videnskaps-akademi i Oslo. II. Hist.-filos. Klasse. 1932*. No. 5. I kommisjon hos Jacob Dybwad. Oslo.

Lienhardt, G. 1993. Frazer's Anthropology: Science and Sensibility. *JASO*, Vol. 24/1, No. 1993: 1–12.

Littledale, R.F. 1906. The Oxford Solar Myth. In Tyrrell, R. & Sullivan, E. (eds.). *Echoes from Kottabos*: 279–290. E. Grant Richards. London.

Lincoln, B. 1975. The Indo-European Myth of Creation. *History of Religions*, Vol. 15, No. 2: 121–145. doi:10.1086/462739

Lincoln, B. 1976. The Indo-European Cattle-Raiding Myth. *History of Religions*, Vol. 16, No. 1: 42–65. doi:10.1086/462755

Lincoln, B. 1981. *Priest, Warriors and Cattle: A Study in the Ecology of Religions*. University of California Press. Berkley.

Lincoln, B. 1986. *Myth, Cosmos and Society: Indo-European Themes of Creation and Destruction*. Harvard University Press. Cambridge, Massachusetts, and London.

Lincoln, B. 1991. *Death, War, and Sacrifice: Studies in Ideology and Practice*. University of Chicago Press. Chicago.

Lindner, S. 2020. Chariots in the Eurasian Steppe: A Bayesian Approach to the Emergence of Horse-Drawn Transport in the Early Second Millennium BC. *Antiquity*, Vol. 94, No. 374: 361–380. doi:10.15184/aqy.2020.37

*The Linga-Purana Part I.*(n.d.). Translated by a board of scholars. Published in: *Ancient Indian Tradition and Mythology*, Vol. 5. Motilal Banarsidass Publishers. Delhi, 1990.

*The Linga-Purana. Part II.* (n.d.). Translated by a board of scholars. Published in: *Ancient Indian Tradition and Mythology*, Vol. 6. Motilal Banarsidass Publishers. Delhi, 1990.

Littledale, R.F. 1906. The Oxford Solar Myth. In Tyrrell, R. & Sullivan, E. (eds.). *Echoes from Kottabos*: 279–290. E. Grant Richards. London.

Long, C. 1993. Cosmogony. In Eliade, M. (ed.). *The Encyclopedia of Religion*. Vol. 3: 94–100. Macmillan Publishing Company. New York.

Lorsch Wildfang, R. 2006. *Rome's Vestal Virgins: Vestal Priestesses in the Late Republic and Early Empire*. Routledge. London and New York.

Lupton, J. 1996. *Food, the Body and the Self*. Sage. London.

Máchal, J. 1918. Slavic. In *The Mythology of All Races*, Vol. III. *Celtic-Slavic*. Marshall Jones Company. Boston.

Magnus, O. 1998. *Historia De Gentibus Septentrionalibus Romæ 1555. Description of the Northern Peoples Rome 1555*, Vol. II. Routledge for the Hakluyt Society. London.

Mallory, J.P. 1989. In *Search of the Indo-Europeans. Language, Archaeology and Myth*. Thames and Hudson. London.

Mallory, J.P. & Adams, D.Q. (eds.). 1997. Andronovo Culture. In *Encyclopedia of Indo-European Culture*. Fitzroy Dearborn Publishers. London & Chicago.

Mannhardt, W. 1865. *Roggenwolf Und Roggerhund*. Verlag von Constantin Ziemssen. Danzig.

Mannhardt, W. 1868. *Die Korndämonen*. Ferd. Dümmler's Verl. Berlin.

Mannhardt, W. 1875. *Der Baumkultus Der Germanen Und Ihrer Nachbarstämme*. Gebrüder Borntraeger. Berlin.

Mannhardt, W. 1877. *Antike Wald-Und Feldkulte*. Gebrüder Borntraeger. Berlin.

Mannhardt, W. 1884. *Mythologische Forschungen*. De Gruyter. Berlin.

Marriott, M. & Inden, R.B. 1974. Caste Systems. *Encyclopedia Britannica*. 15th ed., Vol. 3: 982–991.

Marriott, M. & Inden, R.B. 1977. Toward an Ethnosociology of South Asian Caste Systems. In David, K. (ed.). *The New Wind: Changing Identities in South Asia*. Mouton. The Hague and Paris.

Mathieson, I., Alpaslan-Roodenberg, S. & Posth, C. et al. 2018. The Genomic History of Southeastern Europe. *Nature*, Vol. 555, No. 2018: 197–203. doi:10.1038/nature25778

Mathieson, I., Lazaridis, I. & Rohland, N. et al. 2015. Genome-Wide Patterns of Selection in 230 Ancient Eurasians. *Nature*, Vol. 528, No. 2015: 499–503. doi:10.1038/nature16152

Mattes, J. 2008. *Frühe Kultbauten. Studien Zur Archäologie Sakraler Plätze in Südskandinavien*. Aun 38. Uppsala.

Mintz, S. 1996. *Tasting Food, Tasting Freedom. Excursion into Eating, Culture and the Past*. Beacon Press. New York.

Montelius, O. 1885. *Om Tidsbestämning Inom Bronsålderen Med Särskildt Afseende På Skandinavien*. Kungl. Boktryckeriet. Stockholm.

Montelius, O. 1894. Midvinterns Solfest. *Svenska Fornminnesföreningens Tidskrift*, Vol. 9, No. 1: 68–76.

Montelius, O. 1895. *De Förhistoriska Perioderna i Skandinavien*. Kungl. Boktryckeriet. Stockholm.

Montelius, O. 1899. Solgudens Yxa Och Tors Hammare. *Svenska Fornminnesföreningens Tidskrift*, Vol. 10: 277–296.

Montelius, O. 1910. The Sun God's Axe and Thor's Hammer. *Folk-Lore*, Vol. 21, No. 1910: 60–78.

Montelius, O. 1917. *Minnen Från Vår Forntid*. P. A. Nordstedt & Söners Förlag. Stockholm.

Mueller, H.-F. 2004. *Roman Religion in Valerius Maximus*. Routledge. London.

Müller, M.F. 1856[1909]. *Comparative Mythology. An Essay*. George Routledge. London.

Müller, M.F. 1859. *History of Ancient Sanskrit Literature*. Calcutta.

Müller, M. 1879. *Lectures on the Origin and Growth of Religion as Illustrated by the Religions of India*. Charles Scribner's Sons. New York.

Munkenberg, B.-A. 2004. Monumentet i Svarteborg. In Claesson, P. & Munkenberg, B-A. (eds.) *Gravar Och Ritualer. Projekt Gläborg – Rabbalshede. Bygden Innanför Fjordarna, 3. Kulturhistoriska Dokumentationer Nr 15*. Bohusläns museum. Uddevalla.

Narasimhan, V.M., Patterson, N. & Reich, D. et al. 2019. The Formation of Human Populations in South and Central Asia. *Science*, Vol. 365, No. 6457. doi:10.1126/science.aat7487

Nelson, J.L. 2019. *King and Emperor: A New Life of Charlemagne*. University of California Press. Oakland.

*The New York Times*. 1895a. 22. April. Not Witches, But Faires – A New Explanation of the Strange Tragedy in Tipperary. Retrieved 11 November 2021.

*The New York Times*. 1895b. 6. July. A Witch Burner Sentenced – Michael Cleary Condemned to Imprisonment for Twenty Years. Retrieved 11 November 2021.

Nikander, G. 1916. Fruktbarhetsriter Under årshögtiderna Hos Svenskarna i Finland. *Folkloristiska Och Etnografiska Studier*, Vol. 1: 195–315.

Nilsson, M.P. 1936. *Årets Folkliga Fester*. Hugo Gebers Förlag. Stockholm.

Nilsson, M.P. 1947. Greek Mysteries in the Confession of St. Cyprian. *The Harvard Theological Review*, Vol. 40, No. 3: 167–176.

Noge, A.-S. 2009. Skärvstenshögar Med Människoben i Norra Mälarområdet. *Fornvännen,* Vol. 104, No. 4: 241–252.

Nordberg, A. 2013. *Fornnordisk Religionsforskning Mellan Teori Och Empiri. Kulten Av Anfäder, Solen Och Vegetationsandar i Idéhistorisk Belysning*. Acta Academia Regiae Gustavi Adolphi CXXVI. Uppsala.

Nordqvist, K. & Heyd, V. 2020. The Forgotten Child of the Wider Corded Ware Family: Russian Fatyanovo Culture in Context. *Proceedings of the Prehistoric Society*, Vol. 86: 65–93. doi:10.1017/ppr.2020.9

Nylén, E. 1958. Pryda, Skydda, Binda? Om Gravskickets Mening Och Skärvstensrösenas Problem Med Anledning Av Ett Aktuellt Bronsåldersfynd. *Gotländskt Arkiv 1958*: 23–38. Visby.

Näsström, M.-B. 2002. *Fornskandinavisk Religion. En Grundbok*. Studentlitteratur. Lund.

Obeyesekere, G. 1968. Theodicy, Sin and Salvation in a Sociology of Buddhism. In Leach, E.R. (ed.). *Dialectic in Practical Religion*: 7–40. Cambridge University Press. Cambridge.

Obeyesekere, G. 2002. *Imagining Karma. Ethical Transformation in Amerindian, Buddhist, and Greek Rebirth*. University of California Press. Berkeley.

Oestigaard, T. 2000. The Deceased's Life Cycle Rituals in Nepal. Present Cremation Burials for the Interpretations of the Past. *BAR International Series*, Vol. 853. Oxford.

Oestigaard, T. 2003. *An Archaeology of Hell: Fire, Water and Sin in Christianity*. Bricoleur Press. Lindome.

Oestigaard, T. 2004. Kings and Cremations – Royal Funerals and Sacrifices in Nepal. In Insoll, T. (ed.). *Belief in the Past. The Proceedings of the Manchester Conference on Archaeology and Religion*: 115–124. BAR International Series, Vol. 1212. Oxford.

Oestigaard, T. 2005. *Death and Life-Giving Waters – Cremation, Caste, and Cosmogony in Karmic Traditions*. BAR International Series, Vol. 1353. Oxford.

Oestigaard, T. 2007. *Transformatøren - Ildens Mester i Jernalderen*, Vol. 2. Gotarc Series C, No. 65. Göteborg University. Gothenburg.

Oestigaard, T. 2009. The Materiality of Hell: The Christian Hell in a World Religion Context. *Material Religion*, Vol. 5, No. 3: 312–331.

Oestigaard, T. 2011. Cosmogony. In Insoll, T. (ed.). *The Oxford Handbook of the Archaeology of Ritual and Religion*: 76–88. Oxford University Press. Oxford.

Oestigaard, T. 2013. Cremations in Culture and Cosmology. In Tarlow, S. & Nilsson, L.S. (eds.). *The Oxford Handbook of the Archaeology of Death and Burial*: 497–509. Oxford University Press. Oxford.

Oestigaard, T. 2017. Holy Water: the Works of Water in Defining and Understanding Holiness. *WIREs Water*, Vol.2017. doi:10.1002/wat2.1205

Oestigaard, T. 2021a. *Vinter Og Vår i Vannets Verden: Arkeologi Om økologi Og Jordbrukskosmologi*. OPIA 74. Uppsala.

Oestigaard, T. 2021b. Water and Religion. *Oxford Research Encyclopedia of Anthropology*. doi:10.1093/acrefore/9780190854584.013.477

Oestigaard, T. 2022a. *The Magic of Death. Corpsepower and Indo-Europanisation in Late Bronze Age Sweden*. OPIA 76. Uppsala.

Oestigaard, T. 2022b. *Sacrifice. Theories and Rituals in Nepal*. OPIA 79. Uppsala.

Ostigård, T. & Kaliff, A. 2020. *Likbrud og dødsbryllup. Sjelen, sykdommer og oldnordiske gravskikker*. OPIA 69. Uppsala.

O'Flaherty, W.D. 1994. *Rig Veda*. An Anthology. One hundred and eight hymns, selected. Penguin Books. First published 1981, reprinted 1994.

Olivelle, D. 1987. Rites of Passage. Hindu rites. In: Eliade, M. (Ed.) *The Encylopedia of Religion*, Vol. 12. New York.

Olrik, A. & Ellekilde, H. 1926–1951. *Nordens Gudeverden. Første Bind. Vætter Og Helligdomme*. G.E.C. Gads Forlag. København.

Olrik, A. & Ellekilde, H. 1951. *Nordens Gudeverden. Andet Bind. Årets Ring*. G.E.C. Gads Forlag. København.

Ottesen, J. 2006. Moderne Kremasjoner. In Østigård, T. (ed.). *Lik Og Ulik – Tilnærminger Til Variasjon i Gravskikk*: 47–54. UBAS Nordisk 2. University of Bergen. Bergen.

Pandey, R.B. 1969. *Hindu Samskaras*. Motilal Banarsidass. Delhi. India.

Papac, L., Erneé, M. & Haak, W. et al. 2021. Dynamic Changes in Genomic and Social Structures in Third Millennium BCE Central Europe. *Science Advances*, Vol. 7, No. 35. doi:10.1126/sciadv.abi6941.

Parmeshwaranand, S. 2000. *Encyclodaedic Dictionary of Vedic Terms*, Vols. 1–2. Sarup & Sons. New Delhi.

Parry, J. 1980. Ghosts, Greed and Sin: the Occupational Identity of Benares Funeral Priests. *Man*, Vol. 15, No. 1: 88–111.

Parry, J. 1982. Death and Cosmogony in Kashi. In Madan, T.N. (ed.). *Way of Life. King, Householder, Renouncer. Essays in Honour of Louis Dumont*: 337–365. Vikas Publishing House Pvt Ltd. New Delhi.

Parry, J. 1985a. Death and Digestion: the Symbolism of Food and Eating in North Indian Mortuary Rites. *Man*, Vol. 20, No. 4: 612–630.

Parry, J. 1985b. The Aghori Ascetics of Benares. In Burghart, R. & Cantlie, A. (eds.). *Indian Religion*: 51–78. Curzon Press. London.

Parry, J. 1986. The Gift, the Indian Gift and the "Indian Gift. *Man*, Vol. 21, No. 3: 453–473.

Parry, J. 1987. Sacrificial Death and the Necrophagous Ascetic. In Bloch, M. & Parry, J. (eds.). *Death and the Regeneration of Life*: 74–110. Cambridge University Press. Cambridge.

Parry, J. 1994. *Death in Banaras. The Lewis Henry Morgan Lectures 1988*. Cambridge University Press. Cambridge.

Petersson, M. 2006. *Djurhållning Och Betesdrift. Djur, Människor Och Landskap I Västra Östergötland Under Yngre Bronsålder Och äldre Järnålder*. Riksantikvarieämbetet/Uppsala universitet. Stockholm & Uppsala.

*Life of Numa, Plutarch's Lives*. 1914. Translated by Perrin, Bernadotte. (1847–1920), from the Loeb Classical Library edition of 1914. Heinemann. London.

Possehl, G.L. 1999. *Indus Age. The Beginnings*. University of Pennsylvania Press. Philadelphia.

Possehl, G.L. 2002. *The Indus Civilization. A Contemporary Perspective*. AltaMira Press. Plymouth.

Puhvel, J. 1987. *Comparative Mythology*. Johns Hopkins University Press. Baltimore.

Pyne, S.J. 1997. *Vestal Fire: An Environmental History, Told Through Fire, of Europe and Europe's Encounter with the World*. University of Washington Press. Seattle.

Quigley, D. 1995. *The Interpretation of Caste*. Clarendon Press. Oxford.

Raheja, G.G. 1988. *The Poison in the Gift*. The University of Chicago Press. Chicago.

Raj, P.A. 2001. *"Kay Gardeko?" The Royal Massacre in Nepal*. Rupa & Co. New Delhi.

Ralston, W.R.S. 1872. *Songs of the Russian People as Illustrative of Slavonic Mythology and Russian Social Life*. Ellis & Green. London.

Reich, D. 2018. *Who We Are and How We Got There. Ancient DNA and the New Science of Human Past*. Pantheon Books. New York.

Reichborn-Kjennerud, I. 1928. *Vår Gamle Trolldomsmedisin I*. Skrifter utgitt av Det Norske Videnskaps-Akademi i Oslo. I kommisjon hos Jacob Dybwad. Oslo.

Reichborn-Kjennerud, I. 1933. *Vår Gamle Trolldomsmedisin II*. Skrifter utgitt av Det Norske Videnskaps-Akademi i Oslo. I kommisjon hos Jacob Dybwad. Oslo.

Reichborn-Kjennerud, I. 1940. *Vår Gamle Trolldomsmedisin III*. Skrifter utgitt av Det Norske Videnskaps-Akademi i Oslo. I kommisjon hos Jacob Dybwad. Oslo.

Reichborn-Kjennerud, I. 1944. *Vår Gamle Trolldomsmedisin IV*. Skrifter utgitt av Det Norske Videnskaps-Akademi i Oslo. I kommisjon hos Jacob Dybwad. Oslo.

Reichborn-Kjennerud, I. 1947. *Vår Gamle Trolldomsmedisin V*. Skrifter utgitt av Det Norske Videnskaps-Akademi i Oslo. I kommisjon hos Jacob Dybwad. Oslo.

Rentzhog, S., 1967. Om Skärvsten Och Skärvstensrösen. *Tor*, Vol. XI, No. 1965–1966: 61–82.

Ricoeur, P. 2004. *The Conflict of Interpretations. Essays in Hermeneutics*. Continuum. London.

*Rig Veda*. An Anthology. One hundred and eight hymns, selected, translated and annotated by O'Flaherty, Wendy Doninger. Penguin Books. New Delhi, 1994.

Rijal, S. 1998. *The Traditional System of Iron Working: Technology, Social Context and Rituals of Transformation. An Ethnoarchaeological Study from Eastern Nepal*. M. Phil Thesis in Archaeology, Department of Archaeology, University of Bergen. Bergen.

Robertson Smith, W. 1889. *Lectures on the Religion of the Semites. Fundamental Institutions. First Series*. D. Appelton and Company. New York.

Rundkvist, M. 1994. Skärvstenshögar Med Gravgömmor i östligaste Mälaromrädet. *Fornvännen*, Vol. 89, No. 2: 83–89.

Russell, J.B. 1977. *The Devil. Perceptions of Evil from Antiquity to Primitive Christianity*. Cornell University Press. Ithaca.

Russell, J.B. 1981. *Satan. The Early Christian Tradition*. Cornell University Press. Ithaca.

Russell, J.B. 1988. *Lucifer. The Devil in the Middle Ages*. Cornell University Press. Ithaca.

Russel, J.R. 2002. The Place and Time of Zarathushtra. In Godrej, P.J. & Mistree, F.P. (eds.). *A Zoroastrian Tapestry. Art, Religion & Culture*: 29–39. Mapin Publishing. Ahmedabad.

Saag, L., Vasilyev, S.V. & Varul, L. et al. 2021. Genetic Ancestry Changes in Stone to Bronze Age Transition in the East European Plain. *Science Advances*, Vol. 7, No. 4: eabd6535, 1–17. doi:10.1126/sciadv.abd6535

Sachs, J.R. 1991. Current Eschatology: Universal Salivation and the Problem of Hell. *Theological Studies*, Vol. 52, No. 2: 227–254.

Sachs, J.R. 1993. Apocatastasis in Patristic Theology. *Theological Studies*, Vol. 54, No. 4: 617–640.

Sarianidi, V. 1990. Togolok 21, an Indo-Iranian Temple in the Karakum, *Bulletin of the Asia Institute, Vol.* 4: 159–165.

Sarianidi, V. 2005. *Gonur-Depe. City of Kings and Gods*. Miras. Ashgabat.

Scodel, R. 1984. Tantalus and Anaxagoras. *Harvard Studies in Classical Philology*, Vol. 88: 13–24.

Segal, E. 1997. Judaism. In Cowars, H. (ed.). *Life after Death in World Religions*: 11–30. Orbis Books. New York.

Sharma, S., Rai, E. & Sharma, P. et al. 2009. The Indian Origin of Paternal Haplogroup R1a1* Substantiates the Autochthonous Origin of Brahmins and the Caste System. *Journal of Human Genetics*, Vol. 54: 47–55. doi:10.1038/jhg.2008.2

Shinde, V., Narasimhan, V.M. & Reich, D. et al. 2019. An Ancient Harappan Genome Lacks Ancestry from Steppe Pastoralists or Iranian Farmers, *Cell*, Vol. 179: 729–735. doi:10.1016/j.cell.2019.08.048

Shnirelman, V.A. 1998. Archaeology and Ethnic Politics: The Discovery of Arkaim. *Museum International*, Vol. 50, No. 2: 33–39. doi:10.1111/1468-0033.00146

Shrestha, A.M. 2001. *The Dreadful Night. Royal Carnage at Nepalese Royal Palace*. Ekta Books. Kathmandu.

Singh, M., Sarkar, A. & Nandineni, M.R. 2018. A Comprehensive Portrait of Y-STR Diversity of Indian Populations and Comparison with 129 Worldwide Populations. *Scientific Reports*, Vol. 8: 15421. doi:10.1038/s41598-018-33714-2

Singh, N.K. 1997. *Divine Prostitution*. A.P.H. Publishing Corporation. New Delhi.

*The Siva-Purana Part III*. (1970). Translated by a board of scholars. In Shastri, J.L. (ed.). *Ancient Indian Tradition & Mythology*, Vol. 3. Motilal Banarsidass Publishers. Delhi.

Sjöling, E. 2016. Appendix 2. Ostelogisk Analys Av Brandgravar i Broby, Börje Sn, Uppland. In Ojala, K. (ed.). *I Bronsålderns Gränsland. Uppland Och Frågan Om östliga Kontakter*: 277–285. OPIA 61. Uppsala.

Snorri Sturluson. *Heimskringla, Vol. 1. The Beginning to Olafr Tryggvason*. Translated by Finlay, Alison and Faulkes, Anthony. Viking Society for northern research. University College London. London, 2011.

Solheim, S. 1952. *Norsk Sætertradisjon*. H. Aschehoug & Co. (W. Nygaard). Oslo.

Staal, F. 1983. *Agni. The Vedic Ritual of the Fire Altar*, Vol. 1. Asian Humanities Press. Berkeley.

Staal, F. 1996. *Ritual and Mantras. Rules without Meaning*. Motilal Banarsidass Publishers. New Delhi.

Stausberg, M. 2005. *Zarathustra Och Zoroastrismen*. Nya Doxa. Nora.

Steinsland, G. 1997. *Eros Og Død i Norrøne Myter*. Universitetsforlaget. Oslo.

Stevenson, S.M. 1920. *The Rites of the Twice-Born*. Oxford University Press. London.

Storaker, J.T. 1924. *Naturrigerne i Den Norske Folketro (Storakers Samlinger III)*, by Nils Lid. Norsk Folkeminnelag XVIII. Oslo.

Storaker, J.T. 1928. *Naturrigerne i Den Norske Folketro (Storakers Samlinger IV)*, by Nils Lid. Norsk Folkeminnelag XVIII. Oslo.

Ström, Å & Biezais, H. (eds.) 1975. *Germanische Und Baltische Religion. Die Religionen der Menschheit Bd*, Vol. 19, No. 1. Verlag V. Kohlhammer. Stuttgart.

Stålbom, U. 1994. *Klinga. Ett Gravfält. Slutundersökning Av Ett Gravfält Och Bebyggelselämningar Från Bronsålder Och äldre Järnålder. Östergötland, Norrköpings Kommun, Borgs Socken, Klinga, STÄ 6352, Fornlämning 210*. Riksantikvarieämbetet UV Linköping. Linköping.

Svanberg, F. 2007. Aristokratiska Husgravar Under Bronsåldern. In Artursson, M. (ed.). *Vägar till Vætland. En Bronsåldersbygd i Nordöstra Skåne 2300–500 f.Kr*: 187–222. Riksantikvarieämbetet. Lund.

Svoboda, R.E. 1986. *Aghora. At the Left Hand of God*. Brotherhood of Life Publishing. New Mexico.

Svoboda, R.E. 1993. *Aghora II: Kundalini*. Brotherhood of Life Publishing. New Mexico.

Svoboda, R.E. 1998. *Aghora III: The Law of Karma*. Brotherhood of Life Publishing. New Mexico.

Tachikawa, M., Bahulkar, S. & Kolhatkar, M. 2001. *Indian Fire Ritual*. Foreword, Kashikar, C.G. Motital Banarsidass Publishers Private Limited. Delhi.

Takacs, S. 2008. *Vestal Virgins, Sibyls, and Matrons: Women in Roman Religion*. University of Texas Press. Austin.

Terekhova, N.N. 2008. The Earliest Meteoric Iron Tools to Have Been Found in Russia. In Forenius, S., Hjärthner-Holdar, E. & Risberg, C. (eds.). *The Introduction of Iron in Eurasia*: 129–139. The National Heritage Board & Department of Archaeology and Ancient History. Uppsala.

The Satapatha-Bråhmana. According to the text of the Madhyandina School. Translated by Julius Eggeling. Part V, Books XI, XII, XIII and XIV. In The Sacred Books of the East Vol. 44, edited by F. Max Muller. Montilal Banarsidass Publishers Private Limited. Delhi. 1988.

Thomas, L.-V. 1987. Funeral Rites. In: Eliade, M. (ed.). *The Encylopedia of Religion*, Vol 5. New York.

Thörn, R. 1996. Rituella Eldar. Linjära, Konkava Och Konvexa Spår Efter Ritualer Inom Nord- Och Centraleuropeiska Brons- Och Järnålderskulturer. In Engdahl, K. & Kaliff, A. (eds.). *Arkeologi Från Stenålder till Medeltid. Artiklar Baserade På Religionsarkeologiska Nätverksgruppens Konferens På Lövstadbruk Den 1–3 December 1995*: 135–148. Riksantikvarieämbetet, Arkeologiska undersökningar, Skrifter nr 19. Linköping.

Tillhagen, C.-H. 1977. *Folklig Läkekonst*. LTs förlag. Stockholm.

Tillhagen, C.-H. 1984. *Vardagsskrock*. Bokförlaget Prisma. Stockholm.

Tillhagen, C.-H. 1989. *Vår Kropp i Folktron*. LTs förlag. Stockholm.

Tillhagen, C.-H. 1991. *Folklig Spådomskonst*. Fabel Bokförlag. Stockholm.

Trevelyan, M. 1909. *Folk-lore and Folk-Stories of Wales*. Elliot Stock. London.

Troels-Lund, T.F. 1984. *Att Dö i Norden. Föreställningar Om Livets Slut På 1500-Talet*. Författerförlaget. Stockholm.

Troels-Lund, T.F. 1900. *Sunhedsbegreber i Norden i Det 16. Aarhundrede*. Det Schubotheske Forlag. København.

Turner, A.K. 1995. *The History of Hell*. Harcourt Brace & Company. London.

Tvedt, T. 2016. *Water and Society – Changing Perceptions of Societal and Historical Development*. I.B. Tauris. London.

Tvedt, T. 2021. *The Nile – History's Greatest River*. I.B. Tauris. London.

Tvedt, T. & Oestigaard, T. 2016. Approaches to African Food Production in a Water Society Systems Perspective. In Tvedt, T. & Oestigaard, T. (eds.). *A History of Water, Series 3, Vol. 3. Water and Food: From Hunter-Gatherers to Global Production in Africa*: 1–25. I.B. Tauris. London.

Ullén, I. 1995. Bronsåldersbrunnen i Apalle. In Ullén, I., Ranheden, H., Eriksson, T., Engelmark, R. (eds.). *Om Brunnar – Diskussion Kring Brunnar På Håbolandet*. Riksantikvarieämbetet, Arkeologiska undersökningar, Skrifter nr 12. Stockholm.

Ullén, I. 2003. *Bronsåldersboplatsen Vid Apalle i Uppland. Arkeologi På Väg – Undersökningar För E18*. Med bidrag av Ericsson, P., Eriksson, T., Kjellberg, A-S., Lindholm, P., Wigh, B. & Åkermark Kraft, A. Riksantikvarieämbetet. UV Uppsala. Rapport 1997:64.

Underhill, P., Poznik, G. & Rootsi, S. et al. 2015. The Phylogenetic and Geographic Structure of Y-Chromosome Haplogroup R1a. *European Journal of Human Genetics*, Vol. 23: 124–131. doi:10.1038/ejhg.2014.50

Victor, H. 2002. *Med Graven Som Granne. Om Bronsålderns Kulthus*. Dept. of Archaeology and Ancient History. Uppsala.

Vikstrand, P. 2001. *Gudarnas Platser: Förkristna Sakrala Ortnamn i Mälarlandskapen*. Kungl. Gustav Adolfs Akademien för svensk folkkultur. Uppsala.

Vlastos, G. 1952. Theology and Philosophy in Early Greek Thought. *The Philosophical Quarterly*, Vol. 2, No. 7: 97–123.

de Vries, J. 1956–57. *Altgermanische Religionsgeschichte*, Vols. 1–2. Grundriss der germanische Philologie 12; 1–2. Berlin.

Wadia, A. 2002. The Evolution of the Towers of Silence and Their Significance. In Godrej, P.J. & Mistree, F.P. (eds.). *A Zoroastrian Tapestry. Art, Religion & Culture*: 324–335. Mapin Publishing. Ahmedabad.

Walvoord, J.F. 1992. The Literal View. In Crockett, W. (ed.). *Four Views on Hell*: 11–28. Zondervan Publishing House. Michigan.

Weber, M. 1964. *The Sociology of Religion*. Beacon Press. Boston.

Wegelius, J.O., Wikman, K. & Rob., V. 1916. Om Vidskepliga Föreställningar Och Bruk Förenade Med Julens Firande Hos Den Svenska Allmogen i Finland. *Folkloristiska Och Etnografiska Studier I*: 132–162.

Weinberger-Thomas, C. 1999. *Ashes of Immortality: Widow-Burning in India*. The University of Chicago Press. Chicago.

Welinder, S. 2011. Early Farming Households, 3900–800 BC. In Myrdal, J. & Morell, M. (eds.). *The Agrarian History of Sweden: From 4000 BC to AD 2000*: 18–45. Nordic Academic Press. Lund.

Welinder, S., Pedersen, E.A. & Widgren, M. 1998. *Jordbrukets Första Femtusen år. Det Svenska Jordbrukets Historia*. Natur och kultur/LT. Stockholm.

West, M.L. 2007. *Indo-European Poetry and Myth*. Oxford University Press. Oxford.

Wheelwright, P. 1959. *Heraclitus*. Princeton University Press. Princeton. New Jersey.

Widmalm, S. 2003. Relativism är Granne Med Revisionism. *Axess*, Vol. 2003, No. 5: 23–26.

Wigh, B. 2008. Benens Vittnesbörd. Osteologisk Analys Av Benmaterialet Från Ryssgärdet. In Hjärthner-Holdar E., Eriksson T. & Östling A., (eds.). *Mellan Himmel Och Jord. Ryssgärdet, En Guldskimrande Bronsåldersmiljö i Centrala Uppland. Arkeologi E4 Uppland – Studier*, Vol. 5: 371–389. RAÄ. Stockholm.

Wigren, S. 1987. Sörmländsk bronsåldersbygd. En studie av tidiga centrumbildningar daterade med termoluminiscens. Studies in North European Archaeology 16. Stockholm.

Wilkin, S., Ventresca Miller, A. & Fernandes, R. et al. 2021. Dairying Enabled Early Bronze Age Yamnaya Steppe Expansions. *Nature,* Vol. 2021. doi:10.1038/s41586-021-03798-4

Witzel, M. 2000. The Home of the Aryans. *Münchener Studien Zur Sprachwissenschaft*: 283–338. doi:10.11588/xarep.00000114

Witzel, M. 2003. Vedas and Upanishads. In Flood, G. (ed.). *The Blackwell Companion to Hinduism*: 68–69. Blackwell Publishing Ltd. Oxford.

Witzel, M. 2013. Iranian Migration. In: Potts, D. T. (ed.) *The Oxford Handbook of Ancient Iran*. 422–441. doi:10.1093/oxfordhb/9780199733309.001.0001

Witzel, M. 2019. Early 'Aryans' and Their Neighbors Outside and Inside India. *Journal of Biosciences, Vol.* 44: 58. doi:10.1007/s12038-019-9881-7

Worsaae, J.J.A. 1882. *The Industrial Arts of Denmark. From the Earliest Times to the Danish Conquest of England*. Chapman and Hall. London.

Wright, R.P. 2010. *The Ancient Indus: Urbanism, Economy, and Society. Case Studies in Early Societies*, Series No. 10. Cambridge University Press. Cambridge.

Zaroff. 2019. Some Aspects of pre-Christian Baltic Religion. In: Lajoye, P. (ed), *New Researches on the Religion and Mythology Ot the Pagan Slavs*: 183–219. Lingva. Lisieux.

Zdanovich, G.B. & Zdanovich, D.G. 2002. The 'Country of Towns' of Southern Trans-Urals. In Byle, K., Renfrew, C. & Levine, M. (eds.). *Ancient Interactions: East and West of Eurasia*: 249–263. McDonald Institute for Archaeological Research. Cambridge.

Zguta, R. 1977. The Ordeal by Water (swimming of Witches) in the East Slavic World. *Slavic Review*, Vol. 36, No. 2: 220–230.

Zimmer, S. 2009. 'Sacrifice' in Proto-Indo-European. *The Journal of Indo-European Studies*, Vol. 37, No. 1 & 2: 178–190.

Zimmerman, F. 1982. *The Jungle and the Aroma of Meats*. University of California Press. Berkeley.

# INDEX

Note: *Italic* page numbers refer to figures.